RUSSIA

in
The National
Interest

The National Interest Series

China in *The National Interest*
Owen Harries, editor

Russia in *The National Interest*
Nikolas K. Gvosdev, editor

The National Interest on International Law and Order
R. James Woolsey

RUSSIA

in
The National Interest

Interest

edited by
Nikolas K. Gvosdev

Transaction Publishers
New Brunswick (U.S.A.) and London (U.K.)

Library of Congress Catalog Number: 2003061617
ISBN: 0-7658-0213-9 (cloth); 0-7658-0564-2 (paper)
Printed in Canada

Library of Congress Cataloging-in-Publication Data

Russia in the National interest / Nikolas K. Gvosdev [editor].
    p. cm.
    Includes bibliographical references.
    ISBN 0-7658-0213-9 (alk. paper)—ISBN 0-7658-0564-2 (paper: alk. paper)
      1. Russia (Federation)—Foreign relations. 2. Russia (Federation)—Foreign relations—United States. 3. United States—Foreign relations—Russia (Federation) 4. Russia (Federation)—Politics and government—1991- 5. International relations. 6. Democracy—Russia (Federation)
    I. Gvosdev, Nikolas K., 1969- II. National interest.

DK510.764.R8535 2003

Contents

Introduction:
The Russian Dichotomy

Nikolas K. Gvosdev

When Ivan III adopted the double-headed eagle as his emblem following his marriage in 1472 to Sophia Paleologos, the niece of the last Byzantine emperor, little did he suspect how this strange creature would come to symbolize the clashing and often contradictory imperatives that have shaped the Russian state and Russian society over the past five centuries. Two heads, one body; the eagle can be said to look both to the past and to the future; to the West and to the East; toward the distant Atlantic Ocean and the Euro-Atlantic world (the world onto which Peter the Great desired to "open a window") and out across the expanses of the Eurasian steppes.

In one of his contributions to this volume, Zbigniew Brzezinski posits two questions which affect not only Russia's internal development but its relationship to the larger world: What is Russia, and where is Russia? These are important questions, ones debated in the following pages. Is Russia an advanced industrial country, or a backward country verging on Third World status? Is Russia part of the "community of democracies" or an authoritarian state? Is Russia one of the world's Great Powers or a collapsed and wrecked society? Does Russia's destiny lie as a member of the Euro-Atlantic community, perhaps even a junior chairman of the board, or should it be excluded from the West? Is Russia a crippled empire seeking to resurrect its sphere of influence, or the natural "metropolitan power," the political and economic center for the Eurasian plain?

Befitting a country whose national symbol is a two-headed animal, the answer to the previous questions are all both "yes" and "no." In reality, we cannot speak of "Russia" as a singular entity in the current world. In his groundbreaking work on social capital, economic performance and political reform, Christopher Marsh has demonstrated that there is a real diversity of experience throughout the 89 regions that make up the Russian Federation.[1] Some areas have vibrant civil societies, accountable governments, and prosperous economies; others appear to be trapped in Brezhnev-like economic and political stagnation.

This is why aggregate national measurements and assessments do not provide the observer with the complete story. The Russian Federation may have a gross domestic product that equals that of the Netherlands (or have less foreign direct investment that Thailand)—but what is more important is how and where these resources are concentrated. Thus, certain regions and sectors of Russia function at a level equivalent to what can be found in North America or Western Europe, while others may resemble the poorer countries of southern Asia or sub-Saharan Africa. The Russian military, for example, possesses special forces units and strategic rocket forces that operate at American standards, while simultaneously fielding demoralized conscript infantry battalions with poor quality equipment that have proven, among other things, unable to contain a guerilla insurgency in Chechnya. In higher education, while "certain institutions provide direction and remain at the forefront on knowledge and research ... other institutions are destitute and backward."[2] In the economy, there is "increasing differentiation" in terms of wages and investment between different "sectors of the economy," especially in comparison between export oriented industries involved in the extraction and processing of raw materials, versus a lagging domestic services and manufacturing sectors.[3]

All of this produces a diversity of interests. For the oil and energy conglomerates, integration with European and American markets is the goal. This has produced a business and political class with a stake in bringing the Russian Federation securely within the ramparts of the Euro-Atlantic community. On the other hand, the defense industries, who have little opportunity to export their wares to the advanced industrial democracies, sell their wares to any and all clients able and willing to pay—and the acquisition of advanced weapons systems by India, China, or Iran is not always to the benefit of American national interests.

What is not clear at this point is whether the more prosperous and advanced sectors of Russian society will succeed in pulling the rest of the country upward, or whether the various social crises produced by Soviet impoverishment (declining life expectancy, the rise in disease, especially AIDS, and so on) will drag the country downward. Will Russia's democratic gains be consolidated and extended, or eroded and diminished, over the course of the Putin administration? Will Russia's growing number of shared economic and security interests with the West firmly anchor the Russian Federation within the Euro-Atlantic community, or will Russia become a vague-defined borderland lying between the EU and China? (A related question is whether a possible trans-Atlantic rift between Europe and the United States will cause both Washington and Brussels to bid for Moscow's support.)

This volume attempts to provide answers to some of these questions. Naturally, there is almost no agreement among the broad spectrum of authors represented herein. Yet, a common factor uniting them all is the sense that the United States cannot be indifferent to the future of Russia.

The first section—entitled "Post-Soviet Expectations"—comprises a set of articles written for *The National Interest* during the last days of the Soviet Union and the emergence of the post-Soviet Russian Federation. What makes the pieces by Coral Bell and Fred Charles Iklé more than simply items of historical curiosity is their vision of how a new constructive, strategic relationship between the United States and Russia could emerge from Cold War confrontation. Indeed, if one simply updates the names of the various presidents, they would not seem out of place in today's context. Yet, the reader can also assess the extent to which Iklé's assessment that progress in charting a new security community binding Washington and Moscow might be stymied by a relationship "heavily burdened by the Cold War legacy."

This section also contains Sergei Stankevich's influential essay "Russia in Search of Itself," which still bears reading more than a decade later, as well as responses penned by Leon Aron, Francis Fukuyama, Jim Hoagland and Bruce D. Porter. In addition to highlighting the ongoing tension in Russian thinking between "Atlanticist" and "Eurasian" tendencies, Stankevich's piece and the accompanying commentary sought to explore the relationship between Russia's domestic transformation and its role in foreign affairs.

Part of this debate is taken up more fully in the second section, "Russia: Ally or Adversary?" In his 1996 contribution reproduced in this section, Stephen Sestanovich reminds us that "Since the end of the Cold War, American presidents—first Bush and now Clinton—have treated Russian leaders with exceptional personal courtesy, and with the diplomatic hyperbole embodied in the term 'strategic partnership.'" In other words, Russia was no longer an enemy, but not fully an ally, but existed in a sort of intermediate state, neither fish nor fowl (*ny ryba, ny myaso*, as the Russians might say). It was therefore not clear whether Russia should be considered an emerging ally (and whether this was dependent upon the success of Russia's internal democratic transformation) or a defeated rival. On the Russian side, it became clear that Russia's conception of itself as a great power was not matched by actual resources at its disposal, creating a gap between rhetoric and achievement.

The debate over NATO expansion was symptomatic of this uncertainty. Deprived of its raison d'être in the form of an overwhelming Soviet threat, the North Atlantic Treaty Organization searched for a new role (guarantor of the peace of Europe, preservation of the American tie to Europe, or a hedged bet against a possible revival of Russian imperial tendencies). While seeking to offer Russia a greater role, it also expanded to encompass former Soviet satellites (and ultimately, former Soviet republics). Alexey Pushkov's contribution to this section provides a Russian perspective on the first round of NATO expansion eastward; the reader can assess whether or not the second round has been more successful in assuaging Russian concerns while preserving NATO's viability as a collective security organization.

Zbigniew Brzezinski's "Living with Russia" argues that the long-term integration of Russia into the West is possible only when Russia completes the process of becoming a post-imperial nation-state, warning: "The pursuit of that goal will require patience and strategic persistence." One of his ten commandments in hastening this process observes, "Propitiation of Putin's regime will only delay the desired evolution of Russia into a democratic, Europe-oriented, national Russian state." Robert Legvold, on the other hand, is more sanguine that in a post 9/11 environment, it may be possible for the United States and Russia to develop a true alliance based on common interests. In his second contribution to this section, however, Sestanovich tempers that optimism by noting that real partnership between Washington and Moscow cannot take shape as long as both countries are reluctant to set down the "red lines" that would effectively terminate the arrangement, pointing to Russo-American differences over the last decade over Iran and Iraq as examples.

In the third section, dealing with the Russian reform process, Peter Rutland points out that "Russia has not experienced a more or less clean break with the old system." The selection of authors presented in this section greatly disagree over why this did not occur; was it due to faulty advice from the West or Russia's own inability to construct the requisite institutions? To what extent should a clean break have even been encouraged? Was the so-called "Washington consensus"—the promotion of "radical" economic and political reform, primarily through deregulation and privatization at the expense of evolutionary, systemic change—the correct course of action (and did the Russians fail to implement it correctly, or did their Western advisors knowingly or unknowingly aid and abet in the looting of the Russian state)? Along with Rutland, Zbigniew Brzezinski, Nicholas Eberstadt, and Charles Flickner all address aspects of these questions in assessing the success or failure of the reform process—and of the U.S. role.

One of the most controversial articles ever published in *The National Interest* concerning this question was Janine Wedel's "Tainted Transactions." Wedel discussed the phenomenon of "transactorship"—how the Russian and American officials and advisors tasked with managing Western aid designed to advance Russian reforms instead used their positions to secure advantages for their own network. Wedel's conclusions (as well as her account of events) was vigorously disputed, including by some of those intimately involved in the Russian reform process, which prompted *The National Interest* to offer space for further discussion. Responses by Jeffrey Sachs and Anders Åslund, among others, allow readers to assess the claims and counterclaims made in what is probably one of the most contentious American foreign policy questions of the 1990s.

This section closes with a late 1998 contribution by Dimitri K. Simes, who calls attention to the "de facto intervention in Russia's domestic politics on behalf of President Boris Yeltsin and the so-called 'radical reformers'" on the part of the United States, with negative consequences both for Russia but also for the United States. He then offered an interesting assessment, that "the Primakov government may smooth the transition to the post-Yeltsin era as well."

The December 1999 Duma elections and the 2000 presidential elections saw the emergence not only of Vladimir Putin as Russia's second post-Soviet president but also saw the rise of new political forces—the Kremlin-sponsored "Unity" movement, the "Fatherland-All Russia" bloc, and the "Union of Right Forces." Increasingly, the political mainstream in Russia is characterized by "statist liberals."[4] The "statist-liberals" neither uncritically accepted or unilaterally rejected what the West had to offer. Foreign Minister Igor Ivanov approvingly quoted czarist Minister of Foreign Affairs Sergei Sazonov that "reform must be carried out gradually, so as to be made understandable by the people and not create the impression of a risk-filled experiment."[5] Significantly, many of the pragmatists grouped around Primakov in his cabinet retained their positions in the Putin administration.

"The period of reform is coming to a close," Finance Minister Alexei Kudrin declared in October 2001.[6] If that is the case, then Russia's domestic and foreign policies for the foreseeable future are likely to be shaped by the decisions taken by the Putin Administration. This question is taken up by the fourth and final section of this volume. In his contribution, William Odom highlights the importance of institutions, noting that once a country has put in place a set of institutions—whether formal or informal—not only do they determine the course of development, they are difficult to change. His conclusion is that the "mix" of Soviet and post-Soviet institutions that now characterizes Putin's Russia will keep the country weak and poor, and that as a result, Russia "will not soon return to great power status, either as a liberal democracy or as a dictatorship."

Odom's blunt assessments, in turn, are endorsed or disputed in a collection of short, thoughtful essays penned by, among others, Martin Malia, Jack Matlock, Jerry Hough, Geoffrey Hosking, and Henry Trofimenko. Also in this section, Laurent Murawiec and Clifford Gaddy explore the liberal-reformist current running through the Russian special services for the past two centuries, in an attempt to explore Putin's own political background. Finally, the editor of this volume weighs in with a contribution of his own, exploring the ability of the Putin administration to try and maximize Russia's strategic advantage in Eurasia.

A special afterword to this volume is provided by Paul J. Saunders, director of the Nixon Center (which co-publishes *The National Interest*). Saunders brings revisits the question of Russian-American partnership in the aftermath of the 2003 war in Iraq.

Notes

Nikolas K. Gvosdev is executive editor of *The National Interest* and a senior fellow at The Nixon Center.

1. Christopher Marsh, *Making Russian Democracy Work: Social Capital, Economic Development, and Democratization* (Lewiston, NY: The Edwin Mellen Press, 2000), esp. pp. 81-83.
2. Grigorii A. Kljutcharev and Melissa A. Marsh, "Higher Education and Russia's Dual Transition," in *Civil Society and the Search for Justice in Russia*, eds. Christopher Marsh and Nikolas K. Gvosdev (Lanham, MD: Lexington Books, 2002), p. 134.
3. See especially the April 2003 issue of *Russian Economy: Trends and Perspectives*, issued by the Moscow-based Institute for the Economy in Transition.
4. "Statist-liberals" support political and economic reform within the context of a reconstructed and effective Russian state, a system in which pluralism is regulated with an eye to preserving stability or consensus. See my "Managed Pluralism and Political Parties in Russia," *Analysis of Current Events*, 14:3 (October 2002), especially p. 15.
5. Igor S. Ivanov, *The New Russian Diplomacy* (Washington, DC: The Brookings Institution Press, 2002), p. 4.
6. Remarks made at the U.S.-Russia Business Council, October 5, 2001 (Washington, DC).

Part 1

Post-Soviet Expectations

1

Comrades in Arms: The Case for a Russian-American Defense Community

Fred Charles Iklé*

The strategic relationship now emerging between the United States and Russia opens a new chapter in world history. During most of this century, these two great nations could change their relationship only incrementally, if at all. But since last August, their relations have entered a period of unique malleability, one that offers an epochal opportunity for creative statesmanship.[1]

By far the most promising initiative now would be to inaugurate an American-Russian Defense Community, designed as an evolving program of cooperation that would build progressively closer links between the military establishments of the two sides. Such a relationship with the main heir to Soviet military power would greatly enhance America's security in the coming era, when weapons of mass destruction will spread throughout the world.

As America's foreign policy experts look to the future, they understandably draw on the ideas that served us so well in the recent past. The broad consensus that has emerged on the key goals for the post-Cold War world is constructed entirely out of Cold War concepts. These goals are: to preserve NATO and the alliance with Japan, to continue the policy of peace through nuclear strength, to maintain the "stability" of mutual deterrence, and to redouble our efforts against weapons proliferation. Some want to add a bit of fresh garnish to this platter of old leftovers by postulating an expanded role for the UN Security Council (henceforth supposed to be untrammeled by vetoes). Others draw comfort from the notion that if something like a Stalinist Soviet Union should re-emerge, we could always reconstitute our forces and man the old ramparts again.

---

*Fred Charles Iklé was undersecretary of defense for policy in the Reagan administration and is currently a Distinguished Scholar at the Center for Strategic and International Studies, Washington, DC. This essay first appeared in The National Interest, no. 26 (Winter 1991/92).

Justifiably, warnings of what might go wrong are plenty. From Minsk to Vladivostok, democratic reform is incomplete, the new political structures are fragile, the economy is deteriorating from bad to worse. Attempts might be launched sooner or later to revert to the evil ways of the past. The widespread anxiety about such hazards is now focused on the near term— getting through the Russian winter, avoiding total economic collapse, preventing civil wars among former Soviet republics, and precluding any kind of misuse or accident among the thousands of nuclear weapons. To be sure, traversing the near term is a necessary condition for reaching a better future. But it is not sufficient.

President Bush has moved quickly and prudently to cope with the enormous upheaval in the former Soviet Union, to contain its risks, and to pursue new opportunities. His nuclear initiative in September, in particular, not only reduces present dangers, but opens highly promising avenues for fundamental long-term improvement. The basic transformation of the American-Russian relationship that is so essential for our security, however, cannot be completed within a year or two. Seventy years of Bolshevism and forty years of Cold War have left a hazardous legacy in both East and West—a spiritual, intellectual, and material pollution that will require a purposeful effort over many years to be rendered harmless. The old poisons could become virulent again, like an infectious disease that has lain dormant for a long time.

Danger Signs

Like no other dimension of the emerging American-Russian relationship, the military interaction will remain heavily burdened by the Cold War legacy. On both sides, old habits of the mind, reinforced by old bureaucratic practices, will subtly influence new strategic concepts and new war plans. Throughout the Northern Hemisphere, thousands of military artifacts will remain—armaments, electronic installations, air bases, naval ports, laboratories—that will invest the Cold War apparitions with tangible reality made of hard metal and reinforced cement. Amidst the detritus of the Soviet Union, the Russian Republic is inheriting vast arsenals, huge military forces, and an enormous (although presently crippled) military-industrial complex.

Given this context, we should seek to anticipate how things might go wrong in the evolving military relationship between America and Russia. At first brush, we may find it reassuring to see how military officers from both sides get along with each other. The military harbors less animosity toward its former Cold War adversary than other population groups do. American military leaders are eager to develop cordial and cooperative relations with their Soviet counterparts; to speak to them "as a friend—no longer as an enemy," as General Colin Powell recently told a group of visiting Soviet officers. And the Soviet military has shown that they reciprocate this sentiment.

Underneath this new comity, however, a dangerous dynamic threatens to push America and Russia into a new military confrontation. One way in which this dynamic works is through the growing military strength of other nations that are seen as potential adversaries by Washington or Moscow, and hence as compelling the United States, or Russia, to acquire compensating military strength. For example, many Americans are cautioning against further reductions in the U. S. defense budget, for fear that American forces might not be strong enough later this decade to defeat "another Iraq." Similarly, Russia's new military leaders anticipate that their nation will have to be armed against ever more sophisticated weaponry among (unnamed) nations to the south, and perhaps even against independent armies that are being established by some of the other former Soviet republics. Strategic planners both in America and Russia will surely want to see their own nation's military technology stay well ahead of these potentially threatening new powers.

Alas, with such efforts to arm against emerging "Third World" military threats, America and Russia will stumble into new kinds of arms competition between each other, covering a wide range of weapons developments. And the international arms trade will add fuel to this fire. Because of sharply declining defense budgets at home, arms manufacturers in the United States, Western Europe, and the former Soviet Union are all anxious now to find new markets. The few importers in this buyers' market who are still solvent can demand some of the best and latest technologies. It will not take long for nations acquiring such advanced armaments to be seen—either by Washington or Moscow—as new military threats.

The dynamic that levers America and Russia toward a new military confrontation also includes tensions created by secret and possibly illicit weapons developments. In spite of glasnost, the political transformation in Moscow, and the verification arrangements of recent arms accords, the battle between openness and secrecy is far from over—not only in the Soviet military establishment that is being inherited by Russia and other republics, but in the U.S. military as well.

When the detailed verification provisions of START were finally being settled, it was the American negotiators more often than the Soviet ones who insisted on limiting access for the other side's inspectors. Indeed, protecting the secrecy of certain military technologies had a higher priority for the United States than enlarging the agreed scope for verification. For example, the United States sought to protect technological secrets of its radar-evading "stealth" aircraft.

For the Soviet military, shielding its latest technology from American "espionage" may be less important than keeping other kinds of secrets. Quite likely, the Soviet military establishment still keeps some ugly skeletons in its closet. When former Soviet Foreign Minister Eduard Shevardnadze admitted that the Krasnoyarsk radar station in Siberia violated the ABM Treaty, Soviet military officers still sought to deny culpability. And the story has yet to come out, it seems, on violations of the treaty banning biological weapons.

The old penchant of the Soviet military for pushing to the very edge of what arms agreements allow—and sometimes well beyond—may not have been entirely eradicated by the democratic revolution. Besides, the complexities and ambiguities of recent arms agreements will provide ample opportunity for hard to-prove cheating. In this environment, the cloak of secrecy will do double duty for the self-styled "patriots" in Moscow. It will shield them from American arms control monitors as well as from budget-conscious economists in their own government. Indeed, in the coming years, some Soviet officers and managers of arms industries may seek to perpetuate old practices of secrecy, not as protection from potential foreign enemies, but to keep their parliament and public in the dark about the burden that their military continues to impose on the nation's economy.

Tensions caused by military secrecy could mar American-Russian relations in many ways. On both sides, it is safe to predict, bureaucracies will show great zest and ingenuity in creating confrontational issues about "espionage" and "cheating." Secrecy is a customary companion of military research projects. And it is to be expected that both the American and Russian military establishments will continue to conduct certain research projects whose purpose, at least in part, will be to stay ahead of the former Cold War adversary.

Nuclear Gridlock

Among Americans associated with nuclear weapons research, there is nearly unanimous conviction that the United States must continue to test nuclear weapons, regardless of what happens to nuclear testing in the former Soviet Union. Since the 1950s, Moscow has favored a ban on all nuclear testing, while Washington's position has shifted back and forth between reluctantly considering such a ban and opposing it outright. In prior decades, the American reluctance was due, in part, to the fear that the Soviet Union could easily cheat in ways that would not yield sufficiently unambiguous evidence. Today, the Soviet nuclear weapons establishment is under political pressure not to resume testing for environmental reasons. Should current differences on nuclear testing between Washington and Moscow persist for several years, those in Moscow who want arms spending again to increase will argue that one-sided nuclear testing by the United States is beginning to undermine the Soviet nuclear deterrent.

The hoary dispute about nuclear testing is merely a skirmish in a larger battle—the emancipation of nuclear strategy from Cold War thinking. The warp and woof of nearly all strategic thought—not only in the United States and the former Soviet Union, but also in France and Great Britain—remains the East-West enmity of the last forty years. And this strategic thought remains locked into place in each of these countries by their equally dated nuclear arsenals.

To be sure, we have heard some good news lately. President Bush decided in September to withdraw most of America's so-called "theater" nuclear weapons, and President Gorbachev agreed to reciprocate. In one fell swoop, a large artifact in the Cold War museum of nuclear horrors is thus to be dismantled.

What was the purpose of this artifact? The story reaches back to the early 1950s, when the United States began to deploy theater nuclear weapons for two reasons: as a means of nuclear retaliation less massive than the strategic bomber force, and to give the U.S. Army—which was jealous of the Navy's and the Air Force's nuclear missions—its own nuclear arms. To keep a long story short, since the late 1950s, the various rationales for these weapons have disappeared one by one. In particular, the principal target for American theater nuclear weapons—the Red Army—has gone home.

As these changes occurred, those who believed strongly in the merits of theater nuclear weapons reached for a metaphysical rationale: that nuclear weapons based forward on the territory that might be attacked would provide a more credible deterrent than weapons based in the rear. Here is a reminder that military doctrine based on disconfirmed beliefs can survive for decades.

This brings us to the bad news about the role of nuclear strategy in the emerging American-Russian relationship. Even though theater nuclear weapons will cease to burden this relationship, a Cold War gridlock still persists for "strategic" nuclear weapons—the thousands of nuclear arms on missiles and bombers of intercontinental reach.

During the last four decades each superpower built an enormously elaborate apparatus capable of totally destroying the other and designed so that this cataclysm could be irrevocably unleashed within minutes—on purpose, or (perhaps) by accident. The risk that this supposedly stable system might end in the superpowers' mutual suicide has not yet been eliminated. While the combination locks on nuclear weapons that many people now confidently promote might ameliorate this risk, they cannot eliminate it. A safeguard system relying on codes that would instantly have to be passed to thousands of command posts needs to be renewed and tested from time to time. (The Chernobyl reactor did have safeguards; it exploded because of a mismanaged test of its safeguard system!)

The dangers inherent in this nuclear legacy will continue to create new tensions in the American-Russian relationship. Whenever one side modernizes elements of its strategic forces, the other side will find reason to worry. Military staffs on each side will continue to perform calculations to estimate whether the Other Side (who used to be the Enemy) could somehow launch a first strike without having to fear massive and certain retaliation. On each side, estimates will also be prepared on the number of minutes within which the retaliatory strike would have to be launched before the codes to unlock nuclear weapons could no longer be transmitted to the missile and bomber crews. Such Cold War imagery is likely to persist, like a genetic defect, long after the conflict itself has ended.

Woe and Wickedness

Threats from third nations, competition in military research, and contradictions in nuclear strategy all have the potential to ratchet the United States and Russia toward a new enmity. To make matters worse, as these pressures and tensions do their work, they will be exacerbated on occasion by accidents, mistakes, or mischief—the woeful triplets that always intrude into human affairs.

A future dispute between Washington and Moscow about some secret military research project, for example, might suddenly become inflamed because of an accident that, to Americans, looked like a hostile act planned in Moscow at the highest level—the Soviet shooting down of a Korean airliner in 1983 comes to mind. Disagreements about a new arms program (ostensibly directed against third country threats) might be aggravated by incidents involving "spies" and denial of legitimate access for arms control inspectors. Such incidents, perhaps started by junior officers, could well be magnified by mistakes higher up in the decision chain.

To make matters worse, scattered amidst all these combustible tensions between Moscow and Washington will be plenty of mischief-makers. Like smoldering embers, Bolshevik hatred of the West will linger on in the minds of many senior officials in Russia. In all the former Soviet republics, the older generation had to spend its formative years in a din of anti-Western locutions, distortions, and lies. One recalls that several years after glasnost had swept such old-think aside, then KGB Chief Kryuchkov and Prime Minister Pavlov still gave speeches bristling with hostility toward the West. Although these two men are facing trial as leaders of the August coup, years from now like-minded Bolsheviks might again—or still—occupy positions of influence in the lands that Stalin ruled.

In 1920, Lenin asserted that "the real basis of contemporary international politics is the coalition of all powerful capitalist countries of the world against Soviet Russia"; and Stalin in 1925 foreshadowed the Cold War era by declaring that "the world is now divided into two camps." Two camps—"us" and "them"—who will destroy whom? Paint these old fighting words with lush new colors of Russian nationalism, omit that tedious Marxist theorizing, and you have the core of a new ideology for Russia's unreconstructed Bolsheviks to rally throngs of discontented youths—that essential ingredient for a political mass movement.

If, sometime during this decade, such a political movement were to become influential in Russia or to gain controlling power, much of the enormous

Soviet military establishment would still exist. It will take many years and strong political leadership (both in short supply) to transform a major part of the gigantic Soviet arms industries into genuine civilian enterprises, to deactivate substantial military forces, and to dismantle excess armaments, bases, and military infrastructure.

The American-Russian military relationship would therefore have a decisive influence—for better or for worse—if a reactionary political movement in Russia sought to stir up tensions with the United States. Unless most of the Cold War legacy had been cleared away in the meantime, a new Bolshevik-nationalist-fascist movement could readily gain ardent support throughout the Russian military establishment. A long list of growing American "threats" could easily be compiled: continued U.S. nuclear tests, undiminished U.S. naval superiority, expanded deployment of the "stealth" and precision technologies that won the Gulf War, and the survival of NATO and of most U.S. bases that are "encircling" Russia even though the Warsaw Pact has been abolished.

A Gathering Storm

One recalls that after the First World War, Germany became a democratic nation free of its imperial burdens. During its first four years, to be sure, the new Weimar Republic had a troubled time. It suffered a string of disasters—a Communist putsch, a Nazi putsch, hyperinflation, food riots—the kind of tribulations that people in Moscow are now worried about. During the following five years, however, Germany enjoyed stable democratic government, vigorous economic growth, minimal unemployment, friendly relations with all its neighbors, and a burst of extraordinary cultural creativity. Europe and the world seemed at peace. Suddenly, the Great Depression and its wave of massive unemployment tilted the political forces in Germany (and in Japan as well) in favor of an ideology of violence and expansion.

Yet Adolf Hitler could not have consolidated his power, much less launched his sweeping territorial conquests a mere seven years later, had the German military establishment not been so willing and so well prepared to revert to a policy of imperial expansion. Throughout the seemingly peaceful Weimar years, the German military, stuck in their 1914 mentality, saw the world as divided into two camps—and readied themselves accordingly.

History, of course, will not repeat itself—not exactly. And every lesson from history can be contradicted with another one. Should we heed today the lessons from the 1920s, or the lessons from the 1930s? Were France and Great Britain too slow in the 1920s in weaving closer ties with Weimar Germany, especially with its military? Or were they too slow in rearming themselves in the 1930s? If again "the Russians are coming," how should the United States respond?

The Pentagon's answer today is "reconstitution," by which is meant the rebuilding and refurbishing of America's armed forces. Defense Secretary Dick Cheney has rightly emphasized that such a rearmament effort would entail building "wholly new forces" whose equipment and weaponry would have to be developed long in advance. Much of the equipment that played a crucial role in the American victory over Iraq, Cheney pointed out, "was developed 20 or 30 years ago." Unless the Pentagon keeps funding a wide range of research and development projects, the United States will be ill prepared to rebuild its military strength if it had to meet a global crisis in the future.

In this age of turmoil throughout vast reaches of Eurasia, to maintain a capacity for reconstituting military strength is prudent. But to rely on this capacity as the main guardian of America's security and world peace would be reckless. If the storm should gather again, a rearmament program would not offer a safe haven to which the United States could comfortably retreat.

A policy of rearming would have to gain the cooperation of allies, be guided by agreed strategic concepts, and be supported by the American people. Questions regarding nuclear arms and nuclear strategy would arise at the outset. Conflicting ideas about a policy of nuclear deterrence—which originally emerged gradually during the Cold War and hence rarely stirred up public anxiety—would be hurled into the political arena. Some would want to rely mainly on new defensive technologies, others would want to reconstruct a stable balance between offensive forces; some would want to rearm full speed and without any restraints, others would want to negotiate new arms agreements.

Such discord would revive the profound—and justified—fear of nuclear destruction that has lain dormant since the worst years of the Cold War. Washington's political climate would very likely resemble the Vietnam years during the Johnson and Nixon administrations, rather than the Truman and Eisenhower years when the policies of containment and peace-through-strength could be so successfully launched and promoted with substantial consensual support. The nation's resoluteness and confidence would be sapped by recriminations. Americans and their remaining allies would ask how the victory of democracy that ended the Cold War could have been so foolishly squandered. They would blame their leaders for having failed to build an enduring peace with Russia after the attempted coup, during those few years of great opportunity.

Enough of this nightmare! Our opportunity is not yet lost.

The Problem is the Solution

In 1991, the Union of Soviet Socialist Republics expired, and the autopsy revealed that it died of three chronic illnesses. Most visible in the last few months was its death by terminal imperialism. The world's last empire could no longer hold its independent-minded nationalities together. The second chronic illness was communism. As the world's first "socialist" state, the USSR was afflicted for over seventy years—longer than any other country—with the economic inefficiency, political stultification, and human cruelty of the communist system of government. The third cause of the USSR's demise was militarism. No other industrialized state in the world has for so long spent so much of its national wealth on armaments and military forces. Soviet militarism, in harness with communism, destroyed the Soviet economy and thus hastened the self-destruction of the Soviet Empire.

Of the Soviet Union's three mortal illnesses, militarism poses the greatest danger of being passed on to the successor states; not because Russians (and Ukrainians, etc.) are a particularly militaristic people, but because militarism has become so entrenched in society. Both figuratively and literally it is cemented into the landscape.

The American-Russian military relationship, therefore, presents the greatest challenge for statesmanship. By contrast, economic relations will have much less sway, either to hurt or to help. To help, American economic assistance can play only a small role, since conditions on both sides preclude "another Marshall Plan." To hurt, economic relations are too crushingly one-sided. We need not fear the day when "Russia-bashers" in Congress accuse Russia of flooding the American market with automobiles or computers. The main economic controversy will be about Russia's debt, while lesser trade conflicts might arise as they do with Brazil, India, and other nations.

Similarly, diplomatic relations by themselves are unlikely to cause a new enmity. Mistakes in diplomacy could bring a new Cold War only if accompanied, or followed, by moves in the military sphere—such as Russian security guarantees or arms shipments to an aggressor nation, Russian covert military assistance to terrorists or troublemakers, hints from Moscow of nuclear blackmail, or an outright attack by Russian forces on another nation.

While the military interaction between America and Russia in the coming years is pregnant with danger, paradoxically it also offers the most promising opportunity for building a solid structure of peaceful cooperation. The new, friendly links between Washington and Moscow are still fragile, without roots in the two governments and overly dependent on changing personnel in positions of leadership. For improved relations to become enduring, they must be anchored in institutions that are endowed with steadiness, influence, and continuity.

Proposals for joint activities and common structures between the American and the Russian military establishments do not have to sail against the wind these days. President Bush, on September 27, proposed to Moscow cooperation on storage, transportation, and destruction of nuclear warheads, and discussions on nuclear command and control arrangements. He also foreshadowed proposals for cooperation on early warning against ballistic missiles. President Gorbachev generally endorsed these ideas and mentioned specifically creating a joint system "to avert" nuclear missile attacks. Senior members of Congress have recommended a joint program for destroying nuclear, chemical, and other weapons, and U.S. assistance on converting Soviet arms plants to civilian production. Representatives from Soviet military industries have approached American government officials and business executives for joint ventures to facilitate such conversion. Representatives from the Soviet space program are exploring cooperation with the U.S. strategic defense initiative. And so on.

In the present atmosphere of good will between the two militaries there is no lack of ideas for joint projects. Lacking is a sense of direction—or, more to the point, a sense of destination. Without an agreed destination, all these joint projects will merely provide occasions for good fellowship between American and Russian military people. Without institutional links animated by a common purpose, these fraternal relations offer scant protection against a new enmity. One is reminded of those yellowed photographs from around 1910, depicting German and French, Russian and Austrian generals enjoying lavish picnics together while watching through binoculars their splendidly dressed troops executing a joint maneuver—the better to kill each other in the First World War.

Toward a Defense Community

A clear and ambitious destination should guide the United States and the new Russia in shaping their military relationship. The common goal should be to eradicate the adversarial confrontation throughout the two military establishments. This endeavor will take many years, moving forward step by step through changes in the deployment of forces, their armaments, their exercises and training, and in each side's preparation for war. Great strides have already been made; most significantly, the dismantling of the military confrontation in the center of Europe and, recently, the reductions on both sides in nuclear forces that are kept on alert.

To describe the destination of the evolving military relationship as a "defense community" serves to evoke a useful analogy with the "economic communities" that began to link former enemies in Europe forty years ago, starting with the Coal and Steel Community launched in May 1950 to promote lasting reconciliation between France and Germany. The analogy, of course, must not be pushed too far; and like all enterprises that seek to shape international affairs, the attempt to create an American-Russian defense community might fail.

Failure, though, is more likely for a policy that would cling to the tried and old. Denied a constructive long-term goal, such a policy would lack the calendar to force a process of step-by-step improvement. America and Russia, in their security relationship, would sail ahead without a compass, bobbing and weaving between partnership and confrontation, anxiously focused on some quivering balance of armaments, forever undecided whether to live with each other as friend or foe.

The nuclear arsenals on both sides will provide the lever and the fulcrum to create a defense community. On nuclear arms, Washington and Moscow are accustomed to the idea of cooperation, and America's allies favor, or at least do not oppose, such cooperation. Prudent policy-makers will continue to be burdened with the threat to national survival that lurks behind the continuing "balance of terror." And from time to time, incidents will occur to stir up public anxiety about nuclear war.

The idea that some day, somehow, this latent threat of massive nuclear destruction should be "abolished" is neither new nor the brainchild only of pacifists and left-wingers. When the nuclear age was only nine years old and proliferation had not yet started, even a realist like John Foster Dulles could speak of "nuclear abolition" as at least a distant possibility.[2] Today, in a literal sense, abolition appears to have become impossible. But the political transformation in Moscow has now opened the door to other solutions—although it may not stay open for long. While the United States and Russia cannot abolish nuclear weapons, they can overcome their nuclear confrontation; and in doing so, they will go a long way toward establishing a defense community.

Too much has been made of reducing the numbers of nuclear weapons, and not enough of the need to reduce the adversarial postures of the strategic forces on both sides. Without a fundamental change in these postures, even the most drastic reductions in the number of weapons would still leave America and Russia in a potentially mortal confrontation. Senior defense officials correctly keep reminding us that Soviet missiles could destroy our nation in thirty minutes. This would still be true if the 4,900 nuclear missile warheads permitted by START were halved or even reduced tenfold.

To overcome this confrontation, both sides must abolish the hair-trigger launch procedures of their strategic forces and abandon their constant readiness to unleash nuclear cataclysm. Presidents Bush and Gorbachev have now agreed to take a fraction of their missile forces off alert status, a step decidedly in the right direction. Much more can and must be done. Reductions in alert status already begun can be expanded. Both sides could implement a series of specific measures, in a coordinated fashion, that would make large-scale nuclear attack impossible—short of a clearly verifiable remobilization that would take weeks or months to carry out. The joint warning system suggested by Presidents Bush and Gorbachev would complement such measures. A welcome byproduct of reducing the readiness of strategic forces will be the added protection from civil disturbances in the former Soviet Union that might endanger deployed nuclear weapons.

Nuclear planners schooled in Cold War theories will reject as heresy a nuclear strategy that would be without its thousands of missiles, primed to retaliate instantly against an enemy first strike. The American-Russian defense community, by bringing about a wide-range of military reforms, will make the abolition of the nuclear confrontation both safe and psychologically acceptable. At the end of this road, the remaining, restructured nuclear forces of the United States and Russia will coexist side by side—much like the French and British nuclear forces—without the adversarial concern about the "stability" of mutual deterrence. Are any French generals worried whether their nuclear forces are up to the task of deterring perfidious Albion from launching a first strike against France?

In harmony with this strategic transformation, an old, contentious issue between Washington and Moscow will quietly fade away—NATO's doctrine of using nuclear weapons first to stem a conventional attack by the Warsaw Pact. As the American nuclear advantage kept shrinking, this doctrine kept losing credibility; as the Warsaw Pact collapsed, it lost its purpose; and now, as theater nuclear weapons are being withdrawn, it is losing its chosen instrument.

Instead of the vanished Cold War issue of "first use," the United States, its allies, and Russia will together have to cope with a different and growing problem of first use stemming from the proliferation of weapons of mass destruction. If a "future Iraq" used poison gas or biological weapons against an international peace-keeping coalition, should the United States and Russia respond with a nuclear strike? The answer might not be easy. On the one hand, any use of weapons of mass destruction by some tyrant ought to be deterred; on the other hand, the tradition of not using nuclear weapons since 1945 is of immense value for democratic nations.[3]

The scope of a defense community linking America and Russia should not be confined to bilateral nuclear issues and to issues raised by the global of weapons of mass destruction. The community must also serve to develop a constructive relationship between the conventional forces of both sides. To this end, continued progress in reducing military secrecy is essential, and progress here can have mutually reinforcing benefits. If the two nations no longer see each other as potential enemies, the need for military secrecy between them could nearly vanish; and if military secrecy between them is nearly eliminated, they will have removed a key source of military tension that could cause a new enmity.

A particularly inspiring purpose of the defense community, both for Americans and for the new democratic forces in Russia, is the promotion of democratic practices and traditions for civilian control of the military. These days, such an effort will find open doors in Russia. Most of the military officers now in charge there want their nation to become a modem state with stable civilian control of the armed forces, and the political authorities in Moscow today, of course, share this objective. For the sake of the Russian people, for the sake of world peace, Russia must not become a "giant Burma"—a huge country with a backward civilian economy and a brutal, highly armed military dictatorship.

To construct meaningful institutional links in the military sphere, Washington and Moscow will have to design projects that can benefit from intensive cooperation and, at the same time, are important for the security of both sides. Some of these projects may be temporary (such as the safe disposal of nuclear weapons) and will be followed by new common tasks. Other joint missions will grow in importance and be long-lasting (such as coping with the continuing proliferation of new technologies for mass destruction).

The common military projects that, collectively, will constitute the defense community must not be confused with contrived clusters of bureaucrats, forever in search of a real purpose but always busy with organization charts and acronyms. A sense of urgency in tackling the most dangerous problems will have to be complemented by a sense for organic evolutionary growth. When the European Coal and Steel Community was created, the founders did not seek to establish a common monetary system—it will be forty years later when (and if) such a system materializes.

At this time, four broad missions of the defense community can be identified: First, eliminating the adversarial confrontation of nuclear forces—above all, the hair-trigger posture of these forces. Second, gradually abolishing secrecy between the two military establishments. Third, balancing measures against proliferation with the need to respect the legitimate sovereignty and independence of all nations. Fourth, cultivating responsible civilian control of the Russian military and—in both militaries—a sense of dedication to make the community serve the interests of both nations.

No Hegemony

The more the defense community can promote democratic, civilian control of Russia's military, the less America's allies and friends, in Europe and in Asia, will have to fear an expansionist Muscovite Empire that would again coerce and invade its neighbors. The concept here for a new American-Russian military relationship stands in total contrast to Franklin D. Roosevelt's ill-fated concept for a security relationship with the Soviet Union after World War II. FDR's concept linked up (by necessity) with a Soviet Union that was advancing to conquer other nations, not with a Russia that had recently withdrawn and set other nations free. It was a relationship that floated on air, without any institutional links. It entailed an extreme tightening, not a reduction, in Soviet secrecy, and thus covered up unending Soviet lying. And worst of all, FDR based his attempted new relationship with the Soviet Union on his trust in Stalin's good will.

After the First World War, leading concepts for securing world peace were equally mistaken. The major powers in the 1920s sought, by negotiating several naval treaties, to stabilize a balance in the global strategic armaments of that time—the very purpose of the SALT and START agreements of recent years. After much hostile haggling among technical experts, treaties were concluded that incorporated elaborate definitions and restrictions designed to fix parity (and other ratios) in naval armaments. The goal was to keep the military confrontation peaceful, not to keep the peace by overcoming the military confrontation. Hence, the naval staffs continued to see each other as adversaries (even between the United States and Great Britain!). And seeing each other as adversaries, they modernized their navies and planned for war.

As if to put some icing on this crumbling cake, the major powers of the 1920s tried another concept—renouncing war as an instrument of national policy. Eleven years and five days before Hitler started World War II, the American Secretary of State Frank Kellogg and his French counterpart, Aristide Briand, signed with plenipotentiaries from Germany and a dozen other major powers the Kellogg-Briand Pact, which has since become an object of ridicule among historians.

By contrast, Jean Monnet's idea for a European economic community provides a historic example of a successful concept. Monnet's main goal was to start building a viable, meaningful institution to link France and Germany—nations that had fought three wars in the span of seventy years—and to let other European nations join. "The life of institutions," wrote Monnet in 1955, "is longer than that of people, and institutions can thus, if they are well constructed, accumulate and transmit the wisdom of successive generations."

After World War II, meaningful links between France and Germany could best be established in the economic sphere; after the Cold War, links between the United States and Russia can best be established in the military sphere. Economically, Russia is a supplicant. By contrast, in a military concordat with the United States, Russia can play a global role constructively. However, the national interests that the two nations could now pursue in common through a defense community remain strictly limited. When Russia's economic relations with the outside world gain in importance, its principal partners are likely to be Germany and Japan, not the United States. It is inconceivable that the United States and Russia would ever be seized by a convergent imperialist frenzy, to form a Washington-Moscow axis for global hegemony.

The purpose of the American-Russian defense community will not only remain limited, it will remain fully supportive of the enduring national interests of America's allies. Russia and America will want to eliminate the risk of global nuclear war—the paramount interest of every nation in the Northern Hemisphere. And their new military relationship will also serve to prevent military developments between them that would either threaten America's allies or Russia's national interests and territory. These purposes cannot be achieved by some vast multilateral conglomerate, such as the CSCE or the UN.

America's Atlantic and Pacific alliances have emerged from the Cold War as viable and valued security structures for the new era, linking old allies as well as enemies that fought each other in World War II. America's and Russia's armed forces have never fought a war against each other; they fought together as allies in two world wars. Their day has come to work together for the sake of both their nations and the world at large.

Notes

1. I am referring here to "Russia" in part because that is the pre-1917 name for the nation that stretched from the Pacific Ocean to the Baltic Sea; in part because the Russian Republic, either by itself or in combination with a few other former Soviet republics, will be the most important successor state of the USSR.
2. In 1954, Dulles conveyed to President Eisenhower the thought that even if the United States could break up the Soviet control over Eastern Europe and China, "this in itself would not actually touch the heart of the problem: Soviet Atomic plenty." Secretary of State Dulles mused that the only real solution might be "nuclear abolition." John Lewis Gaddis, "The Unexpected John Foster Dulles" in *John Foster Dulles and the Diplomacy of the Cold War*, Richard H. Immerman, ed. (Princeton: Princeton University Press, 1990), p. 55.
3. This problem has already raised its ugly head during the Gulf War. See McGeorge Bundy, "Nuclear Weapons and the Gulf," *Foreign Affairs* (Fall 1991).

2

Russia in Search of Itself

Sergei Stankevich*

We must discuss the foreign policy of Russia at a time when the country has yet to recognize itself as a state and to shape the attributes of statehood—an army for instance. It does not have borders fixed in accordance with the practice of international law, does not have a sensible and formulated system of national interests on which foreign policy might be built, and has not recognized its particular historical mission.

With us, foreign policy does not emanate from the precepts and priorities of evolved statehood. On the contrary, foreign policy practice, frequently based on search, analogies, and intuition, is helping Russia become Russia. Dealings with the surrounding world are helping shape Russian statehood and helping Russia recognize its interests.

Categorical assertions to the effect that Russia is required to renounce messianism immediately have been heard increasingly often of late. If what is meant by this is a renunciation of the global mentorship of the communist rulers who stinted on neither the money nor the lives of others for the sake of the universal establishment of the totalitarian Utopia, there is no reason to argue with this proposition. But what if we should rush to the other extreme, going so far in our denial of messianism as to jettison the similar sounding, but not identical, concept of mission?

A policy that is built on interests alone is highly vulnerable, and in Russia, in my view, it would be simply disastrous. Aside from interests, a mission—not degenerating into messianism, of course—is needed. It is said that pragmatism

*Sergei Stankevich was state counsellor of the Russian Federation for Policy Issues and an advisor to President Boris Yeltsin. This essay was adapted from "A State in Search of Itself: Notes on Russian Foreign Policy," published in Moscow's *Nezavisimaya Gazeta* (March 28, 1992). This essay first appeared in *The National Interest*, no. 28 (Summer 1992).

should be the leading principle, virtually, of our foreign policy. This assertion is in need of particular reservations and limitations. Pragmatism not balanced by healthy idealism would with us, alas, most likely degenerate into extremes and cynicism. Russia's foreign policy must provide for goals and tasks elevated above opportunistic pragmatism.

Russia's mission in the world, from my viewpoint, is to initiate and support a multilateral dialogue of cultures, civilizations, and states. Russia the conciliator, Russia connecting, Russia combining. A charitable state, tolerant and open within the limits drawn by law and good will, but formidable beyond these limits. A country imbibing West and East, North and South, unique and exclusively capable, perhaps, of the harmonious combination of many different principles, of a historic symphony. Such is my vision of Russia in a renewed world.

This is a perfectly natural role for it, since Russia is in itself, by nature, dualistic. It has always bifurcated and acted as an opponent to itself in order subsequently, negotiating a chain of ordeals, to reach an accord with itself. It is pointless to complain about the nature of this historical destiny. It is very important for everyone who ventures to speak on Russia's behalf to listen closely to the voice of its essence.

Frankly, I would greatly regret it if some Russian version of the strictly rational school of foreign policy were to monopolize Russia's foreign policy. At the same time, were a foreign policy school to emerge combining rationalism and the pragmatic principle on the one hand and, on the other, our innate idealism and sense of Russian mission, I would be prepared to associate myself with such a school immediately. I am not talking about some speculative notions or emotional preferences.

Russia should seriously reconsider its role in the United Nations and use its seat on the Security Council for the realization of its mission, for acquisition of a new status. It would make sense, evidently, having appreciably reduced the quantitative presence of Russia's representatives in the UN structure, to pay considerable attention to the qualitative aspect and to laying claim to specific offices which would help Russia realize precisely its inherent mission. The European organizations of the United Nations, and also the strengthening of the Conference on Security and Cooperation in Europe (CSCE) mechanism, merit special attention. Russia's new role in these structures would help it not only establish itself as a leading European power but also compensate for its present geographical distance from the center of European international life.

As I see it, two lines, which may conditionally be designated Atlanticism and Eurasianism, have emerged in our foreign policy practice of late. Atlanticism gravitates toward the following set of ideas and symbols: to become European, to become a part of the world economy in rapid and organized fashion, to become the eighth member of "the Seven," and to put particular emphasis on Germany and the United States as the two dominant members of the Atlantic Alliance. This is rational, pragmatic, and natural. There is credit, aid, and advanced technology there.

Its opposite trend—Eurasianism—is not as yet as clearly expressed as Atlanticism, but it is already knocking on the door of the tall building on Smolenskaya (Moscow's equivalent of Foggy Bottom or Quai d'Orsay).

At the close of the twentieth century, attempting to resuscitate the idea of Russia's reorientation toward the East and to counteract Russia's Europeanization in its extreme forms would obviously be just as pointless and unproductive as hastily, pulling the Atlantic dinner jacket and bow tie onto Russia's broad shoulders. It is obvious that it is necessary to seek a new balance of Western and Eastern orientations characteristic of the present Russia and our times. Initially, in fact, it will most likely be necessary to pay special attention to a strengthening of our positions in the East, straightening the manifest distortion permitted by the creators of the "common European home" concept. There is no way that the present Russia can escape a combination of old and new realities. The fact is that we are now separated from Europe by a whole chain of independent states. We have become further removed from it geographically and geopolitically, which will inevitably entail quite an appreciable redistribution of our resources, our options, our ties, and our interests in favor of Asia, of the eastern direction. In addition, the development of the domestic political situation, which will inevitably be reflected in foreign policy, is pushing us in this direction also.

There will be a most difficult search for accord, mutual understanding, and cooperation with the Turkic and Muslim components, which have performed a tremendous role in the history of Russia. Our state emerged and grew strong as a unique historical and cultural amalgam of Slav and Turkic, Orthodox and Muslim components. Relations between them currently are on the brink of a fateful conflict. Avoiding this conflict and finding harmony here, a synthesis that will allow Russia once again to feel itself the combining, connecting conciliator, is of categorical importance.

The shaping on and around the territory of the collapsed Union of an appreciably different configuration of strategic interests is confronting Russia with a new historical challenge. We are seeing how the influence of the Muslim world, both geographically close to us and further removed, on our domestic political situation is growing, how zones of influence in the territories of contiguous Asian republics and in the territory of Russia are gradually emerging, and how an arc of crisis (to use the well-known image of the 1970s) from the Transcaucasus through North Caucasus toward the Volga region is progressively taking shape.

Ignoring all this is impossible. Not to understand which dominant powers of the Near and Middle East (Turkey, Iran, Saudi Arabia) are displaying a heightened interest in the arc of crisis is also impossible. We should be preparing to respond purposefully and consistently to the emerging, intricate knot of counter-interests and influences. It is possible, evidently, to talk about a revival of the "Eastern question" in Russia's foreign policy in something close to the classical sense. But we have as yet, alas, no conceptualizers capable of formulating the Eastern question at the modem level, nor are there practical men capable of offering effective answers.

The preservation and gradual strengthening of the special relationship with the states of the Commonwealth of Independent States (CIS)—permeable borders, close economic and cultural ties, allied relations in the military and political spheres—correspond to Russia's long-term strategic interests. But there are distinct limits to the realization of this tendency.

In order to broaden its field of political action as much as possible, Russia must quickly become self-sufficient—that is, Russia must provide itself with all vitally important means and resources from internal sources, or from several independent sources both within and outside the framework of the CIS.

In increasing the volume of treaty relations with its CIS partners, Russia should approach them in differentiated fashion. It will inevitably be necessary to distinguish between those which use the CIS merely as a means of dividing up the Union inheritance prior to a "definitive" parting, and those for whom the Commonwealth is a fundamental historical choice. Concessions to the first in the name, allegedly, of preserving the CIS are pointless and dangerous, and nonviolent competition resulting in agreements beneficial to Russia are more appropriate here. The second group of states, on the other hand, has the right to expect the preference accorded to strategic allies.

There is no need for Russia to insist on unanimity in reaching agreements consolidating its relations with its CIS partners. Better that there should be fewer signatures and more precise meaning, clearer consequences, and higher quality in the case of each document.

It is frequently maintained that Russia's concern for the fate of Russians in neighboring states signifies interference in the internal affairs of the independent states. Russia cannot, in my view, agree with this interpretation. The proclamation of independence and its recognition in international law are only the first step on the long path toward the formation of full-fledged statehood. It is the obligation of a new state laying claim to a worthy role in the international community to come to terms in humane and civilized ways with the legacy of the former era, adopting a solicitous attitude toward people and their fate, and cautiously doing away with the most painful contradictions.

Unfortunately, several states that were formerly a part of the USSR have opted for a different path. Nationalist forces, essentially driven by paranoid ideas of historical or national vengeance, have bestirred themselves there. They are exerting one-sided pressure on the authorities. As fragmented minorities, the Russian communities are not in a position to balance out this pressure, and, as a result, they are falling victim in countries like Estonia and Latvia to discriminatory citizenship legislation which is in fact introducing apartheid practices.

Russia does not have the moral right to remain a passive observer of this process. Responding to any discriminatory decision or action with respect to the Russian population and, more broadly, the Russian heritage (graves, monuments, schools, churches, monasteries, museums) should be the first priority of both our embassies in our "near neighbors" and of our Foreign Ministry.

The attitude toward the Russian population and the Russian heritage of this or that state is a most important criterion for Russia in deciding whether to assign the state in question to the category of friend. The entire set of our bilateral relations—from the question of the fate of the army through the economy and finances—cannot, in turn, fail to depend on the outcome of such a process.

Contrary to all the charges of an "imperial syndrome," such a policy has nothing in common with imperialism. On the contrary, it is for Russia a legitimate and natural aspiration to erase conflicts and harmonize relations on the territory of the former USSR. Furthermore, Russia will invariably take the part of the undeservedly insulted and unjustly persecuted.

Unfortunately, insufficient diplomatic assertiveness on the part of Russia in the sphere in question is leading to a distorted perception by some European politicians of what is happening in the states of the former Union.

We cannot, for example, overlook the speeches in Estonia of Madame Lalumiere, secretary general of the Council of Europe. She made common cause, in fact, with the idea of the separation of peoples into indigenous and nonindigenous in this region. This extremely dangerous idea will never be accepted by Russia and is categorically rejected by the Russian government. We cannot permit a division whereby "nonindigenous" peoples are unequal. We consider such an approach unacceptable on both moral and political grounds.

The subject of the defense of the rights of the populace ethnically connected with Russia will inevitably be a very important topic throughout the negotiating process with the states of the former Union. It is inevitable that Russia will endeavor persistently to incorporate the corresponding provisions in international documents of various levels. In my opinion, at least, it is clearly time for Russia to adopt a tougher tone on this issue than has been the case hitherto—without, naturally, overstepping the bounds of absolutely necessary restraint but, for all that, displaying far greater insistence. For the appeals which have been made thus far have not been heard.

Stability is a priority, a very important value, which must be present in Russia's foreign policy. I would add to this value another: balance, which at the same time is an important condition of stability. Balance both along East-West lines, which we have already mentioned, and along North-South lines. There are gigantic, as yet unutilized, possibilities here. A rapid move into the markets and full-fledged integration into the system of economic relations of such states as the United States, Japan, and the economically developed states of Europe are highly problematical. We are obviously assigned here, for many years to come, at best the role of junior partner who should not be admitted to the inner circle.

At the same time, on the other hand, there are far broader and qualitatively better opportunities connected with other states, other countries of, relatively speaking, the second echelon, which are at a historical frontier similar to ours—that is, at the frontier of historical breakthrough. These are the countries lying to the south of our traditional partners: in Latin America, Mexico, Brazil, Chile, and Argentina; in Africa, South Africa; further in the direction of Europe, Greece; then Turkey; in Asia, India, China, and the Southeast Asia countries.

These states are attempting to accomplish historical tasks similar to ours: integration into the world economy without losing their identity and defending their own interests; transition to a new technology structure; implementation of comprehensive reforms encompassing both industry and agriculture; acquisition of financial, food, and other self-sufficiencies.

Interaction with them, use of the potential available to both parties, movement into their markets, and the use of the potential of our market—these are the opportunities which must not be overlooked. They have thus far, for incomprehensible reasons, remained on the periphery of our foreign policy activity.

The world is changing rapidly, and new intersections of interests and new regional formations with an independent orientation are emerging. All this is affording Russia opportunities to obtain propitious geopolitical positions in key regions, and to rank, in time, among the world leaders.

3

Four Comments on Sergei Stankevich's "Russia in Search of Itself"

*Leon Aron, Francis Fukuyama, Jim Hoagland and Bruce D. Porter**

Leon Aron:

When Italy, unified at last, acquired Rome as its capital in 1870, the great German historian Theodor Mommsen reportedly asked an Italian acquaintance: "What do you intend to do in Rome? You cannot be in Rome without having cosmopolitan projects." Few serious students of Russia ever believed that what seemed like a replay of America's Vietnam syndrome—which, having begun to set in under Gorbachev at the time of the Soviet withdrawal from Afghanistan, intensified in the last two years of the Soviet collapse—would last forever. Stankevich's article confirms the veracity of Mommsen's axiom: In Moscow, as in Rome a hundred years ago, the "cosmopolitan projects" are beginning to stir again under the still thick and heavy crust of isolationism and inward-directedness which formed during the years of disintegration.

Foreign policy is not Stankevich's portfolio: In Yeltsin's cabinet he is in charge of "social organizations" and "political questions." The absence of a formal responsibility for foreign affairs—which, together with national security, are firmly in the hands of State Secretary Gennady Burbulis—liberates Stankevich from circumspection and accounts for the very useful candor of this piece.

---

*At the time these responses were penned, Leon Aron was a resident scholar at the American Enterprise Institute; Francis Fukuyama was a resident consultant at the RAND Corporation in Washington, DC; Jim Hoagland was associate editor and chief foreign correspondent of the *Washington Post*; and Bruce D. Porter was the Bradley Research Associate at the Olin Institute for Strategic Studies, Harvard University. This symposium first appeared in *The National Interest,* no. 28 (Summer 1992).

Regardless of whether he succeeds, Yeltsin's uniqueness and his place in Russian history are secured by his attempt at a massive revision of Russia's national values and priorities. Among several core notions tackled by the Russian president, two are relevant here. First, Yeltsin set out to build a "normal" bourgeois state, a state like any other, whose national security and foreign policies are shaped by national interests, not by national ideology. Yeltsin's historic breakthrough is not so much in de-communization as in the de-ideologization of Russian foreign policy.

Yeltsin's other major revision concerns the comparative weight of domestic and foreign policy considerations in policy-making. For four centuries, the well-being and rights of the Russian citizenry, as well as most of Russia's economic priorities, were defined by, and largely sacrificed to, national security strategy. A domestic political context for Russian foreign policy was virtually nonexistent. Yeltsin is the first Russian ruler to de-link Russian nation-building and foreign expansion and to reverse the traditional causality by attempting to root Russian national security in domestic order.

Both of Yeltsin's revisions are questioned by Stankevich. De-ideologization is found wanting when Stankevich insists on instilling Russian foreign policy with a "mission" and strikes at the "degeneration" and "cynicism" of "opportunistic pragmatism." The primacy of Russia's domestic civilian concerns over those of national security is implicitly challenged by the state counsellor when he, like Russian rulers from Ivan the Terrible through Stalin, claims that national security ("the surrounding world") is helping shape Russian statehood, and, in fact, constitutes the very core Russian national interest.

The operational specifics of the article are not on a par with the conceptual charge of the first few paragraphs. What Stankevich propounds by way of concrete action is nebulous and unoriginal, although largely well meaning. The Slavophile doctrine of Russia's "special" destiny as a bridge or, in the poet Alexander Blok's word, a "shield" between East and West; the imperative of a healthy balance between "Eurasianism" and "Atlanticism" in Russia's emerging foreign policy; the "Eastern," or Muslim, "question" in Russia's past, present, and future; and finally the appeal for self-interested realpolitik in relations with the members of the CIS—all have been bandied about in Russian mass and high-brow media for months.

Perhaps the only noteworthy feature here is the length to which Stankevich goes to express his concern for Russian minorities in the new post-Soviet states. From the pro-Union Communist internationalist Viktor Alksnis, to the proto-fascist Vladimir Zhirinovsky, to Yeltsin's neo-nationalist Vice President Alexander Rutskoy, this legitimate issue has been exploited for political profit by forces largely outside the democratic camp. Devoting almost one-third of the article to Russian *pieds-noirs* is more than a nod to the nationalist right; it is a deep bow. We shall see if it indicates a shift in Stankevich's broader political position—or indeed in that of the Yeltsin administration in general.

Be that as it may, the import of Stankevich's article is not in the operational detail but in the firm, albeit understated, insistence on a set of national values distinct from those advocated by Yeltsin so far. Future historians may well trace to this piece the beginning of the modification of, if not indeed a retreat from, Yeltsin's "rational" revolution in national security and foreign strategy. It may turn out to be the point at which Stankevich's "historic symphony" of the Russian tradition began to compete with the pragmatic jazz of the last ten months of Russian foreign and national security policy, and "historic destiny" began to challenge "rationalism."

This recombination is, of course, inevitable: both history and geostrategy are bound to pull the Russian pendulum away from extreme isolationism. We can only hope that the final product will be benign for Russia and the world.

Francis Fukuyama:

By far, the most significant aspect of Stankevich's piece in *Nezavisimaya Gazeta* is the way in which he talks about the centrality of the need for Russia to protect the rights of ethnic Russians in the other successor states of the Soviet Union, something that has several very immediate and rather troubling consequences. By contrast, the essay's other themes—the need for a new messianism vaguely connected with the UN, the need to reorient toward the Islamic world, collaboration with other "middle-rank" powers—are all fairly nebulous and of uncertain import.

That the protection of Russians outside Russia should be a central issue for Moscow's foreign policy is completely unobjectionable. There are currently some twenty-five million of them, constituting 20 percent of the population of Ukraine and 40 percent of Kazakhstan. Whatever the historical conditions under which these Russians got there, they may well be subject to discrimination and worse in the turbulent times ahead. It would be irresponsible for any Russian government—and for Yeltsin and the "democrats," suicidal—to ignore their interests. The United States and other Western countries are hardly in a position to lecture Russia about "interference" in the "internal affairs" of its neighbors on these grounds, given the fact that we justified invading Grenada ostensibly to protect a handful of U.S. medical students and Panama because the wife of an American officer was sexually accosted.

On the other hand, Russia, just like Germany after 1945, has an imperialist legacy which it cannot simply wish away. It would be impossible for Ukraine, Estonia, or any of the other successor states *not* to see Russian defense of Russians on their territory as an excuse for reassertion of imperial control. Because of such historical memories, the post-1945 Federal Republic has had to tread lightly in defense of the interests of ethnic Germans in Central Europe, an issue that it was spared in many cases only because of the wholesale expulsion of Germans from Poland, Czechoslovakia, etc. after the war. Stankevich seems quite blind to this aspect of the problem. Indeed, he borrows certain phrases from the Russian nationalists, with whom he is at total odds in other respects, as when he asserts that Russia "will invariably take the part of the undeservedly insulted and unjustly persecuted." Not so fast, bro—your neighbors (and the international community) will not see this as an instance of spontaneous altruism.

This will all come to a head sooner than we would like in the Crimea. If the referendum promoted by the Crimean parliament and its Moscow-based backers yields a majority in favor of independence, Stankevich and most of his fellow "democrats" will have to line up in support of it. As far as I can tell, there is scarcely anyone in the democratic camp (save perhaps Mrs. Bonner or Yuri Afanaseyev) who would oppose it, and very many on the nationalist right who would promote it enthusiastically. For their part, even the most reasonable Ukrainians have very little appreciation of the Russians' emotional attachment to Crimea, and virtually no one in Kiev would find independence acceptable. The stage is therefore set for a deadly confrontation that could easily derail the process of democratization in both countries.

Jim Hoagland:

The world turned upside down: that is what Sergei Stankevich describes in his provocative, at times astonishing essay. Without "the precepts and priorities of evolved statehood," Russia must use foreign policy as a tool to "become Russia," he writes. By figuring out how it deals with its neighbors (most of them ex-subjects) and other countries, Russia will figure out what it is.

Stankevich comes as close as a senior official can to acknowledging that his country is caught up in a giant identity crisis for which his government has no clear remedy. The confusion that besets Russia's attempts to provide geographic, ethnic, and national definitions for the old/new entity unearthed by the Soviet collapse gleams through "Russia in Search of Itself."

But there are also, I suspect, immediate concerns at stake. The existence of the essay and the arguments it uses are evidence of a serious debate in the upper reaches of the Yeltsin government about Moscow's relations with the other former Soviet republics in the Commonwealth of Independent States. The piece makes it clear that an incipient power struggle is underway in Moscow.

Stankevich takes direct aim at those in Yeltsin's entourage who would turn their back on Russia's imperial past and former imperial nature to construct a modem, post-colonial, outward-looking Russia. This camp is led by Deputy Prime Minister Yegor Gaidar, Yeltsin's economic specialist, and Foreign Minister Andrei Kozyrev, who made his career in the International Organizations department of the Soviet Foreign Ministry before he broke with the Gorbachev team and joined Yeltsin early on.

Although not named, these two policy technicians are the obvious targets of Stankevich's accusation that Russia's "insufficient diplomatic assertiveness" is undermining and even endangering the Russian populations stranded in other republics. Stankevich comes down in the camp of his fellow politicians who emphasize Russian nationalism and see the Baltic nations and Ukraine as the sources of what Stankevich calls here "nationalist forces essentially driven by paranoid ideas of historical or national vengeance."

Yeltsin has not committed himself in this debate. It is significant that he has done nothing to undercut Gaidar or Kozyrev in their dealings with the other former republics. I can only conclude that Yeltsin shares their view of imperial fatigue as the cause of Russia's current disaster: But I also have to conclude that Yeltsin feels the argument is far from being settled and intends to keep his options open.

Stankevich's fluent English and detailed knowledge of the American political system make him a favorite of American journalists, and give him the air of being the most modern of Russian politicians. But, surprisingly, he adopts in this essay written for a domestic audience a traditional view of his land, arguing that Russia must be a "combining connecting conciliator" between Europe and Asia, "a unique historical and cultural amalgam of Slav and Turkic, Orthodox and Muslim components."

To carry out this civilizing mission, as the French would have put it, to protect Russian minorities and "heritage" on others' soil, to "respond purposefully and consistently to the emerging, intricate knot of counterinterests and influences" in the Middle East—this is a tall order.

Stankevich softens the implications of his message by pointing to the need for restraint and reason. But it is difficult to see how he could accomplish the goals he describes as essential without resorting to methods used by both czar and commissar—without, that is, trying to edge back toward an imperial past that is beyond reach today. It is puzzling that he has written this essay, this way. More puzzling, and more troublesome, is the fact that someone as keen as Stankevich thinks there is an important constituency for this view in Russia today.

Bruce D. Porter:

Sergei Stankevich disavows messianism, yet he broaches a mission for Russia, one vaguely reminiscent of the age-old vision of Moscow as the Third Rome: "A country imbibing West and East, North and South, unique and exclusively capable, perhaps, of the harmonious combination of many different principles, of a historic symphony." A country that will once again feel itself the combining, connecting conciliator. Huh? Play that again, Sergei. Russia the conciliator? Russia the connecting and combining? This is neither idealism, nor a plausible statement of a Russian national mission. It is sheer fantasy and bad history to boot. The only connecting and combining the Russian state has done for centuries has been military conquest and annexation. A country steeped for nearly a millennium in self-isolation, a people with only the most limited knowledge of the outside world, a culture still struggling to rid itself of xenophobia—this is hardly a country that can play the role of world conciliator and harmonizer. It is admirable that Russia finally is striving to shed itself of communist messianism so as to enter the civilized world. That it should pretend to become the connector and harmonizer of the different parts of that world is ludicrous.

If Russia is a state in search of itself, then the search should begin at home, not abroad. Sergei Stankevich argues that only a sense of global mission can help Russia find its national identity. That has been the problem throughout Russian history—striving to find an identity by great deeds on the world stage, rather than by internal healing and renewal.' The Russian state has never represented Russian society. The events of the past five years have narrowed the gulf between state and society, but have not closed it. Boris Yeltsin may be the first Russian leader elected in a millennium, but even now his government rules by decree and the links between it and the people are weak, informal, and tenuous.

Nowhere in Stankevich's essay does he speak of democracy, representative government, constitutionalism, or popular will. Human rights for him are an Estonian issue. Perhaps he regards democracy as a purely domestic affair, yet its absence has been a source of Russian foreign expansionism for centuries. How ironic, yet how telling, that an essay that begins by talking of Russia as the conciliator should end with a diatribe about how it must protect the interests of Russians throughout the CIS, make no concessions to its neighbors, and adopt "a tougher tone. . .than has been the case hitherto."

Stankevich argues that pragmatism not balanced by healthy idealism may degenerate into extreme behavior and cynicism. To the contrary, it is idealism that has ever degenerated into extremism in Russian history. If the Russian people have a weakness, it is a passion for absolutes. Pragmatism has never been their undoing; its absence in the realm of politics has ruined them. Russia indeed has much that it can offer the outside world, but the offering will not be accomplished by the Russian state. It will not come from the Russian political leadership, foreign ministry, or diplomatic corps. Boris Yeltsin will not be the leader of the Russian Magi. He and his government will contribute quite enough to the world by concentrating on the reconstruction of their ravaged country and by acting with responsibility and prudence on the world stage. Russia's real gifts to the world will not be political or diplomatic in nature. They will be cultural, literary, scientific, and intellectual. In these spheres, the Russians are quite possibly the most gifted and talented people on the face of the earth. They have already immeasurably enriched our world with their intellectual and cultural contributions, largely produced in the face of state oppression and persecution.

Even now, Russian citizens still cannot travel freely abroad without an invitation; their channels for expressing their political will or redressing their grievances are primitive; they are condemned to spend their best energies in scavenging for food and consumer goods in an economy still reeling from the inanities of Bolshevist economics. Only when these conditions cease and a genuine liberal democracy is established will the Russians finally be free. The resulting release of the energies, creativity, and talents of a great people will be the real Russian Revolution. Sergei Stankevich's advice to his country no doubt reflects the best of intentions, but he should recall the wisdom of the biblical proverb: Physician, heal thyself.

4

Why Russia Should Join NATO: From Containment to Concert

*Coral Bell**

The shape of the post-Cold War world is beginning to glimmer hazily through the dust of the Gulf crisis. Its outlines suggest some surprising possibilities: diplomatic options that would have seemed unthinkable even a year ago. But then surprise has been the diplomatic order of the day for quite some time now.

For most of the Cold War years, mainstream Western strategists by and large took it as a semi-permanent state of affairs. The central Western diplomatic concept, "containment," had presented the image of a dam constructed to hold back an unremitting permanent pressure. And though the diplomat who proposed that strategy, George Kennan, had originally suggested that it might, after fifteen years or so, result in "the mellowing or the breakup of Soviet power," he did not lay much stress on that element of his analysis. Moreover, since after fifteen years (in 1961–62), the Cold War was just moving into its most dangerous period, with the building of the Berlin Wall in 1961 and the Cuban Missile Crisis in 1962, the original Kennan prophecy of an eventual win for the West was rather shrugged off and discounted. The strategic objectives were tacitly assumed by "insiders" to be the avoidance both of nuclear war and of Western defeat without war: the status quo was expected to be undisturbed save for routing hostilities round the peripheries of the rival power-spheres, in the "grey areas." Mainstream strategic ambitions were thus modest enough, though there were always dissentient voices on the Right calling for more ambitious Western objectives like "rollback"; and dissentient voices on the Left saying that the whole Western strategic enterprise of the Cold War was

*Coral Bell is a senior research fellow at Australian National University, Canberra. This essay first appeared in *The National Interest*, no. 22 (Winter 1990/91).

a mistake, or a crime, or a disaster, or all three. On the balance of evidence, it was a necessity, as well as a success.

What we now see, of course, is rollback, not containment: Soviet political power bowing out of Eastern Europe; Soviet diplomatic and ideological influence being shrugged off in most of the Third World; Soviet troops making their exit from the eastern Lander of the reunited Germany; and, astonishingly, the literal "breakup" as well as the "mellowing" of Soviet power. The Soviet empire, which was the old czarist empire considerably swollen in size and held together by terror and ideology, seems at present to be following the other European empires into history, but by a much faster route. It is the center, Russia itself, which "wants out" of the system as much as the potential peripheral new sovereignties—contrary to what the British, French, Dutch, and Belgian empires found in their own paths to dissolution.

The only direct parallel for the recent Russian transformation of imperial assumptions is that with Portugal in 1974. There, a left-wing revolution replaced the previous political elite, so that what had been a stubborn, bloody-handed determination to hang on to colonial possessions was transformed in a few weeks into an unseemly haste in getting rid of them. Similarly, the current revulsion of opinion against the Soviet ideology seems to have produced a profound and candid eagerness to get rid of all the old regime's works, including its imperial system. Thus one can expect the dissolution process to be much faster than the twenty-five years or so of the British or French imperial dismantlings. (Not that the Portuguese example is much of a recommendation for haste: two of the colonial territories, Angola and Mozambique, fell into prolonged civil wars; a third, East Timor, was swallowed by a neighbor, Indonesia; and a fourth, Guinea-Bissau, by Marxist darkness.)

However, to revert to the contemporary world where, as the West German chancellor said last July, "the future is beginning," prospects by the middle of the decade seem to be of a new central balance of power whose most cryptic member may be Russia, rather than the Soviet Union. Whether as a sovereign entity it proves to be larger or smaller than its present size, Russia will still be a potent as well as longstanding member of the central balance, having been part of it ever since the concept was defined in sixteenth-century Europe. Russia thus will be an experienced player in the game of nations, whose former traditions were by no means entirely lost in the seventy years or so of the Soviet period, and still very much the largest of the European powers in population and resources. It will remain the most formidable strategically too, since even assuming an improbable level of success for START and the other arms negotiations, Russia will probably still have in stock at least 6,000 nuclear warheads on long-range systems, a very large navy, and the other strategic appurtenances of the superpower it recently was. On the other hand, for quite a while it seems likely to be the most economically disorganized and necessitous of the major powers: at least for this decade and possibly much longer.

The social problems that more than seventy years of a command economy and authoritarian politics have engendered are not going to be cured rapidly.

A profound disparity already has defined itself between the strategic rank-order of the major powers and their economic rank-order. The strategic hierarchy for a six-power central balance would still read: the United States, Russia (or the Soviet Union), the European Community (or European Confederation), China, India, and Japan. The economic hierarchy would read: the European Community or Confederation (which by mid-decade may be at least 30 percent larger than the United States), the United States, Japan (by then about 70 percent the size of the U.S.), then possibly China, with India and the Soviet Union bringing up the rear.

Being edged out of the top place in economic clout may be mildly galling for some Americans, but it already has its compensations. For instance, if there is any "Marshall Plan" for Eastern Europe, including Russia, it is the Western Europeans whose surpluses should logically finance it. Similarly, if some analogous project emerges for China, Japanese surpluses are the obvious source. A diminution of American burdens may mean a dilution of American diplomatic ascendancy, but that change is inherent, in any case, in the mutation from bilateral to multilateral balance. The change means that the paramountcy of both the Soviet Union and the United States must be reduced in the new, looser, somewhat more egalitarian diplomatic relationship. The State Department has already had a taste of that change, finding itself distinctly relegated to a "back seat" on the vital deal between Gorbachev and Kohl over a reunited Germany's place in NATO. Economically, rather the same sort of thing happened vis-à-vis Japan at the G-7 meeting in Houston. The Bush policy-makers, especially James Baker, seem to have gulped a bit, but otherwise made no audible fuss. (Of course, it is not Washington that is most sensitive to the possibility that the new Europe may prove to be Germany writ large. That fear roosts in the other European capitals—especially London, as was indicated in the brouhaha over Nicholas Ridley's *Spectator* interview and his forced departure from the Thatcher government. The apprehensions so tactlessly revealed in that incident are very widespread beneath the surface in much of Europe, especially among people over fifty who remember World War II.)

The Balance Then and Now

Yet the balance of *forces* has so far changed much less than the balance of power, which seems rather a reversal of the usual historical sequence. The difference is that the balance of power starts with the balance of forces (existing military hardware, personnel, and deployments) but adds to that relatively straightforward summation several less obvious and less immediate factors: economic, political, ethnic, diplomatic, and ideological. And it is in that group of factors that the recent changes have been so favorable to the West. On the straight "bean count" of weapon systems, some strategic analysts would in fact argue that recent change has been in favor of Moscow. Of course, major weapon systems have a ten-year "lead time," so what is coming off the production lines in the Soviet Union these days is the fruit of decisions made in the Brezhnev era. But while this situation persists, a certain caution about arms cuts and such remains necessary.

Because the transformations in Europe have been so swift, so dramatic, and so benign, most analysis has concentrated on them. But in the world outside Europe (whose problems tend to be airily relegated to second-rate status by NATO policy-makers, despite their having produced all the shooting wars of the Cold War period, and possibly the first of the post-Cold War period), the changes in the central balance and the decline of Russian influence are producing the largest reshuffle in power relationships since the end of the Western colonial empires. Not all these changes are welcome to local players.

In effect, the reduction in central balance tensions has reduced the incentives for both the Soviet Union (or Russia) and the United States to recruit for, or even maintain, their respective groups of strategic "fellow travelers." They are able now to make new cost-benefit analyses of their overall diplomatic relationships, with results in many cases highly disconcerting to the minor powers concerned, whether aligned or non-aligned. There is already quite a group of governments with some reason to be nostalgic for the straightforward days of the Cold War, and there will be more.

All that might have been written before the Gulf crisis. The latest surprise, from world reaction to that ambitious desperado, Saddam Hussein, is the revived possibility of a global concert of powers. I say revived rather than newly arisen, because if one reverts historically to the year before the opening of the Cold War (to 1945 and the creation of the United Nations) that was then still the expectation of the time. The Security Council was designed almost explicitly as a five-power concert, complete with veto power for each of the permanent members. It hardly ever worked in the subsequent forty- five years, of course, because it supposed a level of common assumptions and objectives among the central balance powers that was quite incompatible with the policies of Stalin and his successors. Until the time of Gorbachev and Yeltsin, that is.

In the Gulf crisis, the concert of powers has reappeared, lightly disguised as the United Nations, and speaking the language of UN resolutions and such. There is nothing to be said against that in present circumstances, but it may prove unwieldy and inconvenient as a basis for crisis management in the future, as it has been in the past. In the one parallel case, Korea, the UN aspect of the operation wore very thin quite rapidly. But there is already available some sturdier and more manageable diplomatic scaffolding than the UN for a workable concert of powers. And it exists in a diplomatic structure already conscious of a need for some redefinition of purposes for the post-Cold War period: NATO.

That organization was, from 1949 to 1989, in effect the status quo alliance of the old bilateral balance of power. In that function it had a truly notable success. Sun Tzu, the great Chinese strategist of the third century B.C., reflects that the truly great successful commander is the one who wins the war without actually having to fight the battles. NATO certainly won its war—the Cold War—without having, as an alliance, to fight any of the battles, though individual members of NATO—the United States, Britain, France, Turkey—did fight battles, in Korea and Vietnam and the Falklands and Suez. The same NATO powers, unlike some of their alliance brethren, have been to the fore militarily and diplomatically in the Gulf conflict. Much is to be attributed to the persistence of national traditions in alliance relationships.

Actually NATO has never worked very well in what are called, in the alliance's jargon, "out-of-area issues": that is, conflicts arising beyond the treaty area. That has not been surprising, since the agreement was designed and drafted in 1948-49 to meet the one overwhelming diplomatic and military assumed threat of those years—the possible expansion of Soviet power westward in Europe. But the point is important when we consider the nature and functions of a potential "NATO Mark II," so I will return to it.

As the original organization was the status quo alliance of the original bilateral balance of power, "NATO Mark II" would be the status quo alliance of the emerging multilateral balance. Its basic function would be the same: what would change is the context in which it would operate. And that is already happening, so going along with it is a kind of recognition of the necessities of history.

At this point we need to consider the difference between a balance of power and a concert of powers. A balance of power will change in response to impersonal historical factors like rates of economic development, demographic growth or decline, technology and geopolitics, the flowering and withering of ideologies. All those factors, especially the economic and ideological ones, helped along the mutation from the original balance of 1949 to the emerging multilateral balance of 1989. By contrast, constructing a multilateral concert of powers, based on the pattern of power distribution provided by history, requires something more. It requires bold and sometimes radical or imaginative choices on the part of the decision-makers of the time.

That is why the Gulf crisis seems to me a true catalyst in international politics, especially in the evolving relationship of the central balance powers, speeding up changes in a larger world in which Saddam Hussein himself will have, let us hope, only a brief and marginal role.

The two main decisions that I point to as evidence of this are, first, Bush's decision to invite the collaboration of the policy-makers in Moscow in resolving the Gulf crisis; and second, Gorbachev's decision to accept that bid. Though the declaratory policies of both governments have been put into UN language, and the UN is a useful source of legitimation, especially for minor powers, both those basic decisions have less to do with the UN than with a sort of "grandmother's steps" movement toward a power concert.

In their respective ways, they are equally bold departures from earlier policies. Perhaps this is more consciously the case for the Russians, since the decision meant abandoning what had previously been classed as a useful ally, Iraq, and firmly disappointing the earlier expectations of various would-be revolutionary challengers to the status quo, like the Palestinians. Of course that is pretty much in line with various other Gorbachev policy changes in the Third World, from Angola to Nicaragua and Vietnam. But in this case it has been more explicitly geared to relations with the United States. In fact Gorbachev's aide, Yevgeny Primakov, when departing on his diplomatic mission to the Gulf, said, in effect, that the area was a sort of laboratory for an experiment in collaboration with the United States.

The American departure from previous policy was almost as bold. After all, the United States has devoted itself pretty assiduously over the past two or three decades to keeping Soviet power out of the Middle East and the Gulf, not only as a gesture to Israel (though that has been very important politically) but because of the consciousness that Gulf oil was even more vital to its Japanese and European allies than to its own economy. For geographic reasons, it long seemed likely that if push should come to shove in the Gulf, the Russians would always be able to "get there fastest with the mostest," rather than the Americans. But the changes in the Soviet sphere are modifying even that apparent geographic advantage. For if the "shrinkage" of Russian control and responsibility back toward Russia itself continues, Central Asia will be one of the most affected areas. In an extreme case, rather unpredictable local leaders like those of the Azerbaijanis might have more influence than those in Moscow on conditions near the oil fields. As with Britain in 1907, there might come a time when the Russians will seem like even more useful allies in the Gulf.

A cynical old NATO joke (often attributed to Lord Ismay) maintains that the organization was put together to keep the Russians out, the Americans in, and the Germans down. That has been one of those many truths spoken in jest. The necessity of a permanent tie binding the United States to Europe, more surely than the uncertain commitments of the UN, was seen as a vital part of the reinforcement of deterrence with formal obligations, and with actual troop deployments—the American "trip-wire." Apprehensions about the future of German power were far stronger, and voiced far more freely, when West Germany was being recruited to NATO back in 1954—55, than they have been recently. So the American presence in NATO was in those days seen almost as much as an offset to potential future German power as to existing Soviet capacities.

However, that arriére-pensée about Germany has been much modified over the decades, as NATO has developed the functions of a "security community" to add to those of a military coalition against a nominated adversary. A security community is defined as a group of nations between whom war has been tacitly ruled out as a means of settling disputes. It has much in common with a security blanket, in that it both restrains those who are covered by it in their relations with each other, and reassures them in their relations with the outside world. That result can be achieved even when there is a long historic tradition of enmity, as between Greece and Turkey, who might have been at each other's throats many times in the past few decades were it not that both governments have been conscious of the advantages of NATO membership and the risk of its loss.

Better In than Out

The further extension of that existing Western security community offers the most promising option for NATO if that organization is to avoid obsolescence. It could be done by one quite simple though radical step: the offer of membership to Russia and other major members of the now-defunct Warsaw Pact. If an adversarial relationship with historic roots as deep as those between Greece and Turkey can be restrained by alliance membership, then why not those between Germany and Poland, even Germany and Russia? For that matter, the adversarial relationship between France and Germany has a good deal of history to it, and has been even more completely overlaid by a newer consciousness of a common interest in stability. Most of the Western European members of NATO are also, of course, members of an economic community, but the security relationships came first: 1948-49 for the foundation of NATO, 1957-58 for the Common Market. If the potential gains for stability in what has been historically the very unstable zone of Mitteleuropa (the smaller sovereignties wedged between German and Russian power) it would be more than ample compensation for whatever is lost by such an enlargement of membership.

Actually, the idea is not as new as it may seem. Molotov, Stalin's foreign minister before Gromyko, proposed it from time to time back in the 1950s. The Western powers used to brush it off as just the minister's little joke. Quite rightly, because at that time the challenge to the existing world order did come from the Soviet Union, and NATO was firmly and candidly intent on signaling that it was prepared to resist that challenge, by battle if necessary; after 1954, explicitly by nuclear battle if necessary. And battle did seem possible, or on occasions even probable, through almost four decades.

Not any more, however. In fact, challenges to the world order seem unlikely to come from any of the central balance powers for the immediate future, since all six of them have a lot to lose from global instability. Unfortunately that does not mean a world of peace and harmony, since there are likely to be plenty of challenges from outside the central balance, from regimes and decision-makers with large ambitions or dogmas or theories, and less to lose: new Saddam Husseins, new Ayatollahs, even new Pol Pots. I will return to those issues presently. First, it is necessary to make a case for the proposed expansion of NATO, in terms of the future diplomatic and strategic roles of Russia, Germany, and the United States.

My starting point is the present Russian security elite, and the sequence of traumas it has recently experienced. The generals have already lost the defensive glacis of Eastern Europe, the command and control structure of the Warsaw Pact, and prospectively the forward-deployed troops in East Germany and elsewhere in Eastern Europe. The cuts that they face in conventional weapons as a result of the Conventional Forces in Europe Agreement are enormous, and much larger than those for NATO (about 30,000 tanks, for instance, from the Russian inventory, against about 5,000 from NATO's). Mr. Gorbachev must have recently broken the news that they also face the loss of two or even all four of the Northern Territories, the Japanese islands that were seized by the Russians after World War II and have been reportedly integrated into the radar and sonar defenses of the Sea of Okhotsk, which shelters the vital Soviet last-ditch deterrent force of SLBMs. The START negotiations are moving toward a point at which they promise heavy cuts in other strategic deterrent forces.

Still more trauma, from the point of view of the top brass, is to come. Military goods and services have been absorbing as much as 24 percent of the Soviet GNP over the Cold War decades. If the economic reforms are to work, that must fall toward or below 5 percent. Factories that used to produce tanks and such are already, at least in theory, being turned over to the production of (for example) refrigerators. The peripheral areas of the Soviet sphere that used to produce a lot of conscripts for the Soviet armed forces are ceasing to be willing to do so. They might even be lost to Moscow's military control: at least the fear of that possibility seems to be signaled by the report that nuclear weapons have been pulled out of those regions, back to Russia itself. Most traumatic of all, probably, is the chance that the Ukraine and Byelorussia, which have in the past constituted a vast buffer zone to protect the Russian homeland from attack from the West, might also seek to opt out of Moscow's control.

From the point of view of a strategic analyst, the rate of loss of Soviet strategic assets, as they existed in 1985, is truly staggering. There is still, of course, the long-range nuclear strike capacity, but on past military experience that is only useful for fending off major war. So it is not surprising that the top brass has been sending apparent signals of restlessness, and that consequently rumors of impending military coups have been sweeping Moscow.

It is true that Russia does not have a tradition of military coups, but there is always a first time. The current reforms mean that the prospective careers of many Soviet officers will so down the drain. When Khrushchev, in the early 1960s, proposed strategic changes that also would have ended the careers of many officers, the top brass helped or probably even incited his Politburo colleagues to remove him from power. And that was at a time when the Soviet economy looked a lot more promising than it does at the moment.

Those points are intended to make the case that Gorbachev and Yeltsin may require a visible gain in specifically the security field if they are to continue to get their policies through—policies that undoubtedly are in line with Western interests. The offer of NATO membership would constitute such a security gain. Last July's NATO communiqué, which protested that the Soviet Union was no longer seen as an adversary, was intended as a minor signal of the same kind, and it seems in part to have worked at a difficult moment for Gorbachev in the party congress. But alliance membership would be far more convincing as a gesture of recognition of changed circumstances and assumptions.

Moreover, this is one of the respects in which NATO must appear vastly more significant in Moscow than either the UN or the CSCE (Conference on Security and Cooperation in Europe), which offer the alternative security frameworks. After all, the Soviet Union has been a founding member of both groups, and the average Soviet general does not seem likely to regard either of them as having done much for Russian security. NATO, on the other hand, has been the principle club—in both senses of that word—of the advanced Western powers, and their military elites. It has formalized the one really serious threat that those concerned with Soviet security have faced all their working lives. Admission to its membership would thus be a status symbol for the military and security elite of a sort that neither of the other two international forums can provide. And the military and security elite, in present or foreseeable circumstances, might prove the one Russian group able to replace the present decision-makers by others, as was done in the case of Khrushchev. Anything the West can offer to reduce that possibility seems worth some sacrifice. To put it flippantly, better that the Soviet top brass should be speculating on the chances of a spell of the military high life in Brussels, than on the desirability of the army saving Russia from the radicals and the economists.

The "confidence-building measures" promoted by the CSCE have already had a considerable effect on the growth of détente between NATO powers and those of the Warsaw Pact, but a gesture of this magnitude would of course quite out-do them. All those NATO secrets that the KGB has been so assiduously ferreting out these past forty years would be suddenly thrown open—with reciprocity expected, of course.

Incidentally, recruitment of Russia to NATO would be the only condition under which Poland and the other Eastern European countries could also be recruited, and they may be even more in need of a security blanket than Russia, especially in view of the obvious contemporary tendency for countries which were put together from disparate ethnic groups to fall apart (as, for example, Yugoslavia). The world, especially Eastern Europe, may well be entering a period in which several national states will rearrange themselves into confederations or even looser groupings like commonwealths. In such a context, the mix of reassurance and restraint of an alliance or a security community might prove particularly valuable, even essential.

The second and third sardonic rationales for NATO mentioned earlier (keeping the Americans in and the Germans down) seem likely to be rather more difficult in the post- Cold War period, if NATO is confined to its present membership and to its original primary function. Before the Iraqi crisis, neo-isolationist voices were becoming very audible in the United States, mostly from conservatives like Patrick Buchanan. And they did have a case. In effect, Washington in 1946 had to take up the burden of containment, since no viable European balance of power against the Soviet Union could be constructed at that time in view of the economic devastation and political uncertainties then of Western Europe. Forty years later, a viable European balance of power to contain the far weaker Soviet Union does again seem possible. Two nuclear powers (Britain and France), a large conventional power (Germany), twelve assorted fellow travelers, plus the economic dynamism and ideological elan of Western Europe, ought to more than counterbalance a Russia which is a self-admitted economic failure, unable any longer to control Eastern Europe, probably unable to hold its own contiguous empire together, and lacking any ideological appeal. It still has nuclear strike capacity, but as was pointed out earlier, nuclear capacity does not on past experience seem to translate into anything more than ability to inhibit attack on the homeland of the power concerned. So the case being made before the Iraqi crisis (that America had fulfilled its post-war task and could now bring its forces home and devote its resources to the grave problems of its own society) will be heard again once it is over; probably more bitterly if the costs in Iraq have been heavy and the major allies do not seem to have borne a fair share of them.

If at that point NATO is still confined to its present membership, its leadership might seem logically to fall to Germany, but the ghosts crowding in from history would prevent that from being generally acceptable. If, on the other hand, the membership had been expanded to include the Warsaw Pact powers, Russia would clearly have a claim, and that would prevent the question arising at all, for Washington would be unlikely to feel as much temptation to leave NATO if Russia seemed likely to step into America's shoes. Thus, a valuable element of stability would be preserved. The international system faces so much potential change in the next few years that an abdication of American leadership would overload it with uncertainties.

One of the ghosts of the past that has already been sighted is that of Rapallo: the 1922 treaty which briefly created a special relationship between Russia and Germany, in the days when Stalin was well away in his climb to power in the Soviet Union, and Hitler just setting out on his path to power in Germany. Obviously those are very undesirable ghosts at any feast, but they could be seen lurking in dim comers in the Kohl-Gorbachev agreement. Actually, the circumstances of 1922 and 1990 do have two or three factors in common: Russia needing a lot economically, Germany needing something strategically, and Eastern Europe being a morass of uncertainties. However, the strength of the West is incomparably greater, and it may well be possible to keep it that way, if the right choices are made by contemporary decision-makers.

Thinking the Unthinkable?

There are various objections that might be made to this line of argument: that the Warsaw Pact powers are not part of the North Atlantic (but surely more so than Greece and Turkey?); that it is too soon after the Cold War to recruit the old adversary to the successful alliance (but Japan was recruited only six years after a "shooting war," in 1951, and Germany only ten years after, in 1955, and those adversary relations had generated a lot more destruction and consequent bitterness than the Cold War). But the real parallel seems to be 1815: the recruitment of France just after the Napoleonic Wars to the status quo alliance, which became the Concert of Europe and helped keep the peace for most of the next century.

It could also be objected that America has no experience of, or enthusiasm for, such notions: they could not be explained to the electorate. Perhaps, but American policymakers did put together most of the original draft of the UN Charter, which was largely a concert system dressed up in Wilsonian rhetoric. Besides, Washington has now had forty-five years experience of the costs, financial and human, of leadership in a mostly bipolar system, and has developed a powerful conviction about the desirability of burden-sharing. The easiest way to ensure that the burdens are shared more equitably is to devise a system in which the responsibilities are also shared more equitably. Otherwise there is the risk that American troops might look like mercenaries paid for by the Japanese and Germans, who remain constitutionally aloof from the actual fighting. If the present level of détente and collaboration between Washington and Moscow had developed earlier, when the distribution of power was more bilateral, it would have looked like a potential condominium. And that notion has always aroused a certain amount of apprehension, especially in Europe. In any case, the time for that possibility has passed.

Of course, nations outside the magic circle may well find the idea of a concert of powers rather questionable, especially if they remember its last incarnation in the nineteenth-century Concert of Europe. The objection always made to that system is that while it enabled the great powers to avoid direct hostilities with each other for a century (except for the period of turbulence 1855–70), it thereby gave them a free hand for imperialist acquisitions in what is now called the Third World. That may be true, but it is unlikely to be repeated in the twenty-first century. For the theory that economic prosperity and welfare are to be secured by the direct control of territory or resources is by now totally discounted. No nation has had more expansive territory or more resources at its disposal than the Soviet Union (or the czarist empire that was its previous incarnation). But the Russian people have never exactly been shiny with prosperity in either phase of their history, and their present situation is truly miserable. Conversely, the Western Europeans have never done better economically than since they lost their assorted overseas empires, and found instead their present community. So it would be difficult to make a case on recent historical experience, that either contiguous empire (Russia) or overseas empire (Britain, France, Holland, Belgium, Portugal) does much for the living standards of the metropolitan power. Prosperity does not even require size, witness Hong Kong, Singapore, and Taiwan.

Far from the evolving multilateral balance presenting a temptation to new imperial adventures, it could have the opposite effect of enabling the major powers to shrug off their former interest in Third World societies. During the Cold War decades, the United States and the Soviet Union were in the situation of the "anchorman" in a tug-of-war: recruits to the "team" were sought or bought for whatever weight they carried, even if the regimes concerned were politically repellent, strategically marginal, ideologically incompatible, and economically disastrous. Competitive bidding between the adversaries did of course enable the countries concerned to secure assorted benefits, though those benefits were often of a dubious sort: advanced weapon systems from both superpowers, for instance, or Western loans in the 1970s, which were not productively used and merely created heavy debt burdens later. With a multilateral central balance, and not much adversary tension between its members, competitive bidding for the support of peripheral powers should be almost nonexistent. A few commodities, like oil, which are largely produced in Third World countries, might theoretically provide a focus of central balance rivalry, but even that seems unlikely. In the present Iraqi crisis, for example, all six of the central balance powers see their respective interests in the same terms: preventing the flow of oil being blocked or its control taken over by a regional bully who would thereby be able to set world prices.

One might on the whole assume that the declining diplomatic leverage of Third World countries could mean decline in their capacity to secure economic aid, especially in a world in which the competitive demand from Eastern Europe and the Soviet area will be so strong. In a phase of history in which the true division is that between the capital rich (very few) and the capital hungry (very numerous), capital will tend to go where the returns seem most promising. And in a lot of cases that will be Eastern Europe: better infrastructure; eager, skilled, but low-paid work forces; more sophisticated technologies; markets in need of practically everything.

The end of the Cold War might also for a while be diplomatically discomforting for Third World countries in another sense: it will undermine the basis of the doctrine of non-alignment. That doctrine assumed a high-tension bilateral adversary relationship between two superpowers. In a world of six great powers, with no single well-defined central adversary tension, the advantages of avoiding alignment or alliance are hard to see. In fact, the cultivation of a "special relationship" with one or other of the central balance powers would seem to hold more prospect of economic advantage, and diplomatic or even military protection where necessary. More visible already is a sort of compensating ideological benefit for Third World countries that can perhaps be translated into economic and political betterment. Through the decades of the Cold War, and indeed most of the period since 1917—especially when the Soviet Union looked as if it was doing well either strategically or economically (and there were long phases when that assessment was promoted to the Third World by Western journalists and academics)—the bright young would-be leaders of the Third World have been under almost a compulsion to adopt some elements of Leninist theory, especially his theory of imperialism since it offered a rationale for their own drives for power. It also offered an apparent "solution" for the problems of national poverty and backwardness: a command economy governed by a one-party autocracy, as in the Soviet Union. That pernicious illusion ("nationalism painted red," in M. N. Roy's words) set the ideological tone for a great many Third World political elites as they emerged from the British and other Western imperial systems. One can see it as much in the Zimbabwean elite emerging in 1974 as in the Indian equivalent in 1947. But in a world in which it is now possible to carry in Moscow a banner reading "72 Years of Getting Nowhere," and in which it is clear that neither economic nor ethnic problems were solved by the Soviet model, they will have to look elsewhere: to their indigenous traditions, or to Western ones. Some, like Cuba and perhaps North Korea, may be unable to do so until the present leadership is gathered to its ancestors, but many, even perhaps Vietnam, may be able to move away from the old fallacies quite fast. And that should allow more prospect of economic advance. So also should the winding down of regional and domestic conflicts which borrowed some of their momentum from the Cold War. Again that process is already very visible: in Angola, Mozambique, Namibia, Nicaragua, maybe finally Cambodia and Afghanistan. The central balance powers have little to gain in such strife-torn societies, save expensive dependents: they have, rather, a joint interest in stability, so long as their relations with each other remain on an even keel. To sum up, what Third World societies may lose economically in the post-Cold War society of states, through loss of diplomatic leverage, they may retrieve through the dispelling of some very destructive ideological illusions.

That argument has assumed a rather harmonious, even concert-like, relationship between the six central balance powers. Is such an assumption justified? There is a lot of evidence to support it, at least for the final decade of this millennium. The great central adversary tension of the past forty-five years, that between Russia and the West, seems unlikely to revive in such a span of time, assuming continuance of present trends. In fact, a notable irony of the Western victory in the Cold War is that it has produced a situation in which perhaps the most vital and endangered single Western interest is now the continuance of a benign evolution of events in Russia. That is, evolution toward a market economy, pluralist politics, an agreed and peaceful devolution of power to the other fourteen erstwhile Soviet republics, the maintenance of secure central control over the nuclear stockpile (which may still run to about 30,000 warheads), maintenance of competent authority in the nuclear power stations, maintenance of enough political control over military authority to see the arms cuts through, the hardware dismantled, the men demobilized. The factor most likely to disrupt all that would be the eviction of the present leadership from power: hence my argument that Western effort (even sacrifice) is warranted to keep the present evolution on track. There is a parallel between the West's situation vis-à-vis Russia at present, and vis-à-vis Germany and Japan in 1945. Adoption into the Western alliance system worked out well in those two cases.

Until the emergence of Saddam Hussein, Japan almost seemed to be replacing the Soviet Union as the fashionable chief menace on the American horizon. The view provided in some quarters of "Japan as Number One," diplomatically as well as economically, has been (fortunately) deflated by the Gulf crisis. The real vulnerability of the Japanese situation, even economically, has again become obvious. Of the six central balance powers, Japan is least well endowed with the variety of assets that make for a durable great power.

Europe is quite a different proposition: the one true potential competitor for the United States at the top of the economic hierarchy, and even the top of the strategic hierarchy in time. But not yet. For the rest of this millennium, the arguments about the "widening" versus the "deepening" of the Community will keep it busy, and it may be a decade before it develops enough joint political will to make a confederation, much less a federation. China once seemed likely to be able to secure the role and advantages of the "balancer" power when the prospect was of a five-power balance with the strongest tension still that between the United States and the Soviet Union. However, as long as the present Chinese leadership survives and remains determined to resist political liberalization (cultivating market economies and political pluralism), China will be the most isolated, ideologically and politically, of the six, since the other five are all either pluralist or aspiring to be. India seems likely to be the hegemonic power of the Indian Ocean region, as well as the Indian subcontinent, but is neither strategically nor economically at odds with the other five. Like Europe, it has a lot of internal reconciliations and adaptations to make. Thus, for the immediate future, Washington is less challenged as a focus for decision-making for the society of states than it was in the days of the bilateral balance. Then it had a dangerous-seeming rival, at least strategically, and even ideologically, during the earliest decades. Now its other potential challengers are all still some distance down the track. The crucial decisions at present must be Washington's. The Iraqi crisis has made that much clearer than it was six months ago.

The status quo alliance in the society of states is like the protagonist in a classic Greek drama—capable of speaking through many masks. At the moment the convenient one is the United Nations, but the difficulties with that are already being illustrated by the situation of Israel. By sheer weight of numbers, the UN is likely to remain dominated by the Third World. The CSCE, on the other hand, is governed by consensus, so even the smallest powers like Malta can hold up decisions for months, and it is too much based on harmony-of-interest assumptions. NATO, by contrast, has always been run on great power management, is tough-minded, conflict- conscious, and never likely to underrate the importance of military power. The scaffolding for the new world order will no doubt come from all three, but some of the sturdiest timber could be NATO's.

Much will depend on the outcome of the Iraqi crisis, seen as the exemplar of the sort of crises the society of states is most likely to face in the foreseeable future. James Baker's remark that "the line drawn in the sands of Kuwait was a line drawn in time" may prove true in a larger sense than anyone expected.

.

Part 2

Russia: Ally or Adversary?

5

Dual Frustration: America, Russia, and the Persian Gulf

Stephen Sestanovich*

Iran and Iraq loom larger than ever in Russian-American relations. At a time when the number of issues on which Moscow and Washington disagree is dwindling, these two are still contentious enough—despite Russia's "yes" vote in the UN Security Council on November 8—that officials and commentators on each side regularly suspect the other of ill will and bad faith.

It's not a new problem. Long before President Bush found Iraq and Iran to be part of an "axis of evil," they were already the subject of acrimonious exchanges between Moscow and Washington. American policymakers have frequently asked their Russian counterparts how they can expect to maintain friendly relations with the United States and with states that support terrorism, threaten American friends, and violate their own international commitments by seeking weapons of mass destruction.

Worse, Americans accuse Russia of helping Iraq and Iran. When Russian diplomats shielded Iraq from international pressure in the late 1990s, Madeleine Albright used to call them "Saddam's lawyers." And the U.S. government continues to believe that Iran's effort to build nuclear weapons and long-range missiles gets a boost from Russian technology and expertise. This is no minor irritation: the acquisition of weapons of mass destruction by regimes deeply hostile to our interests has become America's pre-eminent national security concern, and Russian policies that make it harder for the United States to address this concern are not easy to ignore.

*Stephen Sestanovich is a senior fellow at the Council on Foreign Relations and professor of international diplomacy at Columbia University. From 1997 to 2001 he was ambassador-at-large and special adviser to the Secretary of State for the former Soviet Union. This essay is adapted from a monograph that was published by the Stanley and the Century Foundations. This essay first appeared in *The National Interest*, no. 70 (Winter 2002/03).

The extraordinary near-alliance forged by President Bush and President Putin after September 11, 2001, ought to help the two sides to work together on these issues. But the legacy they must overcome is daunting. The United States, under Democratic and Republican administrations alike, has raised Iran and Iraq with the Russians over many years, when relations were good and when they were shaky. It has treated them as matters of the highest priority and as everyday diplomatic nuisances. It has sometimes offered to pay a high price for resolving them, at other times no price at all. Russia's response to all this has changed little over time. It has usually resisted putting pressure on either country, and only rarely restricted its relations with them. While expressing hope that neither will acquire nuclear weapons, it has usually betrayed a kind of fatalism about the outcome.

As we face the prospect of another Persian Gulf war, a closer look at the past is in order, if only to understand why years of American effort have not gotten us the results we sought. Renewed confrontation with Iraq may actually create an opportunity for Russia and the United States to put this disagreement behind them for good. (Washington has already offered Moscow more substantial inducements to cooperate than ever before.) Success may open up a chance for a breakthrough on Iran, as well. But none of this will come to pass if the United States does not give the Russians a better sense of what its tolerances are and how our relations are likely to develop if we cannot cooperate. Otherwise, the Bush-Putin partnership could become an inadvertent casualty of war.

Iraq, the Last Time Around

Since the Persian Gulf War, Russia and the United States have played out their disagreements over Iraq largely within the UN Security Council. Here the war of 1991 gained an international mandate, peace terms were laid down, and disputes about enforcing them took shape.

These disputes were at their peak between 1997 and 1999, when Saddam Hussein challenged the UN inspection system created at the end of the war to deny Iraq weapons of mass destruction. After two years of confrontation, inspectors of the United Nations Special Commission (UNSCOM) were ousted from Iraq, and UNSCOM itself was forced to disband. Its much weaker successor, UNMOVIC (United Nations Monitoring, Verification and Inspection Commission), was not even able to enter Iraq.[1]

The Iraqis would not have been able to overthrow the UN disarmament regime but for divisions among the permanent members of the Security Council. From 1997 on, whenever Iraq sought to dilute UNSCOM's authority, replace its leadership, change the composition of its staff or restrict its activities inside Iraq, it enjoyed consistent Russian support. Moscow insisted that Iraq had gone far to meet UN disarmament requirements and deserved to know that intrusive inspections would soon give way to less onerous "monitoring" and eventually to a full lifting of economic sanctions.

Two motives appeared to guide Russian policy. The first was political—to constrain U.S. actions, preserve Russian authority, keep the Iraq question in the Security Council and maximize U.S. isolation if Washington acted unilaterally. The second motive was economic—to reap the material benefits of being Iraq's chief protector against American pressure.

Russian success was significant, but incomplete. The confrontation between Iraq and UNSCOM was punctuated in December 1998 by four days of British and American bombing, which Moscow could neither prevent nor counter. Nor did Russian support free Baghdad from the UN sanctions regime and indirect regulation of the Iraqi economy. Yet even this halfway result brought Moscow substantial benefits. The United States and Britain punished Saddam, but they did not take Iraq off the Security Council agenda. Indeed, once the bombing stopped, their diplomats went back to negotiating UNMOVIC's mandate. Russia's veto continued to give it influence with both sides. On the economic front, Russia profited handsomely from the continuing standoff. The oil-for-food program, created in 1996 to help the Iraqi people, perpetuated UN oversight of Iraqi trade; but because it allowed Iraq to choose its partners, it was an effective tool with which to reward Russia for its support. Between 1997 and 2000 Russian-Iraqi trade quintupled.

Saddam offered Russia even larger pay-offs down the road. At the beginning of its campaign against UNSCOM, Iraq signed a major exploration and development contract (valued at around $12 billion) with the Russian oil company LUKoil. Unlike increased trade, of course, these benefits could only be realized if sanctions were lifted; the same was true of Russia's desire to collect its $7–8 billion in Iraqi state debts. Both gave Moscow further reasons to keep pressing for an end to sanctions.

In the late 1990s, accumulating Russian-American disagreements stoked a conviction on both sides that meaningful cooperation, not to mention real partnership, could not last. As one of the most important issues on which the two sides disagreed, Iraq was part of this downward trend. Yet what is striking about the evolution of Russian-American relations in this period is how limited the impact of Iraq turned out to be. American officials wanted to keep discord over Iraq from having negative side effects; they called this "managing our differences," and considered it a mark of maturity in Russian-American relations. Russia, too, clearly wanted to avoid paying a price in American enmity for the support it gave Saddam.

Domestic politics provides part of the explanation for Iraq's marginal impact on relations between Russia and the United States. Both presidents were politically vulnerable and had more pressing matters on their minds (Clinton, impeachment; Yeltsin, the political turmoil that followed Russia's financial crash). Other international issues, like the Balkans, evoked a much stronger domestic response. Iraq, by contrast, was an issue for foreign ministries.

Yet the main reason that Iraq did not cut deeply into Russian-American relations was that American aims were so limited. The Clinton administration treated confrontation with Saddam as a test of core international principles— non-proliferation of nuclear weapons, respect for multilateral obligations, great power solidarity against rogue states and terrorists—but it was not willing to push matters to a decisive conclusion. American use of force did not aim to make Saddam comply, only to make his actions costly. No one thought a brief show of force would change Iraqi behavior, get inspectors back in, alter Russian policy, or, least of all, dislodge the Ba'ath regime. President Clinton had just signed a bill making Iraqi "regime change" the goal of U.S. policy, but airpower alone was clearly not going to achieve it, least of all in four days. When this episode was over, the administration paid little further attention to Iraq.

Because America's ends were limited, so were its means. During this period no U.S. official ever offered a serious quid pro quo for Russian support; or warned of the consequences of not cooperating. Measured against the priority that Iraq has now acquired, these omissions may seem strange, but as part of a strategy that did not aspire to solve the problem, they were not strange at all. The most obvious economic inducements that Russia sought were those associated with an end to sanctions. But because it was unwilling to do what was needed to disarm Saddam or overthrow the Ba'ath regime, the United States came to rely more heavily on keeping sanctions in place. They were what remained of a tough U.S. policy.

As for warning Russia of the negative consequences of backing Iraq, this was hard to make credible. Russian-American relations were already troubled, and the Clinton administration wanted to salvage what was left, not subject the relationship to still greater stress. More important, pressure tactics against Russia would have been inconsistent with American strategy toward Iraq itself. Washington itself was not trying for a knockout punch against Saddam Hussein, and there was thus no sense in telling the Russians that they were to blame when we ourselves fell short.

Iran: The "Bill and Boris" Formula

Iran and Iraq—two Persian Gulf states seeking weapons of mass destruction—posed similar problems for Russian-American relations in the 1990s, but Washington's strategy for dealing with Russia on Iran was completely different from its strategy on Iraq, and left a deeper imprint on Russian-American relations.[2]

The first difference involved the scale of the problem, and its priority. American officials, who sometimes felt personally deceived by their Russian counterparts, claimed that Russia was helping Iran acquire long-range ballistic missiles and nuclear weapons. As a result, Russia's relationship with Iran was much more than a divisive diplomatic issue for the United States. It became a source of uneasy second thoughts about Russia's post-communist evolution, and about the overall wisdom of U.S. policy. (Assistance to Iran put Russia in very disreputable company. Its policy toward Iraq, after all, was similar to France's; its policy toward Iran was similar to North Korea's. This was no small difference.)

Because stopping Russian assistance to Iran was a higher priority than Iraq, it required a different kind of communication. Harsh words between foreign ministers would not be enough. The U.S. message on Iran aimed both higher— at an explicit "Bill-and-Boris" commitment to fix things—and wider, since so many institutions of the Russian state (and actors outside it) were working with Tehran's weapons programs. A solution had to start at the top, but could not succeed without the cooperation of officials at lower levels, too.

Such an effort called for deploying serious leverage, and the result was a third difference between the U.S. handling of Iran and Iraq. The Clinton administration offered large economic inducements to re-orient Russian high-tech industry—whether the huge Ministry of Atomic Energy or individual missile specialists—away from business with Iran toward more wholesome ventures with the West. American officials conjured images of vast cooperation, but when carrots alone did not work—and when Congress threatened to act on its own—the administration made use of sticks as well. Sanctions were imposed in mid-1998 and again in early 1999 on Russian entities that had helped the Iranian nuclear and missile programs, and were repeatedly threatened thereafter.

To stop Russian assistance to Iran, American policy sought the extra torque it lacked over Iraq. No other issue was said to threaten the Russian-American relationship so fundamentally, was tied so closely to mutual confidence between presidents, was so incessantly discussed by officials at all levels, or was linked to such large material inducements. It would be hard to draw up a cleaner textbook case in which outwardly similar and highly important issues were handled so differently.

Why, then, was the result so similar? Russian export-control laws and regulations were tightened, and some glaring cases of freelance cooperation appeared to end (especially when the U.S. government provided specific information about them). Yet no moonlighting Russian missile engineers were arrested, no Iranian middlemen were expelled for misusing their diplomatic status, and the largest item of Russian-Iranian cooperation—a nuclear power reactor being built at Bushehr—continued to provide effective cover for illicit assistance. By the end of the decade, the U.S. intelligence community judged that Iran continued to benefit from Russian help.

In the effort to stop Russian assistance to Iran, each tool of U.S. pressure proved blunter than it should have been. The very claim that Iranian nuclear weapons proliferation was a matter of high priority was doubted by Russian officials, who seemed to view American warnings about assistance to Iran as essentially a way of fending off partisan domestic attacks on the Clinton administration. The Russians retorted that it was not their job to save the president from his critics. Similarly, they read American forecasts of deep damage to Russian-American relations as an invitation to engage in a joint effort to manipulate Congressional opinion. They always wanted to know what minimum set of actions would defuse pressure for a while, not how to solve the problem for good. These perceptions were wrong, but they were not altogether unreasonable.

The administration's use of inducements was also problematic. The Russians needed to be convinced that their performance alone would determine whether they got the carrots they wanted. They saw instead that corporate lobbying successfully blocked the use of sanctions whenever it was likely to hurt American business. The administration's own message about the link between performance and payoff was inconsistent. Thus, Vice President Gore's stiff warning to Prime Minister Yevgeny Primakov in November 1998 ("You can have a piddling trickle of money from Iran or a bonanza with us, but you can't have both."[3]) coincided with a proposal for major new assistance to Russia under the Nunn-Lugar program.

Finally, the assumption that a presidential handshake could stop Russian assistance to Iran proved mistaken and out of date. By the late 1990s, Boris Yeltsin lacked the interest, energy, aptitude, and maybe even the power to meet such a complex political and institutional challenge. And American appeals to him, and to the grand goal of Russian-American partnership, no longer had their old motivating force. Russian assistance to Iran seriously eroded mutual confidence, but so did financial meltdown and scandal, Kosovo, NATO expansion, national missile defense and other first-order disagreements. The circuitry of relations between Moscow and Washington had reached overload. They did not become manageable again until each country's transition to new leadership was complete.

Bush, Putin, and Saddam

Since President Bush's "axis of evil" speech, the United States and Iraq have again been on a collision course. But Washington has no longer to take all-out Russian opposition for granted, a strategic transformation made possible by a series of changes in Russian politics and foreign policy.

The first of these changes, of course, is the strong rapprochement between Russia and the United States and the unprecedented, unequivocal endorsement of U.S. military action that came with it. That President Putin would also distance Russia from Iraq was made possible by a second change—his complete authority over Russian foreign policy, based on his extraordinary personal popularity and reputation for a bristly attentiveness to Russian national interests. Yeltsin believed that denouncing every American military action made him look tough; Putin sees that ineffectual public tantrums would make him look weak.

Similarly, when Putin says Russian diplomacy must serve economic interests, no one accuses him of putting foreign policy up for sale. He enables low motives to win respect as high principle. When American pressure on Iraq resumed, Russian spokesmen started issuing public reminders of Russia's economic stake in the matter. Iraq had never before been bargained over like this, but U.S. officials got the hint. Russia, they promised, would be rewarded for support.

The broader evolution of Russia's economic elite has also pushed policy toward accommodation with the United States. Riding a four-year surge in oil production, leading Russian business figures now say that their prime goal is to gain access to Western markets; they profess to be tired of being bottom-feeders dependent on semi-illicit ties with the world's rogues. For businessmen with such an outlook, Putin's alignment with Bush did not sacrifice the Russian corporate bottom line—it strengthened it.

Together these changes ruled out the reflexive pro-Saddam stance Russia had adopted in the past. Saddam might face defeat, but Putin would not let it become his defeat as well. Some commentators even wrote of the risks for Russia in standing by Iraq too long. Russia, they said, might find itself empty-handed and isolated when the war was over: What kind of hard-boiled defense of the national interest would that be?

As such talk showed, the hardening of U.S. policy against Iraq had narrowed the benefits that Baghdad could offer Moscow. Yes, by taking advantage of a crisis it might be possible to push Russian-Iraqi trade a little higher, but the larger economic interests that Russian officials have been invoking—the repayment of Iraqi debt to Russia and the long-term development of Iraq's energy potential—can best be advanced by working with Washington, not with Ba'athi Baghdad. (In fact, Saddam cannot bestow these benefits even if war is averted, since they depend on the lifting of sanctions, to which the U.S. administration will clearly not agree.)

Much of Russia's recent handling of Iraq has seemed to follow from such calculations. Putin has avoided personal identification with Iraq, declined to meet with Saddam's longtime deputy, Tariq Aziz, and authorized official contact with Iraqi opposition figures. At the end of last summer, when Iraqi diplomats began touting a draft ten-year economic agreement, Russian officials quietly declined to sign. Meanwhile, Russian oil companies talked up cooperation with the United States. From LUKoil's CEO, Vagit Alekperov, came the (probably false) claim that the United States had promised to honor the contract he had signed with Iraq in 1997; his rival at Yukos, Mikhail Khodorkovsky, urged the Russian government to get assurances that Washington would prevent too big a drop in postwar oil prices. Putin actually joked that he was not trying to squeeze more out of the West in some sort of "Oriental bazaar." No one believed him.

The most telling sign that Russia does not want to go down with Saddam was, of course, its vote for UN Security Council Resolution 1441, warning Iraq of "serious consequences" if it did not meet its disarmament obligations. After two months of diplomatic stalling, and of seeming to want above all to stay America's hand, Russia positioned itself to blame Saddam if war broke out. Between 1997 and 1999 Russia's abstentions and endless haggling in the Security Council had clearly encouraged Baghdad to flout its obligations, knowing that Moscow would continue to front for it no matter what. Joining a unanimous Security Council vote in November 2002 sent a completely different message: You're on your own.

Yet for all the seeming clarity of this message, Russia will face continuing choices as Iraq's confrontation with the United States unfolds. And Moscow will have many motives to try to tie the Bush Administration down. There will be the unavoidably gray areas of UNMOVIC's mandate and findings. There will be those who say that Russia cannot defend its authority in the UN Security Council—a last residue of Soviet great power status—by supporting the United States, only by checking it. There will be the example set by France, Germany, and other European critics of U.S. policy. There will be the chance to wheedle concessions from Washington on Georgia and Chechnya. Putin may even believe that protracted haggling will further bolster his image as a tough advocate of Russian interests.

Above all, Moscow will keep its options open if it is not sure of the direction and conviction of American policy. The United States, after all, has sought Russian support by offering inducements on which it can make good only if it wins outright. Until it is clear that the United States will prevail, Russia risks more by aligning itself prematurely with the United States than by standing aloof. Were American policy to unravel and Saddam to stay in power, what reward would Russia then claim, and from whom? Putin no more wants to tie himself to an American failure than to an Iraqi one.

In the 1990s, American influence with Russia was limited by the fact that Washington clearly did not intend to go all the way. The same is true today. A U.S. policy that is not determined to solve the problem actually revives Saddam's leverage with Moscow.

Finally, Putin's choices will be affected by how he reads their likely impact on what has been his supreme foreign policy achievement—a partnership with the United States that elevates Russia's international status. Last time around, Russian policymakers knew that their handling of Iraq would have no material impact on their relations with the United States. Washington had made clear it would not link the two. In the current confrontation, however, no goal of U.S. foreign policy is more important than success against Iraq. For all their improvement, Russian-American relations cannot be insulated from this issue. If, when it's all over, the administration feels that it has been critically held back by Russian policy, it will hardly be able to shrug off the disagreement as it did before. Has President Putin told President Bush he doesn't want Iraq to harm U.S.-Russian relations? If so, it's surely true. But has President Bush told President Putin that they will be just as good friends if this disagreement keeps American policy from succeeding? If so, it's almost surely false.

Iran Today: "Bill and Boris" Again?

Before George W. Bush took office, his supporters and spokesmen insisted that in dealing with Russia on Iran he would show a sharper edge than his predecessor and make Moscow see that cooperation in other areas would depend on solving this critical problem. But it didn't happen, and the main reasons are not hard to discern.

Despite its criticisms of the Clinton record in handling this issue, the new administration wanted most of all to engineer a smooth withdrawal from the ABM treaty, and for this reason, far from featuring a sharp edge, initial meetings between Bush and Putin accentuated the positive. Lest they spoil the tone, other contentious issues would have to wait. After September 11, a still more powerful reason to put Iran to one side arose—and it was not just that the war on terrorism came first. Putin's quick show of support made the entire idea of Russian-American partnership credible again. Senior American officials assumed that the two countries now had key parallel interests, and that with a bit more time their new ally would do the right thing on Iran.

For his own reasons, Putin did seem to be fashioning a new approach to Iran. He fired Yevgeny Adamov, his minister of atomic energy (seen by U.S. officials as an incorrigible liar about cooperation with Iran), abandoned Moscow's support for Tehran's claim to an equal share of Caspian Sea energy, and proposed a multilateral force that other Caspian states might join for protection against Iran. After Bush's "axis of evil" speech, too, the Iranian foreign minister's visit to Moscow was abruptly cancelled; Putin, it seemed, did not want to see him.

Officials in both countries, then, had reason to think that the ingredients of a solution to this problem might be at hand. Putin faced fewer bureaucratic obstacles to a policy shift and seemed ready to stand up to Tehran; with both Congress and the media ignoring Russian assistance to Iran, Bush was also free to maneuver. Most important, in both Moscow and Washington there was new interest in a formula that would allow each side to claim it had achieved its core objective. Privately, senior U.S. policymakers acknowledged that the Bushehr nuclear power plant was not a prime proliferation danger in itself, but rather that it provided a cover for transfers of really dangerous assistance. If the Russians would stop all sensitive transfers to Iran beyond Bushehr—and stop making excuses for themselves and the Iranians—an agreement might be possible.

For their part, highly placed Russians admitted privately that Iran was working on nuclear weapons and long-range missiles, and that this called for strict and tightly enforced limits on future Russian-Iranian cooperation. If, they said, the Americans were prepared to stop trying to roll back all Russian nuclear cooperation with Iran, focus on what was truly dangerous, and lubricate an understanding with a major expansion of Russian-American nuclear cooperation, then this long-running dispute would be over.[4]

"They're saying all the right things!"—this was the cheery assessment of American officials before the Bush-Putin summit of May 2002. Yet the meeting and its aftermath were a severe setback. Far from confirming a new approach, Putin embarrassed Bush at their joint press conference by refusing to confirm "assurances" that Bush had just claimed to have heard from him in private, moments before. Instead, Putin launched into a spirited defense of nuclear cooperation with Iran, and charged that American companies were guilty of giving Tehran dangerous technologies. U.S. officials bravely insisted that the private discussions had gone better, but Russian officials showed no signs of a new policy. In July, in fact, they announced plans to build as many as five more reactors after current work at Bushehr is completed.

Why did high hopes for a breakthrough come to so little so quickly? Ironically, one part of the answer was the new atmosphere of Russian-American relations. With less public heat on the issue, and no threat of Congressional interference, U.S. officials had hoped that Putin would push for a solution without fear of seeming to yield to U.S. pressure. But the lack of pressure also implied that the United States now cared less about the whole issue. Wittingly or not, the Bush administration may have come to believe in the very solution that the Clinton administration did—mutual trust between presidents as a lever to override narrow bureaucratic or economic interests. Far from thinking they should reciprocate because the administration had become so reasonable, Russian officials may have concluded that Washington was looking to retreat from a failed policy.

Similarly, although the Bush administration had described a long and impressive list of material inducements intended to elicit a change in Russian policy, it had not persuaded the Russians that getting these benefits depended on changing their own policy. The American effort to pick up the pieces after the summit showed this problem vividly. Perhaps, the president's advisors admitted, Putin had not gotten a clear message in Moscow, but he would definitely hear straight talk at their next gathering, the G-8 summit in Canada. When that meeting rolled around, however, the leaders spent their time discussing a new $20 billion aid program to improve the security of Russian nuclear materials. They barely touched on Iran. Demands for better behavior were now being downplayed in favor of offers of new assistance, just as the Clinton administration had done in 1998 when it veered from sanctions to aid increases over just a few months' time.[5]

In seeking a breakthrough in the long dispute over Russian assistance to Iran, the Bush administration has had many advantages: a strong overall relationship, an effective Russian leader to deal with, and an array of powerful material inducements to offer. The administration has not treated Iran as a make-or-break issue of Russian-American relations, and it will understandably not do so until its confrontation with Iraq is over. At that point, assuming that Putin has avoided putting himself at odds with the United States, there is likely to be a further surge of confidence between Moscow and Washington— and this will create an even better opening for a serious discussion of assistance to Iran. Yet the administration must remember that, for all the advantages of the U.S. position, it has so far been unable to convince the Russian side to take the problem seriously enough to solve it. Getting it to do so will not be easy. In its dealings with two administrations on Iran, Russia's preference has always been for partial solutions—at best—that only stored up trouble for Russian-American relations in the future. If the administration wants to change that preference, it will have to show that more hangs in the balance than has ever been true in the past.

Russia's Fatalism

Over the past decade, most of the issues that were thought to have the potential to sink Russian-American relations for good did not do so. Almost all of them have in fact faded into insignificance. Iran and Iraq, however, are likely to have far greater staying power. Not only do the Persian Gulf and Middle East seem certain to remain first-order preoccupations of American national strategy for years to come, but Moscow and Washington continue to have different approaches to the issue that has lately animated the U.S. government more than any other—the spread of weapons of mass destruction.

The American approach to this problem has become, especially since September 11, increasingly absolutist. The prospect of having hostile states vault the nuclear threshold is viewed as a fundamental threat, to which the right policy response is to make use of all available instruments of pressure—stopping nuclear cooperation with offenders, branding them as pariahs, using force in extremis to block their progress or to disarm them. The Russian outlook has been more fatalist—less fearful, more resigned, less determined. Proliferation, in this view, is hardly good, but it may be inevitable. If so, the right response is to preserve one's influence with those who acquire such weapons, deter their use and not let oneself become a target.

The United States has never had a better opportunity than it has now to draw Russian policy away from this fatalism. We need to seize it, for the more absolutist our own approach, the more we need others to work with us. Absolutism—trying to solve a problem outright—is not the same thing as, and is not served by, unilateralism.

Given Russia's circumstances, of course, fatalism has something to be said for it, and absolutism may seem like overreaching. But only at first glance. The record of recent years suggests the high costs—for both the United States and Russia—of pretending that partial solutions are complete ones. It can't be lost on Putin that if Yevgeny Primakov had not let Saddam defy the United Nations four years ago, Russia would not be in the awkward fix it's in today, trying to decide which way to jump when war comes. From the Russian standpoint, North Korea's recent sensational disclosure that it has defied its 1994 agreement to foreswear a nuclear weapons program must be equally unnerving. For Putin knows that Russia is, in a sense, the sponsor of a still looser arrangement with Iran, and that Russian help is already implicated in subverting it. Does he like the prospect of being briefed by George Bush, at some point in the future, that Iran has taken the North Korean path?

To change Russia's fatalistic calculus, the United States has to suggest the results that will follow from such scenarios in the future, and from continued inability to cooperate in the interim. But it must also suggest the possibilities that greater cooperation would open up—not only in slowing or stopping proliferation, but in the consolidation of Russian-American relations. If America's new absolutist goals are at the center of its national security policy, then they need to be at the center of its relations with Moscow as well.

Notes

1. For an account by UNSCOM's second chairman, see Richard Butler, *The Greatest Threat: Iraq, Weapons of Mass Destruction and the Growing Crisis of Global Security* (New York: Public Affairs Press, 2000). Kenneth Pollack's *The Threatening Storm* (New York: Random House, 2002) provides an inside view of U.S. policy.
2. For inside accounts, see Strobe Talbott, *The Russia Hand: A Memoir of Presidential Diplomacy* (New York: Random House, 2002); and Robert Einhorn and Gary Samore, "Ending Russian Assistance to Iran's Nuclear Bomb," *Survival* (Summer 2002).
3. Talbott, *The Russia Hand*, p. 295.
4. For a cogent version of such a proposal, praised by many Russian and American officials, see Einhorn and Samore, "Ending Russian Assistance to Iran's Nuclear Bomb."
5. Under Secretary of State for Arms Control and International Security John Bolton tried to set the record straight in Congressional testimony in October, saying that poor Russian performance on Iran would block the new aid. But it will take more than one statement to make this linkage credible.

6

All the Way:
Crafting a U.S.-Russian Alliance

Robert Legvold*

Russia and the United States both stand on the verge of fundamental foreign policy choices likely to change dramatically their mutual relationship
and, quite possibly, much more besides. For Russia, the choice centers on how
thoroughgoing an alignment with the West it should pursue; for the United
States, the choice centers on how thoroughgoing should be the independent
assertion of its power. Choosing in the Russian case depends on how fully the
leadership persuades itself, and then the Russian political class, that a changing international environment requires a change in the Russian approach—
one that cuts free from habitual fears and addresses factors crucial to national
welfare and progress. Choosing in the U.S. case has less to do with the elite's
conception of international challenges than with the scope and methods of
dealing with them. If the Russians make a dramatic conceptual choice, the
effect on U.S.-Russian relations could be profound and positive. In contrast, if
the United States makes a particular strategic choice, the effect on those relations could be major and negative, and the potential for a truly beneficial U.S.-
Russian alliance may be lost.

   Understanding why this is so and what is at stake requires a deeper look at
what has happened to Russian foreign policy in the year since September 11,
2001. Dramatic as Vladimir Putin's instantaneous support for the United States
was, and important as Russian cooperation in the campaign against global
terrorism has been, it is the basis of this shift that should focus our attention.
Putin's foreign policy is no tactical foray. Rather, he and his domestic allies
have settled a critical ambivalence that plagued the country's foreign policy

*Robert Legvold is professor of political science at Columbia University and editor of
Thinking Strategically: The Major Powers, Kazakhstan, and the Central Asian Nexus (The
MIT Press). This essay first appeared in *The National Interest*, no. 70 (Winter 2002/03).

before September 11, one that had left Russia torn between competing images of the outside world.

Until then, for many within the foreign policy establishment and, it seemed, a part of Putin himself, the international setting remained a traditionally menacing place. It was a world where the state of military balances mattered; where the assertion of U.S. power constituted a challenge to be thwarted; where NATO's expansion toward Russian borders assumed first-rank importance, and its actions over Kosovo posed a direct threat; and where the virtues of a longed-for multipolar order served as standard mantra. Yet for others, including another part of Putin, the world was increasingly engulfed by globalization, and there, amid the tyranny of global capital flows, the refinement of trading agglomerations and an information and communications revolution, the fate of Russia's own transformation would be decided. This was a place of geo-economics, not geostrategy; a place of arbitrage and export, not power plays and arms races.

It is this second world that President Putin now stresses, and thus it is clear in retrospect that his aligning Russia with the United States in the struggle against Al-Qaeda and the Taliban was but an eye-catching manifestation of a more basic strategic decision to throw Russia's lot in with the West. By so doing, Putin not only put an end to much post-Cold War uncertainty and equivocation, but also reconciled himself to what can only be a junior partnership with the United States—one in which Russia's ability to contest objectionable U.S. policies may be no greater than that of any U.S. ally, and perhaps a good deal less than some.

For those Russians still of the old view, Putin's concessions appear not merely misguided, but treasonous. In May, the leader of the Communist Party, Gennady Zyuganov, condemned a policy that "threatens the very existence of the country." In his angry recital:

> Reliable allies have been sold out. Russian bases in Vietnam and Cuba vital for our country's security have been closed. American soldiers have appeared in Central Asia and in Georgia. Soon U.S. aircraft will land at the airfields of Latvia, Lithuania and Estonia. The CIS and Russia have already been proclaimed as within the sphere of the U.S. vital interests. The strategic encirclement of Russia is being completed with the full consent of Mr. Putin and his team.[1]

But Putin and his critics are ships passing in the night. Not only does the president no longer share even partially their view of the threats posed by the outside world, he has adopted an entirely different foreign policy agenda from theirs. This is not to deny that Putin's new direction has roots in the period before September 2001 or to suggest that all his concerns over NATO, the U.S. nuclear posture or manifestations of U.S. unilateralism have evaporated. But it is important to recognize how different is the order of tasks on which he is fixed from that of two or three years ago.

Russia's New Agenda

Vladimir Putin's overriding priority is to synchronize his domestic and foreign policy agendas, which inevitably means featuring economics. Not by chance has the focus of Putin's last two "state of the union" addresses to parliament been devoted overwhelmingly to domestic issues, with only a few fleeting paragraphs on foreign policy—and even these few paragraphs have had mainly to do with economic issues. In this year's address, for example, he opened his comments on foreign policy by discussing the World Trade Organization and closed by stressing that "a fundamental feature of the contemporary world is the internationalization of the economy and society." Russia, he said, "no longer [has] a choice of whether or not to integrate into the world economic space."

This shift in priorities radiates throughout Russia's foreign policy, and has three critical effects. First, it diminishes the urgency and immanence of alternative preoccupations. NATO's evolution and activities lose their centrality; the massive U.S. military advantage, its imperious approach to designing the strategic nuclear regime of the future, even the arrival of U.S. troops on former Soviet territory, all loom less large; and the need to watch, catlike, for any encroachment on Russia's strategic positions in bordering regions shrinks.

Second, the reordering of priorities leaves room for Russians to rethink old assumptions. Rather than accent latent traces of U.S.-Russian rivalry—including a not-so-latent strategic competition within post-Soviet space—those of the new perspective emphasize instead that "Russia's and the United States' geopolitical interests don't contradict each other; in fact, they tend to coincide."[2] Looked at objectively, they argue, by bringing down the Taliban regime and forcing Al-Qaeda on the run, the United States did what Russia could not do for itself—reduce the security threat from its south. On other pressing security issues, too—the spread of weapons of mass destruction, fighting terrorism, enhancing energy security, or even stabilizing Russia's northeast frontier in Asia—Russia and the United States have common interests that ought to lead to common endeavors. This is not just talk. The weakening of old fears and the incipient rethinking of security interests have already given rise to more constructive approaches to issues that once vexed U.S.-Russian relations. For example, the trade-off between the new NATO-Russia Council and a new Russian equanimity in the face of further NATO expansion would not have been possible if not for the shift in Russian attitudes that preceded them. Nor, almost surely, would the Moscow Treaty have sufficed to offset the unilateral U.S. abrogation of the ABM Treaty and its determination to do with its strategic forces as it chooses.

Third, because of the fundamental turn in Russian foreign policy, the basis for a radically different U.S.-Russian relationship now exists. In short, Putin's new agenda permits a new and positive U.S.-Russian agenda. No longer, say partisans of the Putin approach, need Washington and Moscow concentrate on preventing the negative; the two countries can now combine strengths to pursue a positive joint security agenda. After all, Putin rallied to the U.S. side so swiftly after September 11 not merely because he sensed an opportunity, but because he felt that his own earlier drumbeat of concern over international terrorism had been vindicated. Beyond the problem of terrorism, supporters of Russia's new approach envisage the United States and Russia as partners managing what Dmitry Trenin calls "strategic stability" in the twenty-first century. This has to do less with the nuclear balance between the two powers and more with the need to counter "the growing danger of further proliferation of WMDs and their use in regional crises," most of which are nearer Russia than North America. Trenin sees Russian-American cooperation in developing theater missile defense as part of this effort, and trends in official circles, too, are moving in this direction.[3]

Putin has also put energy partnership squarely on the new agenda. Beginning with a February 11 *Wall Street Journal* interview, he has stressed Russia's potential as a reliable alternative to traditional Middle Eastern sources of oil and natural gas. Rapid movement in this direction, from the May Moscow summit through the Houston "energy summit" in September, reflects genuinely reinforcing interests. If its oil production goes from today's 7.7 million barrels per day to a planned 9.5 million by 2010, Russia will need the U.S. market; and the United States, even were it to commandeer Iraqi oil fields, will need Russia's help to stabilize international oil markets.

Finally, Russians apply the word "partnership," albeit somewhat more gingerly in this case, to evoke the two countries' common stake in seeing China safely integrated into the international community. Some stress the importance of promoting China's continued domestic evolution into a responsible and predictable actor on the international stage. Others focus on guaranteeing a strong Russian presence in its own Far East, lest Chinese power too easily flow across the border. But either way, addressing the challenge of China forms another key area of potential U.S.-Russian cooperation.

In this sense, the new arrangement between Russia and NATO is but a prototype of the relationship Putin and his allies have in mind. The promise of this venture owes as much to the new agenda being addressed as to the new mechanism by which Russia is to be included. In the struggle against global terrorism, the effort to control weapons of mass destruction and the management of regional conflicts—the heart of this new agenda—NATO, as both sides understand, needs Russia. The mechanism of the NATO-Russia Council, therefore, has an intrinsic value that its predecessor, the Permanent Joint Council, lacked, designed as it was to deal primarily with Russian discontents. Not surprisingly, therefore, "NATO at 20" in the half year of its existence is already off to a far more constructive start than the PJC. It is seriously at work on assessing terrorist threats, planning airspace management and joint training exercises, discussing problems of crisis management, considering theater missile defense, and coordinating efforts to secure fissile material wherever possible (as was demonstrated by U.S.-Russian cooperation in removing more than 100 pounds of enriched uranium from Serbia's Vinca nuclear reactor last August).[4]

False Perils

Where are the obstacles to an effective Russian-American alliance? What could prevent President Putin's preferences from carrying the day?

Three hazards, alone or in some combination, compose the typical answer. The first is opposition at home. Putin's new course has been very much at his own initiative, and while he is supported by narrow though powerful strands of the political elite, skepticism remains among a broad spectrum of the Russian political and analytical community. Second, many have assumed that Putin cannot persist if his concessions are not reciprocated or rewarded by the U.S. side, and this, it is argued, the Bush administration has failed to do. And third, others suspect that Putin himself endangers a far-reaching change in U.S.-Russian relations by mistakenly assuming that he can have his cake and eat it too: that he can pursue improved bilateral relations with the United States while continuing to cut deals with Iran, Iraq and North Korea that ignore important U.S. interests.

Dangers do exist, but not in these forms. Putin's new course does face opposition at home, but deep-seated resistance to the essence of the policy is confined to increasingly marginal political groupings such as the Communist Party and pockets in the bureaucracy. Bureaucratic obstinacy, particularly in the military and among some in the foreign ministry, can nick the policy and distort this or that element of it. It is true, too, that support among a broader portion of the political class has been tepid, but this is not because its leading voices have a better idea. Less do they object to the broad thrust of the policy than to specific aspects of its implementation.

Putin, however, so towers over the Russian political scene that little of this threatens to knock him off course, and he does have allies among the business elite and the key economic ministries. Only if Putin's general political position disintegrates will critics of his foreign policy have an opening, and that is only likely if Russia slides into serious economic difficulty. While not out of the question, economic trouble on this scale appears improbable any time soon.

The second concern—that the new policy will reap too scant an American payoff—ignores two factors: Putin has not framed the policy as a horse trade, but has made clear that he seeks a larger, overarching set of changes; and the Bush administration has responded at this level. As Defense Secretary Donald Rumsfeld said in an October 24 interview, "The Cold War is over. The time now is one of cooperation between the two nations, not as it was of rivalry or competition."[5] The clearest expression of what the administration has in mind came in a June 1 speech by Richard Haass, the director of the State Department's Policy Planning Staff. "U.S.-Russian relations," he said, "are of course still evolving from a Cold War relationship dominated by efforts to prevent what we could do to one another to a new post-post-Cold War one based on promoting what we can do with each other." He emphasized that the "most important and challenging task at this stage is to define a long-term positive agenda for the bilateral relationship," one that "has to be about more than eliminating old Cold War threats and fighting terrorism, important as those are. The relationship must be based on new opportunities for cooperation." As to those new opportunities, Haass' list is not much different from the Russian list: energy cooperation, the economic development of the Russian Far East, cooperation in Central Asia, and what Haass termed "the large and demanding multilateral agenda" extending from "managing regional crises such as those in the Middle East and South Asia" to "transnational challenges such as HIV/AIDS, drugs, and human trafficking."[6]

The third concern—that Russian maneuvering or double-dealing in its ongoing policies toward Iran, Iraq and North Korea will intrude—misconstrues this dimension of Russian policy. Russia's rapprochement with the West, historic as it is, does not and cannot mean that Russia will abandon its interests in relations with these three countries—or, for that matter, with China and India—just because they are not to U.S. tastes. But, if the argument here is correct, Putin will pursue these interests within the limits of what the traffic will bear in quest of his larger foreign policy objectives.

As a case in point, while Putin wants to protect long-term Russian economic interests in Iraq, including LUKoil's majority stake in the 11 billion-barrel Qurna oil field, and while he means to subject U.S. action as much as possible to UN Security Council oversight, he will not likely fall on his sword to prevent the United States from moving militarily against Iraq. Similarly, while Putin, the Ministry of Atomic Energy and the Russian domestic nuclear industry are eager to complete the $800 million Bushehr reactor in Iran (and perhaps follow-on projects as well), they seem likely to insist on the return of spent fuel to Russia and the promised international inspection regime pursuant to those projects. If Tehran balks, the deal may well come unglued. In sum, what might be thought of as "out of area" issues in a future U.S.-Russian alliance may well raise difficulties, just as such issues have often troubled NATO partners over the years. But if a common agenda conforms to core national interests on both sides, and if indeed national interest is the main currency of mutual understanding between Moscow and Washington, then these issues need not destroy the larger partnership.

Real Perils

If not these commonly assumed perils, then what does threaten Putin's new course and the prospect of a radically recast U.S.-Russian relationship? An initial threat arises from the impediments to Russia's rapid integration into international economic institutions, but that is the easy part. Beyond that stand three vastly more formidable challenges.

As to this initial impediment, it is clear that Putin may struggle to find second gear. Entry into the World Trade Organization will require wrenching decisions affecting the economic interests of powerfully entrenched actors within Russia—indeed, whole industrial sectors such as aluminum, steel, civil aviation, food processing and pharmaceuticals. It will also require the revision of a vast range of legislation: as many as a thousand laws are at issue. Promoting Russia's integration with (not into) the European Union promises to be still more difficult. At every turn, the process will involve potentially disruptive "two-level games," to use the political science term, which is to say that national leaders will have to engage external and domestic parties simultaneously. Even a two-level game between the United States and the EU over, say, steel quotas, is fractious enough—and that is when all players on both sides are familiar to one another and the game has long since been legitimated. When such players and games are neither familiar nor legitimated, it is likely to produce far less modulated political effects—as can already be seen, for example, in both the WTO talks and the Russian-EU dialogue.

Difficult as these processes will be, they are far less demanding than the three larger challenges at hand. The first of these concerns the fate of political trends within Russia itself. One need not share the bitter view of many Russian democrats that Putin's turn toward the West rests on a Faustian bargain to appreciate how fast the idea of a deep and durable partnership with Russia will shrivel if Russia's advance to democracy falters.[7] The notion that Putin has rushed to the U.S. side in order to secure a free hand in Chechnya or a free pass from Western criticism in repressing civil liberties both claims too much and does too little to explain the shift in Russian foreign policy. Still, the basic issue of what Russia is to be, not merely what it wants to do, remains. The simple historical fact is that the United States does not have enduring alliances with major powers that are not democracies.

Putin's notion of "managed democracy" does not turn him into a despot or even an autocrat-in-the-making; it only suggests that the ultimate foundation for Russian-American partnership is yet to be established. The communiqués that Putin and Bush sign speak of common interests and common values. Common interests there are; common values are yet to be fully demonstrated. In the meantime, frictions over human rights violations by an overzealous Russian intelligence agency, government intimidation of the press and media, and, in particular, brutality in Chechnya will undermine the sense of true partnership engendered by cooperation in other spheres. The alternative—Washington's looking the other way—would be worse, however. For the United States to soft-pedal Russian shortcomings in order to protect Moscow's cooperation in, say, the war on terrorism would implicitly, albeit unintentionally, derogate the very idea of a more substantial U.S.-Russian alliance. Democrats in Russia have long seen Russia's integration into the West as critical to eventual democratization in their country. But for Russia to be integrated into the West there must be convincing and sustained progress toward democracy. Putin, in his foreign policy, has gone a long way toward integration. Ultimately, however, if he means to complete the journey, his policies at home must be reinforcing.

The second of the three grand challenges cuts to the heart of the broad, basic foreign policy choice facing the United States. It has to do essentially with the ends to which U.S. power is applied, and the extent to which they incorporate or, alternatively, disregard the ends allies would have the United States pursue. Russia is no longer the focal point of the U.S. foreign policy agenda, and certainly the Bush Administration will not accord Russia a veto over critical American decisions anymore than it accords a veto to Germany or France. Nevertheless, as with other U.S. allies, how the administration sets its course, as much as what course it sets, will do much to define the limits of Russian policy. Much of the Russian foreign policy elite has come to accept that U.S. primacy in the first part of the twenty-first century is overwhelming and likely to endure. Most also believe that the Bush Administration will be ruthless in using its power—not against Russia, but against the states that it sees as immediate dangers. Those states would be, first, Iraq, but then in short order Iran, maybe Syria, perhaps even Saudi Arabia (and, if things go very wrong there, Pakistan). Because they see Iraq as only a first step, they conjure up images of spreading disorder to their south; of outcast regimes redoubling their efforts to acquire nuclear weapons; and, coupled with U.S. determination to preserve unchallengeable military superiority, an intensifying U.S. military competition with China.[8]

Were such a U.S. policy to unfold, the strong tendency within this elite would not be to press Russia's leadership to take the lead, or even to join in directly resisting U.S. policy. Rather the push would be to stay clear of entanglement with U.S. policy to the extent possible, and here is where the problem would arise for Putin's new course. It is not that an unrestrained U.S. policy would render Putin's alignment with the United States untenable because of the domestic opposition it would engender; it is more that Putin himself would demur. Washington must therefore understand that the essence of the problem, as Russians see it, no longer arises so much from the fact of U.S. preponderance or even from its tendency toward unilateralism. The essence resides in the ends to which U.S. power is put and the discomforting sense that these may not serve Russia well. To the degree that the Bush administration ignores this side of the problem, or reduces it to calibrating mere multilateral gestures against unilateral actions, it will constrain severely Putin's option of deciding in favor of a deepening relationship with the United States.

The last of the three major perils rests at the conceptual level. It is inauspicious when the most elaborate and sophisticated—indeed, the only elaborate and sophisticated—assessment of a radically different U.S.-Russian relationship comes from the level of an assistant secretary of state. Haass' June 1 speech echoes the spirit of comments made by President Bush, Secretary Powell, Secretary Rumsfeld and National Security Advisor Condoleezza Rice on various occasions, but none, including the President in his five meetings with Putin, has yet provided a conceptually coherent outline of the outcome America seeks. The Joint Declaration signed by the two countries at the May Moscow summit promises that "we are achieving a new strategic relationship." It commits the two sides to "cooperate to advance stability, security, and economic integration, and to jointly counter global challenges and to help resolve regional conflicts." But there is little evidence that the administration has a clear notion of this new strategic relationship, either of what its conceptual anchor or primary purpose should be or, therefore, how to define its success or failure.

The Core of Cooperation

The new agenda in U.S.-Russian relations, constructive as it is for now, still falls short of its historic possibilities. Viewed in proper perspective, the evolution under way in Russian foreign policy, if fostered, opens the prospect of going beyond temporary cooperation all the way to a genuine alliance. The point is not a formal treaty, but a psychological leap by which each side comes to trust the other as an ally, to believe that on the most vital international issues they have a common purpose and that where there is disagreement, it is between friends, not opponents. It is a reach, but it is a wise reach.

If this idea seems far-fetched to some, it is, first, because the revolution occurring in Russian foreign policy is not yet clear to them, even as the suspicion of Russian double-dealing still looms large in the back of many peoples' minds; second, because so few have thought through what such an alliance would be about; and, third, because the new direction in Russian policy seems still fragile, appearing to be virtually one mortal man's work.

On the last score, were Putin gone tomorrow, the thrust of the new Russian policy would doubtless lose some momentum, but it would not collapse. Putin, after all, is not so much inventing a policy that transcends events as he is adjusting to realities that no Russian leader can escape. In the end, whether an alternative leadership would pursue an accommodation leading to a U.S.-Russian alliance depends more on the course of U.S. policy than on the vagaries of Russian politics.

So what might animate a U.S.-Russian alliance? The core focus can and should be stability and mutual security in and around the Eurasian land mass. This focus operates through three geographical lenses: Russia itself and its near European periphery; Russia's south; and China's western periphery.

First, as Alexander Vershbow, the current U.S. ambassador in Moscow, puts it: "Russia is the most important key to the stability of Eurasia," without which neither Europe nor Asia—two regions in which the United States has vital interests—can "be stable and prosperous."[9] As long as Russia respects the sovereignty of the former Soviet republics, the United States has every reason to cooperate with Russia in stabilizing and aiding those states. In this regard, as well as others, alliance does not mean condominium; U.S.-Russian collaboration must not imply a readiness to decide matters over the heads of Russia's neighbors. On the contrary, an alliance's purpose would be to strengthen their sovereignty and vitality. A key example of the subtle way in which the revolution in Russian foreign policy makes this kind of alliance possible concerns Belarus. Putin's new agenda has led to a sharp cooling in Russia's relations with Alexander Lukashenka's regime. As a consequence, a leadership that flouts the values on which modern European security is based is increasingly isolated, the prospect of a Russian-Belarusian union has faded, and Ukraine's fears of encirclement have eased. Although not perfectly parallel, U.S. and Russian interests in Belarus, Ukraine and Moldova now converge sufficiently to make promoting stability and successful reform there a matter of common U.S. and Russian ground.

Second, to borrow the formulation of Alexei Bogaturov, in the twenty-first century no longer is peninsular Europe or Northeast Asia the critical "strategic rear" of the United States, but the vast turbulent region stretching from eastern Turkey to western China and along Russia's south.[10] As the United States girds to cope with the threats emanating from this area, no country brings more value as a potential ally than Russia. As things stand, the United States has backed into Central Asia with military power as part of the war against terrorism, and in the process it has offered quasi-security commitments to its new partners, almost certainly without careful consideration of their wider implication.[11] Central Asia forms the unstable core of Inner Asia; it is an area—the only one in the world—surrounded by four nuclear powers, two of whom recently teetered on the brink of war. It contains multiple points of friction—from Kashmir to the Fergana Valley to northwest Kazakhstan to China's Xinjiang province. Each of these points is capable of bleeding into a larger conflict, and of strengthening WMD proliferation and terrorism. It is populated by regimes whose stability is universally suspect, and contains wealth—particularly in energy resources—that will make it increasingly important to both Asian and European consumers.

Not only are the United States and Russia directly but separately implicated in the stability of this region, but China is as well. This raises the third aspect of a U.S.-Russian alliance to enhance Eurasian stability. China will be a decisive actor in Inner Asia, not the least because it forms an integral part of the region. Unfortunately, China enters through its underdeveloped northwest territories, including Xinjiang—precisely where it feels most vulnerable. In part because of this sense of vulnerability, and in part because of the general state of Sino-American relations, China has not welcomed the arrival of American military power in Central Asia. On the contrary, while excusing a temporary deployment in the context of a war that it supports, China's leadership has opposed an extended U.S. presence there as an element of a hostile encirclement stratagem.

Russia and the United States have good reason to act jointly, not only to enhance their common stake in regional stability, but to draw China into a constructive dialogue over the role all three will play in Central Asia. Russia, with the Shanghai Cooperation Organization, is already engaged in such an effort. Talking to the Russians about U.S. military activities in Central Asia (and Georgia) builds mutual confidence by promoting transparency, but it is not so far-fetched to imagine a far more ambitious trilateral dialogue among Russia, China, and the United States. Much as the United States and its European allies share assessments of threats at the edges of Europe, plan for coordinated action, and struggle to create the necessary machinery to carry it out, so can and should Russia and the United States do the same in Eurasia with Chinese participation when appropriate.

High Stakes

Russia and the United States allied against the new century's primary strategic threats, particularly those emanating from within and around the Eurasian land mass, would have much the same significance in the emerging international order as key U.S. alliances have had in the past. Even more so will this be the case if the alliance is underpinned by Russia's successful integration into the international economy and its safe passage to democracy.

Not insignificantly, movement toward alliance also has the advantage of blocking movement in the opposite direction. This is a rare moment in history. For the time being, and almost uniquely in the last three centuries of international politics, strategic rivalry among the major powers has disappeared. None of them defines any of the others as a primary security threat; none strains to amass military power against another; and none labors with alliances intended to thwart aggressive designs assigned to another. Given its weakness, Russia could not, even if it wished, turn itself into a global rival of the United States anytime soon. Within its own neighborhood, however, it is less disadvantaged. If events flow in the other direction, if Putin or someone to follow decides that alignment with the United States is not worth the candle, this key region could be one of the first places where this historic blessing begins to fade.

It is not difficult to imagine what such rivalry could be about. An incipient jostling between the United States and Russia in the post-Soviet space began in the 1990s, complete with competition over energy pipeline routes and the mutual nurturing of alignments with favored states, leading in turn to the polarization of regional groupings (such as GUUAM and the collective security cluster within the Commonwealth of Independent States).[12] While these trends have dissipated, none has disappeared, and in some Russian quarters they simmer unabated, sustained by U.S. troops on former Soviet soil and the impending enlargement of NATO across former Soviet borders.

Additionally, without a great deal of imagination one can conjure renewed trouble over strategic military developments. This is and will remain a nuclear world. While U.S. attention is rightly focused these days on preventing outlaw states and groups from arming themselves with nuclear and other weapons of mass destruction, ultimately the nuclear superstructure will be determined by the major nuclear powers. Currently, U.S. preponderance has permitted the United States to dictate the shape of the U.S.-Russian nuclear relationship, and Putin has prudently bowed to an outcome he cannot prevent. In the process, he and parts of the Russian security establishment are coming to accept the possibility of working with the United States and its NATO allies on the future role of missile defense.

But these are opening gambits in an ongoing process, leading in unknown directions—probably into space and the uncertainties that competition there will bring, and to a set of Chinese responses that will further complicate the Indo-Pakistani nuclear nexus and perhaps draw Japan across the nuclear threshold. The United States may for some time enjoy technological leads, permitting it by means of its own choosing to cope with the threats that lie ahead. In the modern era, however, history has been hard on states that assumed they could unilaterally impose a security order of their own devising and make it last. If, on the other hand, Russia is America's ally and not merely a reluctantly compliant foil, the United States would have much more leverage in designing a nuclear regime drained of competitive pressures among established nuclear powers, and thus more capable of circumscribing the behavior of new and would-be nuclear states.

In this light, it cannot be a good thing when Russians who are the strongest advocates of cooperation with the United States find it necessary to defend the Moscow Treaty by trumpeting effects that scarcely contribute to a more stable strategic nuclear regime. Sergei Rogov, for example, the director of the Institute for the Study of the USA and Canada, praises the agreement for proving again that Russia remains the only nuclear interlocutor the United States deems worthy of engaging; for restoring Russia's MIRV option; and for exempting Russia's large store of tactical nuclear weapons from arms control at a time when, because of weaknesses in conventional capabilities, "present Russian military doctrine puts much greater stress on nuclear containment than the Pentagon."[13]

Moving the U.S.-Russian relationship to the level of a true alliance will not be easy, considering that the two countries have only allied three times in a century and a half, and then only briefly during wartime. Nor should the idea be embraced without eyes wide-open, weighing fully its implications and recognizing its requirements. The changes under way in Russian foreign policy, however, make such a relationship thinkable, and think we should, for the stakes are high. Consider how different the world would be in twenty years if a democratic and economically revitalized Russia is a genuine partner of the United States, addressing side by side fundamental threats to international comity and welfare. Consider how much safer the world would be if no great power is locked in strategic rivalry with another, and no combination of them is lined up against one or more others. And consider how much more success-ful the United States would be if its ends and methods are increasingly seen by other major players as wise and fair.

Whether any or some of this comes to pass will depend in no small measure on what is made of the current historic opportunity in U.S.-Russian relations. So, we are brought back to the fundamental choices facing Russia and the United States. We are about to see how far Russia is prepared to go toward a deep and lasting partnership with the United States, and how much the United States is prepared to do to make it possible.

Notes

1. Zyuganov, "Our Defensive Shield Is Going into Ruin," *Sovetskaya Rossiya*, May 18, 2002.
2. Andrei Piontkovsky, "Problems for the Foreign-Policy Elite," *Russia Journal*, March 15–21, 2002.
3. Trenin, "Sealing a New Era in U.S.-Russian Relations," *Moscow Times*, May 27, 2002.
4. In this regard see Graham Allison and Andrei Kokoshin, "The New Containment: An Alliance Against Nuclear Terrorism," *National Interest* (Fall 2002).
5. Rumsfeld interviewed by Valeurs Actuelles (Paris), November 1, 2002, p. 35.
6. Haass, "U.S.-Russian Relations in the Post-Post-Cold War World," Remarks to RAND Business Leaders Forum, New York, NY, June 1, 2002.
7. For an example of this view, see Dmitry Furman, "The Flight of the Two-Headed Eagle," *Obshchaya gazeta*, May 30, 2002.
8. See, for example, "Remarks at a Round Table on Iraq, Georgia, Bush Doctrine, and Russian-American Relations," *Mosfilmovskaya*, October 2, 2002 (as reported by the Federal News Service at www.fednews.ru).
9. Vershbow, "Russia, the United States, and the Challenges of the 21st Century," Remarks at the Moscow School of Political Studies, July 22, 2002.
10. Bogaturov, "Russia-U.S.: Is It Rapprochement or a Political Game?" *Vek* (May 2002).
11. Note A.J. Bacevich, "Steppes to Empire," *National Interest* (Summer 2002).

12. GUUAM is the acronym for the joint undertaking among Georgia, Ukraine, Uzbekistan, Azerbaijan and Moldova intended to coordinate security and economic interests among these five states. Although Uzbekistan withdrew this past year, the group remains something of a counterpoise to Russian-led enterprises within the larger region.

13. Rogov, "Is It Surrender or Transition to Partnership?" *Nezavisimoye Voyennoye Obozrenie*, May 24–30, 2002.

7

Living with Russia

*Zbigniew Brzezinski**

The progressive inclusion of Russia in the expanding transatlantic community is the necessary component of any long-term U.S. strategy to consolidate stability on the Eurasian mega-continent. The pursuit of that goal will require patience and strategic persistence. There are no shortcuts on the way. Geostrategic conditions must be created that convince the Russians that it is in Russia's own best interest to become a truly democratic and European post-imperial nation-state—a state closely engaged to the transatlantic community.

Of the major Eurasian entities (the European Union, Russia, China, and Japan), only Europe and Japan can be said to recognize fully their fundamental stake in international stability. The case is somewhat more ambiguous with respect to China and Russia, which still favor more or less drastic alterations in the distribution of global power. But both are also cognizant of their limitations and aware of their interest in cooperating with the West. China is so inclined largely because it is an ongoing economic success; Russia because it is not. China thrives on foreign investment; Russia fears potential threats from its immediate south and east, and senses the diminished utility of its nuclear forces. China is self-confident; Russia is self-conscious.

Hence, both Russia and China may be susceptible to a strategy aimed at their inclusion in cooperative international structures. To that end, two Eurasian power triangles must be steadily managed and, over time, more directly connected: one involving the United States, the European Union and Russia; and the other involving the United States, Japan and China.[1] For that linkage to be effective, the constructive engagement of Russia is essential.

*Zbigniew Brzezinski, former national security adviser to the president, is counselor and trustee of the Center for Strategic and International Studies and Professor of American Foreign Policy at the School of Advanced International Studies, the Johns Hopkins University, Washington, D.C. This essay first appeared in *The National Interest*, no. 61 (Fall 2000).

To be sure, neither America nor, even less, Europe can by itself seduce or transform Russia. Russia's epiphany must come from within, much as was the case earlier in the twentieth century with the collapse of the Ottoman Empire and the emergence of the modern Turkish state. But both America and Europe can help create not only a congenial but a compelling context for desirable change. And for that reason, despite justifiable short-term pessimism regarding the outlook of Russia's current political leadership, there is a reasonable basis for longer-term optimism.

The Historical Setting

The emergence of a democratic, Europe-oriented, post-imperial, and national Russian state would provide historically relevant and strategically stabilizing answers to the two questions that haunt politically minded Russians today: what is Russia, and where is Russia? These questions are being posed in an environment bordering on social catastrophe and in a context of geopolitical vulnerability.

One cannot underestimate the cumulative damage inflicted on the Russian people by seventy years of communism. Russia's current condition should not be judged by the superficial glitter of Moscow or St. Petersburg, the primary beneficiaries of Western financial inflows, or by occasional ups and downs in Russian growth rates. The painful reality is that the communist experiment has bequeathed to the Russian people a ruined agriculture, a retarded and in many places primitive social infrastructure, a backward economy increasingly facing the risk of progressive de-industrialization, a devastated environment, and a demographically threatened population.

To measure precisely the cumulative effects of that legacy is impossible. They are both massive and enduring. Russia's current crisis coincides with the collapse of the five hundred year-old Russian Empire, which had expanded in the Soviet era into an even larger communist empire. The domestic crisis threatens the well-being of the Russian people; the imperial collapse, while posing a potential geopolitical challenge, confuses, tempts and frustrates the country's political elite—an elite that for decades was not only doctrinally stupefied, but at times also lethally purged.[2] That elite grew accustomed to the privileges and satisfactions of Russia's global status, a status for which today there is no solid foundation. The last ten years have compounded rather than resolved these challenges. Russia's relative openness has made the Russian people quite aware of the truly enormous gap separating their condition from that of their West European neighbors. The increasingly widespread awareness that a densely populated China next door is also doing incomparably better is an additional source of anxiety. Finally, for a state long accustomed to thinking of itself as America's principal rival, it is galling to contemplate the fact that Russia's GDP, measured in terms of purchasing power parity, is only about one-tenth of America's, roughly half of India's, and somewhat less than Brazil's.

It must also be troubling for informed Russians to learn that last year China benefited from more than $43 billion in direct foreign investment (bringing the 1992–99 total to about $350 billion)—and that the much smaller post-communist Poland was the beneficiary in 1999 alone of $8 billion in such investment—while only $2–3 billion was directly invested from abroad in Russia during the same period (making for a meager total of $11.7 billion over 1992–99). Flagging foreign investment derives in part from Russia's poor international economic image. In the 1999 Global Competitiveness Report, Russia was ranked last among the fifty-nine countries surveyed (China was 32, Zimbabwe 57, and Ukraine 58). In a comparative assessment of corruption in ninety-nine states, Russia was placed at 82 (behind Armenia).

It is telling that there have been no major domestically funded investments in Russia over the last ten years. By 1997 overall capital investment in the production sector had fallen to about 17 percent of the 1990 level, and only lately has risen slightly. Moreover, it has been estimated that it would take roughly $25 trillion over the next twenty-five years to renew Russia's industrial infrastructure, which, on average, is three times older than that of the OECD countries. Indeed, even with sustained economic recovery proceeding at an annual rate of 5 percent, Russia would still account for only about 2 percent of the world's GDP by 2015. By contrast, the United States and the EU together will account for approximately 45–50 percent, and Japan and China combined for probably another 25 percent or so. The qualitative gaps in technological innovation and economic competitiveness between Russia and its western neighbors may be wider still.

The social picture is even bleaker. Some 70 million Russians live in urban areas affected by levels of pollution that exceed U.S. maximum contamination levels by a factor of five or more. About 75 percent of Russia's consumed water supply is polluted by U.S. standards. Russia's health system, long a source of pride, is malfunctioning, with many hospitals (especially in non-urbanized areas) lacking hot water and unable to meet even minimal hygienic standards. Some 100,000 cases of tuberculosis have been registered, and only about 40 percent of all recent births have resulted in fully healthy babies. According to one study, some 20 percent of Russian first graders have been diagnosed with some form of mental retardation. Male life expectancy has declined from approximately sixty-four years in 1990 to about fifty-nine years in 1999 (alternative data suggests the figure might be about 61 years, still very low by Western standards). The World Health Report 2000 on national health systems ranked Russia's at 130, barely ahead of Sudan's.

Indeed, Russia's population has dropped from 151 million in 1990 to about 146 million in 1999—with annual deaths in recent years exceeding births by slightly more than 50 percent (about 2 million deaths and 1.3 million births per annum). While economic recovery and an improvement in public health programs could eventually slow the steep population decline, some demographic studies anticipate that Russia's population could dip below 135 million by the year 2025. Then, too, many Russians are moving out of the exposed northern and far eastern extremities of Russia to the more secure central region west of the Urals, thereby reversing long-standing efforts to settle the sparsely populated northern and eastern peripheries.

Russia, then, is confronted by a menacing combination of demography and geography. Its far eastern neighbor, China, not only has a population of some 1.2 billion, but an economy that in GDP terms is already four times larger than Russia's. It is also no source of geopolitical reassurance for Russia that Japan's economy is about five times larger than its own; and that to the west an expanding European Union is taking shape, with an economy already approximately ten times the size of Russia's and a population of some 375 million. Moreover, the much more prosperous Europe is allied to the United States, which has a population twice that of Russia and a GDP more than ten times as large.

To the south prospects are, if anything, even more ominous. That area is currently organized into nine states inhabited almost exclusively by Muslims. Their combined population totals about 295 million, not counting the population of the Europe-oriented Turkey, which is about 65 million. An additional 20 million Muslims currently live within Russia's borders. At current birth rates, by the year 2025 the Islamic population living immediately to the south of Russia could number as high as 450 million (not counting the projected 85 million Turks).

It is probable that most of the neighboring Muslim countries will be economically weak, enhancing the likelihood that they will also be politically volatile. Their populations—composed in the main of the younger generation, which is restless, increasingly nationally self-conscious and more intensely Islamic in self-definition—could prove quite susceptible to extremist appeals. Unless handled with great skill and genuine moderation by their formerly imperial neighbor, their political awakening could acquire a fervent anti-Russian cast, of which the Russian mishandling of Chechnya might be only a harbinger.

Much, therefore, depends on the performance of the current Russian political elite—an elite that is strikingly different in composition and outlook from its post-communist counterparts in Central Europe. Russia's current leadership includes no former political dissidents, not even one. Moreover, in Central Europe the anti-communist opposition—Solidarity in Poland, Sajudis in Lithuania and Charter 77 in Prague—represented a critical mass that was subsequently capable of undertaking democratic reforms. In most Central European states, the Communist parties also quickly converted themselves into social-democratic ones, generally supportive of reforms and of closer ties with both NATO and the EU.

In contrast, the current Russian political elite is largely an alliance of former *apparatchiki*, criminalized oligarchs, and the KGB and military leadership. Their renunciation of the Soviet past has been perfunctory: the retention of a mausoleum in the middle of Moscow honoring the embalmed corpse of the founder of the GULAG neatly encapsulates their mindset. Indeed, President Vladimir Putin's new team is composed of individuals who, with no exception, could now be serving in the higher echelons of the Soviet government (particularly the KGB) if the Soviet Union still existed. Putin's own political lineage is quite suggestive in that regard. He is a third-generation *apparatchik*: his father was a Party functionary, while his grandfather even served on Lenin's and then Stalin's personal security detail.

The present Kremlin leadership matured in the Soviet Union's waning years. By and large, it no longer believed in the crudities of Soviet ideology, but it relished Soviet power. The fall of the Soviet Union was for most of its members not only a historical shock but a calamity that could have been, and should have been, averted. While many of them dried their tears with profits derived from the kleptocratic dismantling of the state-owned economy, they nonetheless felt deprived by Russia's loss of international status. Putin captured their pent-up feelings at his inaugural when he spoke nostalgically of Russia as "a great, powerful and mighty state."

In rebuilding a Russia "which commands respect in the world", Putin's good tactical sense dictates that outright hostility to the West is to be avoided. Indeed, some accommodation with the United States is desirable, particularly in order to draw it into an anti-Islamic alliance in the event that Russia's problems in the south spin out of control. President Clinton's easy seduction into the anti-Chechen camp, in 1995 and again in 1999, offers a case in point. Russia's residual nuclear capability also provides the basis for a special dialogue with the United States, thereby enhancing Russia's prestige and perhaps even creating the impression of a special relationship.[3]

Russia's selective accommodation with the United States can be pursued in parallel with carefully calibrated efforts to cultivate anti-American sentiments in Western Europe, in order to dilute Western resolve regarding any further expansion of NATO and to exacerbate existing cleavages within the Euro-Atlantic community. Traditional diplomacy in dealings with Berlin and with Paris can also be exploited to fuel European rivalries, in order to impede the emergence of a politically more integrated EU, tied to NATO, on Russia's western frontiers. In any case, a détente with the West is the sine qua non of continued Russian access to needed Western financial assistance.

Above all, a breathing spell in relations with the West is needed if Russia is to achieve Putin's central goal: the restoration of a powerful Russian state. To the present rulers, the appearance of a dozen or so newly independent states following the Soviet Union's collapse is a historical aberration that should be gradually corrected as Russia recovers its power. Although it would appear that they realize that the end result may not be a single imperial state, they seem determined to attain the gradual subordination of the post-Soviet states within the framework of the Commonwealth of Independent States in a way that limits their practical sovereignty in the key areas of security and external economic relations.

That aspiration is the root cause of Moscow's vehement opposition to any Western economic presence in the space of the former Soviet Union. The Kremlin's attitude in this regard is still based on the old Leninist zero-sum approach: it is better for the non-Russian areas not to develop economically if such development entails a Western presence. That is why direct access of the newly independent states to the global economy through multiple pipelines from the Caspian Sea region is viewed by the current Russian elite with almost as much hostility as that shown toward Ukraine's flirtation with NATO. As one Russian Foreign Ministry official put it,

> The significant volume of funds already invested or planned by American companies for investment in Caspian oil business is defining a tendency toward a build-up of a political, and on its heels a military, U.S. presence in the Caucasus. In essence, without prior consent, the incorporation of the Caspian region into the sphere of "the United States' vital interests" is taking place.[4]

Note particularly the quaint insinuation that Russia's "consent" is required for Western investment in the newly independent states.

Strategically, Russian policy toward what the Kremlin calls "the near abroad" has essentially three prongs. The first is to exercise pressure on both Georgia and Azerbaijan, increasing their vulnerability to eventual destabilization after their current presidents depart from the scene. Second, Ukraine's return to some sort of a special "Slavic" relationship with Moscow should be encouraged, with the Russo-Belarusian "union" providing a model of the "brotherly Slavic solidarity" to which Ukrainians should aspire. Third, pressure is to be applied to prevent the Baltic states from joining NATO, on the grounds that they were once "legally" a part of the Soviet Union.[5]

In brief, the Kremlin's current occupants believe that the "mighty" Russian state should be much more than a national state coexisting with others within the former Soviet space. Although most members of the current elite realize that economic recovery is a necessary precondition for regaining historical grandeur, some also place special emphasis on Russia's military power as the basis for its claim to global status. Not surprisingly, that view is strongly held within the top Russian military leadership and was explicitly reflected in the new military doctrine adopted in December 1999. Top military leaders are also particularly strong proponents of re-established Russian political power in a new "Eurasian union."[6]

It would appear, therefore, that the current elite is more preoccupied with the restoration of a dominant Russian state than with a historic reorientation of

Russia. As a result, there is an obvious disconnect between the leadership's ends and the country's means. Contemporary Russia is simply too weak to sustain regional domination while nostalgically reclaiming superpower status. Despite numerous internal shortcomings, the new post-Soviet states are determined to retain their independence. It would take an enormous effort, far beyond Russia's present means, to subordinate them. Moreover, it is unlikely that the West, even were it inclined to accept some of Russia's regional aspirations as legitimate, would remain entirely passive if the independence of, say, Ukraine or Georgia—not to speak of the Baltic states—was threatened.

Further, Russian proponents of reliance on military power greatly underestimate the economically draining effects of any renewed arms competition with America, and overestimate the political leverage that Russia can exercise through its essentially one-dimensional strategic capability. The fact is that Russia—already spending about 5 percent of its GDP on the military—cannot compete with the U.S.-pioneered revolution in military affairs. And while its nuclear weapons can serve as a deterrent, they are not an effective political tool; their value is gradually being diminished by nuclear proliferation, especially in Russia's immediate neighborhood.

A prolonged delay in providing realistic answers to the two questions that confront post-imperial Russia—What is Russia? Where is Russia?—could prove calamitous. Social mobilization on the basis of nationalism can only be a short-term remedy. Russia, underpopulated and socially deprived, could become entangled in flaming collisions with the Muslims in the south and more vulnerable to Chinese territorial encroachments in the east, while also antagonizing Europe (and America) to the west. An "alliance" with China would only subordinate Russia to China without solving its problems.

As a result, it may be only somewhat hyperbolic to suggest that the ultimate consequence of any prolonged failure to confront the full implications of Russia's menacing geopolitical context and of the debilitated state of its society could be the emergence not of "a Europe to the Urals" (as once envisaged by General de Gaulle), but eventually of a beleaguered and imploded Russia only to the Urals.

A Decalogue on Russia's Geopolitical Condition

1. Russia's economy is about one-tenth the size of America's, and its indus trial plant is about three times older than the OECD average.
2. About 70 million Russians live in urban areas with levels of pollution five times higher than U.S. maximums, and about 75 percent of Russia's consumed water is contaminated.
3. Only about 40 percent of all recent births in Russia have resulted in fully healthy babies.
4. Russia's population has dropped from 151 million in 1990 to 146 million in 1999.

5. Russia's immediate neighbor to the east, China, has a total population of 1.2 billion; to the west, the EU has 375 million; and to the south live approximately 300 million Muslims.

6. China's economy is already four times larger than Russia's, while foreign investment in China during the last decade has been thirty times higher than in Russia. The EU's economy is ten times larger than Russia's.

7. Unlike post-communist Central Europe, the current Russian political elite is an alliance of the KGB-military leadership with former *apparatchiki* and criminalized oligarchs; all the current top Russian leaders could be serving in the Soviet government if the Soviet Union still existed.

8. The present Russian government has made it clear that its central goal is the restoration of Russia's power and not democratic reform.

9. Russia desires an accommodation with the West in order to gain a free hand in dealing with the new states in the former Soviet space.

10. Defiance of demography and geography could embroil Russia in conflicts menacing to its future as a major territorial state.

For Strategic Direction

In considering Western policy toward Russia, we would do well to reflect briefly on the collapse of the Ottoman Empire and the subsequent emergence of the Turkish national state. That experience is more pertinent to Russia's dilemmas than either Germany's and Japan's after 1945, or Great Britain's and France's after they ceased to be empires.

Unlike Germany and Japan, Russia was neither occupied and subjected to political "re-education" by the Cold War's victors, nor treated to large-scale social reconstruction under their direct supervision. For most Russians, the outcome was more ambiguous and confusing. Most at first did not feel defeated; many later felt deceived; few were receptive to Western tutelage.

Like the Russian Empire, the Ottoman Empire was territorially contiguous. Both Ottoman and Russian imperial elites drew many members from the subject nationalities. The boundaries of what was specifically Russian or Turkish territory were not very precise. In both cases, the empire was not a remote reality overseas but a seamless extension of the homeland itself. Hence, the sudden loss of empire was both more searing and directly disruptive.

In contrast to the efficiently repressive Soviet Russia, however, the long, slow decline of the Ottoman Empire spawned a significant minority of dissident intellectuals and young officers determined to model Turkey on the West European nation-states. The Young Turks, first organized in the late nineteenth century, gained increasing political influence, especially in the wake of the military defeats suffered by the Ottoman rulers. Some of them at first sought to re-create a modernized version of the old empire. But the defeat suffered in World War I prompted the next generation of reformist leaders, notably Kemal

Pasha (who later became known as Atatürk), to embrace the concept of a modernized, post-imperial state, patterned on the European nation-states. In short order, the Swiss civil code, the Italian penal code and the German commercial code were adopted, and—very important to note—irredentist claims, derived from the imperial past, were explicitly renounced.

Three timely conclusions can be drawn from the emergence of the modern national Turkish state: first, Turkey would not be contending today for membership of the European Union were it not for the fact that Atatürk and his bold reformers represented a critical mass capable of effecting a psychological break with the past; second, this effort would not have endured if the West had continued to spurn Turkey; and, third, the process of historical self-redefinition is necessarily a prolonged one, to be measured in decades, not years, and is likely to be punctuated by periodic setbacks.

These conclusions contain important lessons for Russia. Although Putin displays a picture of Peter the Great in his office, his reliance on a KGB entourage and his professed admiration for his KGB predecessor, Yuri Andropov, indicate that Putin is no Russian Atatürk. His geopolitical mindset reflects the thinking of the last Soviet generation and not of the first post-Soviet generation. Nonetheless, a new outlook is being nurtured beneath the existing political surface in the much more open conditions of post-Soviet Russia. And if only for actuarial reasons, the next generation of Russian leaders is unlikely to be the product either of the KGB or of the *apparat*.

That generation will come of age at a time when Russia's past imperial and global status will have become a distant memory rather than an entitlement. This inevitably will create a different global outlook. The next generation of leaders is much more likely to include graduates of Western universities and businessmen with genuine international (but not criminal) exposure, sharing a more widespread desire for Russia not only to be like the West but to be a part of the West. Not least, the Russian public will increasingly demand that its overall lifestyle begin to match at least that of Central Europe, and that Russians not be deprived of free access to the enlarging Europe next door. In short, a critical mass supportive of a genuine break with the past is taking shape.

To encourage that process, Western aid to Russia should be continued. But such assistance should not be directed to the central government. Russia is wealthy enough to be able to address its basic problems through its own resources, and Western aid has the tendency to perpetuate the worst inclinations in the current elite. Also, since financial aid is fungible, its diversion to military programs and operations (such as those in Chechnya) is a likelihood. Instead, Western aid should concentrate on helping Russia's nascent NGOs, which promote the emergence of a new, younger and more open-minded political elite—an elite that understands its own interest in a society based on the rule of law.[7]

The United States should also expand its ongoing visitor programs for younger Russian political and economic aspirants. In 1999 the Library of Congress initiated a program to bring to the United States some 2,000 younger Russian local officials for visits designed to acquaint them with the complexities of American democracy. This initiative deserves to be enlarged tenfold, and it should be complemented by a similar program for the newly independent states. After World War II, tens of thousands of young Germans and Japanese were made familiar with American democracy, with an immensely beneficial impact. Younger Russians, especially from outside Moscow and St. Petersburg, should have the same opportunity.

However, the reorientation of Russia's outlook will be delayed if Russia's current political leadership gains the impression that its priorities can be successfully pursued, especially in the space of the former Soviet Union. That such illusions and nostalgia tend to be self-perpetuating makes it all the more important that Western policy both engage Russia and drive home the need for a basic redefinition of Russia's role in Eurasia. To facilitate Russia's historical transformation, Western support for the consolidation of the new states—especially Ukraine, Georgia, Azerbaijan, and Uzbekistan—must be sustained.

Admittedly, the necessary strategic balance will not be easy to strike. In fact, some Russian sources have claimed that Clinton administration officials at times have encouraged Russian efforts to regain a dominant position in the former Soviet space.[8] Even the internationally condemned Russian assault on Chechnya did not produce a single noticeable U.S. response, on the grounds that it would be contrary to the policy of "engagement." It may unfortunately be the case that, during the latter phases of the Clinton administration, the one-sided U.S. emphasis on the West engaging Russia—but not on Russia engaging the West—could delay by some years the day when Russia comes fully to terms with its current historical condition.

To hasten rather than delay that moment, the transatlantic community must patiently keep the grand option of an ever widening and deepening association open to Russia, while persistently reinforcing an environment that discourages any Russian efforts to turn back the geopolitical clock. Only then may the next generation of Russian leaders—no longer the products of the Soviet era and more likely to represent a new critical political mass—draw the sole realistic conclusion to the dangers posed by their country's internal malaise and external vulnerability: namely, that in order to recover Russia must opt for the West. What is more, Russia must do so unambiguously and unconditionally as a post-imperial state. Russia's imperial baggage cannot be dragged into Europe. Russia cannot be at once imperial and European.

To prepare the ground for that historic choice, it is crucial that the West signal clearly that the continued enlargement of the EU and of NATO does not exclude a priori the possibility of Russia's eventual participation. Although President Clinton gave such a signal in his "Charlemagne" speech in Aachen in June 2000, he does not speak for the EU or even for NATO. A formal statement to that effect should be made, perhaps jointly by both organizations. Clearly, a truly democratic Russia that desires to be part of the West should have the option of becoming, in some mutually acceptable fashion, associated closely with both the EU and NATO. The precise modalities need not be spelled out now; in fact, given Russia's present condition and orientation, any effort to do so would be counterproductive. But the option should be held out.

In the meantime, a strategic setting favorable to that prospect should be fostered. Steps can be taken to enhance gradually the role of the Euro-Atlantic Partnership Council, which sponsors joint security programs between NATO states and Partnership for Peace members. While the United States in particular should be alert not to fall into the trap of becoming Russia's ally against the Muslims (or the Chinese), the serious possibility of conflicts spreading like grass fire throughout Central Asia might, over time, dilute Russia's hostility to greater Western involvement in the region. Moscow might then view more favorably not only greater economic access to the region, but also a larger role for peacekeeping by the Organization for Security and Cooperation in Europe (OSCE) and eventually perhaps even by NATO.

The EU's forthcoming expansion to Central Europe, even if somewhat delayed, is bound to include Poland and eventually the Baltic states. In that context, discussions with Russia regarding a possible special EU status for the Kaliningrad region could prove fruitful, not only resolving the region's persisting economic problems but also initiating closer EU-Russia arrangements. The same is true regarding the EU's ongoing efforts to promote Baltic regional cooperation that embrace both the St. Petersburg and Kaliningrad provinces of Russia.

In the meantime, President Clinton's initiative in inviting Russia to join both the EU and NATO has given greater urgency to the task of enlarging both. In fact, it is altogether unrealistic to contemplate Russia's inclusion in either structure without Central Europe's full and prior inclusion. It is equally unrealistic, and even risky, to envisage delaying Central Europe's full membership until Russia either grants its permission or itself opts for Europe. That would be tantamount to granting Russia an indefinite veto, with the likely effect of stimulating the Kremlin's geopolitical aspirations regarding the Baltic states and Ukraine. The bottom line is that the consequence of any inclination to make NATO enlargement contingent on Russia's permission is a prescription for the perpetuation of geopolitical ambiguity on the western fringes of Russia, which will impede Russia's own internal evolution. Indeed, Russia's willingness to acquiesce to the further eastward expansion of NATO, particularly regarding the Baltic states, is a litmus test of the sincerity of any declared choice by Moscow in favor of a European and a transatlantic connection.

Constructive initiatives toward Russia thus will only be credible if they are matched by tangible steps toward the enlargement of both the EU and NATO.

That dual enlargement is desirable in itself, and also because it eliminates the risk of a possible collision between competing notions of "Europeanism" and "Atlanticism." Moreover, several European countries immediately to the west of Russia—the Baltic states especially—want to be, and have the right to be, part of both the EU and of NATO. The next president of the United States should therefore urge our allies to move promptly on the admission of any democratic European state that meets the criteria for NATO membership, even before the year 2002 (the date previously set by NATO for the consideration of further enlargement).

The enlargement of NATO, in any case, has already proven beneficial for Europe's security, including Russia's. Most notably, it has made post-Cold War Europe more stable, anchoring Germany more solidly in its middle rather than making it a "border state," as some German leaders feared might happen after reunification. NATO enlargement has consolidated a sense of security among the new members and promoted better relations between them and their non-member neighbors. It has encouraged aspirant nations to improve their treatment of minorities and to settle their territorial disputes. It has also stimulated closer Polish-Ukrainian cooperation, reinforcing Ukraine's declared interest in its eventual association with the West. Last but not least, Romania and Bulgaria, because of their desire for membership, acted decisively during the Kosovo conflict to prevent the unilateral deployment of Russian para-troopers into Pristina—a deployment that could have precipitated a risky collision between Russia and NATO.[9]

The West should not be timid in affirming that Russia's acquiescence to the expansion of the EU and of NATO will hasten the day when Russia itself will be able to choose a more comprehensive association. Its precise form and extent will have to be negotiated, but a constructive Russian response should also prompt both NATO and the EU to begin a systematic review as to what kind of a shared security system, spanning "Vancouver to Vladivostok," might be both feasible and desirable. The enhancement of the OSCE, and its transfor-mation from a "European" to a "Eurasian" framework, could likewise become timely; and NATO itself may eventually become a core element of a transcon-tinental security system.[10] Given a positive Russian attitude, it may not be too early to initiate informal exploratory discussions regarding these longer-range prospects in the context of the NATO-Russia Joint Council, a step that would enhance the Council's significance and also gratify Moscow.

Thus, step-by-step, a linkage of the two critical global security triangles—involving the United States, the European Union and Russia; and the United States, China and Japan—may be constructed. That process may be hastened by the ongoing revolution in military technology, which raises the serious possibility that the more than forty year-old reliance on mutual deterrence may have to be fundamentally revised in favor of some form of strategic de-fense. Given that such a development bears directly on the immediate security interests of the three nuclear NATO powers, as well as of Russia and China, a comprehensive dialogue among them will become necessary beyond any bilateral U.S.-Russia discussions. That need will itself generate pressures for a standing Eurasian security forum.

It is important to reiterate that, while it should be the policy of the United States to engage Russia in an ever-closer relationship with the West, such policy should not be confused with one-sided courtship. Effective engagement should strive to create a geostrategic setting in which the Russian elite itself comes to realize that Russia's only option is its best option: to become genuinely "engaged" to the West.

It takes only a little imagination to conjure how beneficial it would be for Russia if one day the Kremlin startled the world by announcing that it welcomed the enlargement of the EU and NATO to include all those who wished to join, and that Russia itself hopes to qualify for membership of both. Such an epiphany would liberate Russia from its ominous geopolitical context and create favorable conditions for its acutely needed social rehabilitation.

The policy of effective engagement should be deliberately designed to make that choice Russia's only choice.

A Decalogue of Strategic Guidelines

1. The lessons of the collapse of the Ottoman Empire are highly relevant to Russia's contemporary dilemmas.
2. Turkey's historic self-redefinition was made possible by the presence of a reformist critical mass and by the West's eventual responsiveness.
3. The next generation of Russian leaders may provide the critical mass needed for a decisive, post-imperial choice in favor of the West.
4. To that end, Western financial assistance should concentrate almost exclusively on the advancement of a new democratically minded elite through the promotion of grassroots democracy and expanded visitor exchanges.
5. Propitiation of Putin's regime will only delay the desired evolution of Russia into a democratic, Europe-oriented, national Russian state.
6. Support for the newly independent states will help to advance the historical self-redefinition of Russia.
7. The EU and NATO should formally propose Russia's eventual association, and both the EU and NATO should explore with Russia specific initiatives to that end, including a special EU status for Kaliningrad.
8. In the meantime, both EU and NATO expansion should continue, thereby eliminating any geopolitical ambiguities or temptations in the areas immediately west of Russia.
9. A transcontinental security dialogue on strategic doctrine, building on a closer NATO-Russia connection, eventually could link the two key Eurasian security triangles.

10. Effective engagement cannot be pursued through one-sided courtship but only by shaping a decisive geopolitical context, in which a choice for the West becomes Russia's only viable option.

Notes

1. See my "Living With China" and "Living With a New Europe" in *The National Interest's* Spring 2000 and Summer 2000 issues, respectively. "Living with China" is also a chapter in *China in The National Interest* (Transaction, 2002).
2. Few in the West fully appreciate the scope of Stalin's purge of the social elite. In one chilling example from the Soviet archives, the NKVD's Moscow headquarters set quotas for the number of people to be immediately arrested and shot. That quota for Moscow in the fall of 1937 was 5,000; for Leningrad 4,000; for Vladivostok 2,000; for Sverdlovsk 4,000, etc. Subsequently, some of the NKVD regional offices submitted appeals, requesting increases in their quotas!
3. The current Russian leadership seems more skilled than its predecessors in influencing Western policymakers and opinion shapers, apparently relying more on the KGB's intelligence apparatus, those trained by the Soviet Institute on the USA, easy access to Western centers of influence enjoyed by Russian oligarchs holding dual citizenship, and even on hired public relations firms. It stands to reason that the Russian leaders are not indifferent to the outcome of U.S. presidential elections and may be sensitive to the West's thirst for electoral campaign funds.
4. S.I. Chernyavskiy, "Washington's Caucasus Strategy," *Mezhdunarodnaya zhizn* (January 1999).
5. Disturbingly, the official position of Russia is that the Baltic states in 1940 gained "admission" to the USSR. See, for example, the official statement of the Russian Foreign Ministry, February 2, 2000.
6. A good example of such thinking is the doctoral dissertation of the influential head of the Defense Ministry's Main Directorate of International Military Cooperation, General Leonid Ivashov, titled "Evolution of Russia's Geopolitical Development" (May 2000).
7. For a compelling case for a much more discriminating Western aid policy toward Russia, see Michael McFaul, "Getting Russia Right," *Foreign Policy* (Winter 1999-2000), pp. 65-7.
8. "Off the record, State Department officials often talk unequivocally in favor of a Russian sphere of influence in Eurasia." Andrei Kortunov, "The U.S. and Russia: A Virtual Partnership," *Comparative Strategy* (October-December 1996), p. 347.
9. See Zbigniew Brzezinski and Christopher Swift, "Russia and the Kosovo Crisis" (Washington, DC: CSIS, October 1999), pp. 14–16, 19.
10. The case for the further expansion of the EU was made in my "Living With a New Europe." On expanding the OSCE from a European to a Eurasian organization, see my "Living With China." It should also be noted that the EU has initiated strategic consideration of a long-term security relationship with Russia, through its "Common Strategy of the European Union on Russia" of June 4, 1999.

8

Geotherapy: Russia's Neuroses, and Ours

Stephen Sestanovich *

> *"An ambition, inordinate and immense, one of those ambitions which could only possibly spring in the bosoms of the oppressed, and could only find nourishment in the miseries of a whole nation, ferments in the heart of the Russian people. That nation, essentially aggressive, greedy under the influence of privation, expiates beforehand, by a debasing submission, the design of exercising a tyranny over other nations: the glory, the riches which it hopes for, consoles it for the disgrace to which it submits. To purify himself from the foul and impious sacrifice of all public and personal liberty, the slave, upon his knees, dreams of the conquest of the world."—The Marquis de Custine, Russia in 1839*

During the Cold War, Americans by and large forgot Custine, perhaps the grumpiest tourist and most scathing vilifier of Russia who ever wrote. Locked in conflict with a totalitarian state, we thought that the main reason the Soviet Union made trouble for us, and for the world at large, was that it was not a democracy. Take away Bolshevik ideology, the command economy, and the power of the Politburo, and you'd be a long way toward normalcy. Dissolve the Warsaw Pact, slash military spending, give the non-Russian republics their independence, and it would be hard to see what we might fight about. Adopt a constitution, end censorship, respect religious freedom, hold elections, then hold more elections: Could a country that did all these things really be a threat?

Apparently, yes. Political institutions, we are now told, solve much less than was once imagined. They do not address deep psychic and socio-cultural torments, and legions of new Custines have begun to argue that for Russians

---

*At the time this piece was authored, Stephen Sestanovich was vice president for Russian and Eurasian affairs at the Carnegie Endowment for International Peace in Washington, DC. This essay first appeared in *The National Interest*, No. 45 (Fall 1996).

no torment is deeper than that of being a fallen superpower—unless perhaps it is that of being a fallen superpower while also undergoing the transition to a market economy. In any case, the pain is excruciating and is said to be relieved only by an increasingly belligerent foreign policy, ideally by re-establishment of the Soviet Empire. As for other countries, they need to understand the deep roots of this affliction, while resisting any thought that the tools of modern medicine can ameliorate it. Foreign policy, says one authority, is not a realm of "psychological engineering." Russia, says another, is not our "patient."[1] (These authorities, it will be seen, do not always follow their own advice.)

Nations do have neuroses. If an unhappy past is one of the causes, Russia must have at least its share of them, and probably more. But for all its pseudo-historical depth, the current psychiatric school of analyzing Russia's politics and policies tells us very little about what is going on there. As a result, it cannot be a proper basis for formulating policies of our own.

The Diagnosis

An exceptionally diverse group of analysts and political commentators subscribes to some version of the diagnosis just set forth. It is embraced by those who were the most ardent critics of the Soviet order and those who are trying their best to restore it, by lowly working journalists and eminent former officials. Despite their differences, they agree on this: Russian imperial consciousness is not dead. To the contrary, writes Richard Pipes, perhaps our greatest historian of Russia, the loss of empire "has produced bewilderment and anguish."

> [N]othing so much troubles many Russians today, not even the decline in their living standards or the prevalence of crime, and nothing so lowers in their eyes the prestige of their government, as the precipitous loss of great-power status.[2]

Anatoly Lukyanov (once one of Gorbachev's principal lieutenants, then one of his principal betrayers, and now a leader of the revived Russian Communist Party) seconds this view. "We communists," he has said (this is an admission he would hardly have made in the old days, when good communists despised bourgeois liberties), "always understood perfectly well that the Soviet man, the citizen of Russia, had fewer political rights than a European. But that shortfall was compensated for by the sense of belonging to a great nation, a great state." Yeltsin undid this formula, thereby making Russian democracy vulnerable to a communist revanche.

He took away that sense of world importance. Any party which takes advantage of this today will be on top. That is why the communists have so many patriotic slogans, slogans of statehood, of nationhood.[3]

The reason that popular government does not mean peace, in short, is that the people don't necessarily want peace; they want to be on top again. As Henry Kissinger has put it, "[W]hat passes for Russian democracy too often encourages an expansionist foreign policy." Yeltsin can hardly let the Communists be the only ones to tap the people's mood, so he ends up taking positions that "differ only in degree from those urged by Zyuganov," his Communist challenger in the June presidential race. As one measure of how domestic political pressures work, Russia is now inclined "to conduct adventurous policies in Asia for no other purpose than to augment its prestige."

For Kissinger, this mad preoccupation with "ancient glories" is no mere election-season phenomenon, but something more durable—and more dangerous. "Foreign policy," he announces, "has emerged as the *deus ex machina* for Russia's elite to escape present-day frustrations by evoking visions of a glorious past."

A *deus ex machina*, of course, always transforms the story of which it is a part, and Russia will be no exception. Chrystia Freeland, who writes from Moscow for the *Financial Times*, worries that what she calls Yeltsin's "shift to the nationalist camp" will prove to be "a dangerous watershed in Russian history." It means nothing less than that he has "abandoned the effort to forge a new post-communist and post-imperial identity." Instead of endlessly pretending that their past was so great, she feels, Russians should "undergo a process of national repentance." This self-examination is the only way back to political health: "[B]efore they can construct a new, democratic national myth, Russians must confront their murderous communist past."

For Zbigniew Brzezinski, Russia's need to take "a hard look in the mirror" is more than a mere scholarly conclusion. It should be the core of U.S. policy. After all, "democracy and modernization begin with self-education." Unfortunately, what he sees in Russia today, even among its democratic leaders, is a "self-deluding obsession with power and status." Getting the Russians to listen won't be easy, he acknowledges, but we have an obligation to tell them—"calmly, frankly, and firmly"—the truth about what ails them and about what it will take to recover.

Toward a Second Opinion

It is difficult to think of a time when so much distinguished pundit-power has been devoted to putting an entire country on the couch. Consider the psychiatric vocabulary that runs through the discussion. There is "anguish," "loss of status," "identity" and a "sense of belonging," "repentance," and "self-deluding obsession."[4] Russia, once a country that needed a revolution, now seems to need something even more profound: professional help. It's not enough to be free, you also have to be cured.

The mere fact that our leading foreign-policy commentators have started to talk like therapists does not, of course, prove that they are wrong. But the mode of analysis is, to say the least, a little unusual—not least because it is so often combined with a vehement insistence that U.S. policy toward Russia must not be, as Henry Kissinger himself put it years ago, "a subdivision of psychiatry." Let us therefore try to verify the diagnosis.

The geotherapists assert the following four propositions. First, that public opinion creates irresistible pressures, to which Russian leaders have to respond, for an expansionist foreign policy. Second, that the Russian elite retains a strong imperial mindset and, in particular, is determined to regain control of the old Soviet Union. Third, that Russian leaders are dangerously preoccupied with questions of prestige and status, and believe that in the past these were their country's proudest asset. And fourth, that the indulgent attitude of the West, and above all the United States, toward Russia, even when it defies us, is making all these pathologies worse. (There are, it has to be said, some differences among the various commentators who argue this case. Some feel more strongly about one proposition than another. But we will be in a better position to decide how seriously to take these little nuances once we see whether even one of the propositions stands up.)

Evaluating these four claims should not be hard. A patient in such terrible shape is going to give daily proof of how much is wrong with him. If Russia really were as sick as this, we should find useful evidence everywhere we look—in domestic struggles for political power, in the conduct of foreign policy, in the strategic concepts embraced by officialdom and the intelligentsia. Do we?

The Traumatized Public

The Russian political system lacks legitimacy; it can't deliver bread, only imperial circuses; expansionism, and expansionism alone, diverts the popular mind from its misery. For symptoms of this problem, we can start with the recent presidential campaign—a political event that in many countries does bring neuroses to the surface. Boris Yeltsin, it should be remembered, ran for re-election on the basis of a dual strategy, and it was often a quite unedifying sight. On those issues where the Communists had him on the defensive, he pandered and dissembled. Hence his promises to pay all back wages and to end the war in Chechnya. At the same time, on those issues where he had *them* on the defensive, Yeltsin turned up the pressure. Hence his lurid evocations of the Communist past and policy initiatives, like his decree on private land ownership, that were meant to frame the election as a choice between politicians who accept the new order and those who don't.

Now, where did imperial nostalgia fit into this strategy? Leave aside for the moment the fact that those candidates who put nationalist themes at the center of their campaign lost badly, and that exit polls put the number of voters who were swayed by foreign policy at only 2 percent.[5] If the geotherapists were right about the country's mental state, we should have seen Yeltsin scrambling to prove that he is part of the revisionist patriotic consensus. Instead, we saw him use foreign policy as a tool to demonstrate the differences between himself and the Communists, and to remind voters of what they *don't* want to retrieve from their "glorious" past.

The issue was not simply a matter of rhetoric and mood, but of conflict between the legislature and the executive. On March 15, 1996, the Russian parliament passed two Communist-sponsored resolutions annulling the acts under which the Soviet Union was dissolved in 1991. It declared that the agreement to create a Commonwealth of Independent States (CIS) in place of the USSR "did not and does not have legal force," and charged that the officials who had "prepared, signed, and ratified" this decision had "flagrantly violated the wish of Russia's people to preserve the USSR."

With this bold move, the opposition clearly thought that they had Yeltsin trapped. On the one hand, he could hardly endorse a resolution that personally denounced him. On the other, opposing it would put him on the wrong side of a supposedly super-charged issue. As things turned out, however, the Duma's action proved to be the moment when Yeltsin's campaign got on a winning track for good. It gave the president and his allies their first, best opportunity to persuade voters that the Communists really were bent on restoring the old order. Yeltsin called the resolution "scandalous" and, showing that he had no fear of seeming too attentive to foreign opinion, immediately instructed Russian diplomats to tell other governments that the vote would have no effect.

There is a Moscow witticism that goes: Anyone who does not regret the collapse of the Soviet Union has no heart; anyone who wants to restore it has no brain. The Communists bet that people did not really believe this; they lost the bet. The March 15th resolution and its aftermath certainly put a question mark over the idea that the loss of empire has left Russians in a state of "bewilderment and anguish." But it is, admittedly, only a single incident. Perhaps the Duma's action was too bald, with too many overtones of restoring communism intact? Perhaps for this reason the Russian people weren't quite able to respond to it as they might have liked, with honest imperial relish?

Fortunately, there is other evidence to work with. In the course of the election campaign, Yeltsin *did* pander on some foreign policy issues. Even before the Duma's March 15th resolutions, his advisers openly acknowledged that he intended to respond in some fashion to the electorate's presumed unhappiness with the state of relations among the former republics of the USSR. These initiatives, they said, would keep the Communists from monopolizing popular discontent. And sure enough, at the end of March and beginning of April, Yeltsin unveiled new agreements with three of these states: a quadrilateral "Treaty on Deepening Integration in Economic and Humanitarian Spheres," signed by Russia, Belarus, Kazakhstan, and Kyrgyzstan; and a bilateral treaty between Russia and Belarus, which created "a qualitatively new phase in relations" between them. The closer one looks, however, the less these agreements, and the public response to them, seem like proof of a growing appetite for empire. As they scrutinize the menu, Russians appear quite undecided about how hungry they really are, and eager to make sure they don't overeat.

Both integration agreements were replete with commitments to advance this or that concrete interest, such as increased trade and investment, joint efforts in science and technology, coordination of education policy and veterans benefits, etcetera. The quadrilateral treaty, in particular, was precisely the kind of diplomatic "breakthrough" that Russians long ago learned not to take seriously. As for the "union of the two" with Belarus, the real question was whether the agreement marked the first big break in Russia's reluctance to cooperate too closely, on the grounds that it would be too expensive and slow down Russia's own economic stabilization program. There was, in fact, some reason to see the agreement as something new: Russia had for the first time agreed to a monetary and a customs union. And yet the conditions for implementing the agreement remained extremely stiff. For "integration" to take effect, Belarus has to bring its economic reforms and policies fully into line with Russia's—and this is virtually inconceivable.

There was perhaps no better confirmation (even if indirect) of Russian skepticism about the new relationship than the speech given by the president of Belarus, Alyaksandr Lukashenka, at the treaty signing ceremony in Moscow. Sensing that this was his best chance to speak to the Russian people about the agreement, he devoted the bulk of his remarks to refuting the idea that only Belarus would benefit from it, at Russia's expense. ("That is not so. It is a lie, to say the least," he fulminated. "Belarus has never been dependent on anyone and has never been a parasite.")

Lukashenka did not seem aware that the Russian soul is possessed by demons that drive the country toward integration whether it will benefit or not. He appeared to believe that he actually had to defend the treaty on the humdrum ground of interest. Accordingly, he spoke of all the goods that Belarus produces for the Russian market, of the revenues it used to supply to the Soviet treasury, of the value of coordinated national policies on such matters as "finding employment, health care, acquisition of property, housing construction, and so on."

After the April agreements were signed, there was a typical bit of Moscow squabbling about who deserved the real credit for this gigantic achievement. Was it the Duma, as the Communists insisted, that had pushed Yeltsin in this direction? Or had the president, as his aides rebutted, been deeply committed to integration for a long time? This was precisely the sort of struggle for political advantage that could bolster the geotherapists' case. Except for one thing: The controversy seemed to evoke no public interest. It lost its fizz almost immediately, and the politicians turned to other issues, where it really mattered who got the credit.

An Imperial Elite?

The fact that reconstituting the Soviet Union has been a bust politically makes it hard to defend the first of the geotherapists' propositions. There is no identifiable pressure from jingoist public opinion that radicalizes all policies until they "differ only in degree." But we can hardly be certain that Russia has sworn off empire just because its people are not imperialists. The elite may have its own, very different aspirations, and lack of popular support will not necessarily keep them from being realized.

This second proposition is a bit harder to put under the microscope. The Russian ruling class is far more diverse than ever before—politically, economically, regionally, generationally, ethnically, and in other ways as well. It is therefore quite artificial to speak of what *the* elite thinks. (This was beginning to be true even in the last years of the Soviet era.) All the same, there are many organizations purporting to express what they claim is a hard-boiled centrist consensus, and none does so more convincingly than the Council on Foreign and Defense Policy (CFDP). The group is a self-styled analog to our own Council on Foreign Relations in its heyday, a comparison made credible by the former's success in bringing together corporate leaders and experts on international affairs. Its members—among whom ambitious insiders, trimmers, and climbers are very well represented—know exactly what is respectable and what is not.

Last winter and spring, the CFDP conducted a series of meetings to discuss a draft report—"theses," they were called—on the issue of integration. The document went through three versions, was greatly expanded, heavily revised, and published in May under the signature of forty-four bankers, industrialists, journalists, and policy wonks. In its final form (bearing the title, "Will a Union be Reborn?"), it represents the most revealing statement to date of elite opinion about Russia's relations with the other former Soviet states.[6]

The most arresting passage in the CFDP "theses" is the repudiation of the idea of recreating the USSR, which is labeled "an extremely reactionary utopia." Pursuing it, says the report, will only weaken Russia and cause much bloodshed.

> However humiliated the national consciousness of the Russians may be, today Russian society is absolutely unprepared to pay the price of a lot of blood to make up for geopolitical losses.

To be against a restored communist imperium and against bloodshed is not, of course, to be against re-building Russian power. The CFDP believes that the collapse of the Soviet Union left Russia with much less international influence, and it proposes to try to increase it. But how? Bloodshed, it turns out, is just one constraint among many; so is cost.

> The new Russian political and economic elites are oriented more toward economic rather than military-political domination in the territories of the former USSR (the latter is more troublesome and more costly).[7]

"Economic domination," it should be said, doesn't mean a readiness to subsidize poor countries; Russia had its fill of "donorship" in the old days. For the CFDP, the main way to make Russia a "magnet" for the rest of the CIS is through "the successful development of Russia itself, the continuation of democratic and market reforms, and the beginning of an active policy of economic growth."

The CFDP prides itself on being hard-headed and unsentimental, just like the "establishment" (a current Russian vogue word) that it claims to represent. Accordingly, while it favors the goal of "rapprochement and integration," it can't help pointing out the emptiness and stupidity of many proposals for achieving this goal. Russia's relations with the rest of the former Soviet states, for example, should not be over-institutionalized: grand designs are silly. The CFDP "theses" propose instead

> to shift the center of gravity of activities in the space of the former USSR away from the highest level—the establishment of superstructures, the signing of treaties and agreements and the like—to support for specific projects of interaction in the cultural, social and above all economic spheres: the exchange of debt for ownership, the creation of financial-industrial groups, the facilitation of financial transactions, the establishment of joint banks, and so forth.

When it comes to achieving "economic domination," what these hard-headed, unsentimental folks say they want is "a common market for goods and services," and their reasons have a distinctly familiar, un-imperial ring. "Openness of markets," they note, "helps to create jobs in all states, alleviating the political and psychological consequences of the disintegration of the USSR."

To be sure, there is also a strong military side to the program. The CFDP definitely supports defense cooperation with CIS states. But it opposes the reflexive broadening of Russia's ambitions and commitments just because it sounds tough and because some neighboring states (for reasons that may not serve Russian interests at all) are willing to cooperate. The "theses" specifically object to creating "a system of collective defense" for the CIS.

It is one thing to organize specific cooperation in several areas (air defense, ABM defense, border service, training of officer cadres, supply, etcetera), but it is another thing to create an alliance costly for Russia that will be perceived by many neighbors as a threat and not only not increase but rather decrease Russia's defensive possibilities.

So, a multilateral alliance seems to be out. And even bilateral ties—no matter how close the state's historic connection to Russia is—may not make good strategic sense:

> [U]nder present conditions a military alliance with Belarus may be used by the adherents of a very rapid expansion of NATO, an alliance with Armenia may harm Russia's interests in Azerbaijan, and an alliance with Kazakhstan may cause a certain amount of concern in China. For this reason it is advisable to build alliance relations "from the bottom up" under conditions of maximum possible transparency and in dialogue with neighboring countries.

The core judgment of the CFDP's report is that, over the long term, closer relations between Russia and the former Soviet states are probably inevitable. But its core recommendation is that Russia should aspire to "leadership, instead of control." Trying to accelerate the process will accomplish nothing, and may even slow things down.

It used to be said of U.S. policy in the Western hemisphere that Americans would do almost anything for Latin America except hear about it. The Russian elite spends so much time talking about its former Soviet neighbors—and the discussion is so full of cautions, hesitations, and fine print—that one is tempted to ask: Is there anything Russia will do for the "near abroad" except hear about it?

The Matter of Pride

Let us turn to the third element of Russia's allegedly neurotic politics—the preoccupation of its leaders with their country's international status. Brzezinski sees them as "obsessed by the notion that Russia be hailed a great power." And Kissinger, in describing the consequences of Russia's "almost paranoid sense of insecurity," speaks of "adventurous" policies that he claims have no other purpose than "prestige."[8]

In ordinary Russian discourse on foreign policy, the question of prestige does come up in a way that is, at first sight, quite different from what one encounters in an American context. A bureaucratic document produced for President Clinton by the staff of the National Security Council, for example, would not ordinarily speak of protecting the prestige of the United States as a major national interest. Yet last spring *Nezavisimaya Gazeta* devoted three full pages to the publication of just such a document, "The National Security Policy of the Russian Federation, 1996-2000," prepared by the staff of Yeltsin's Security Council. It declared, among other things, that securing and protecting Russia's "international status" were right at the top of its foreign policy goals:

> Russia's most important national interest at a global level is its active and full participation in building a system of international relations in which Russia is assigned a

place corresponding in the highest degree to its potential political, economic and intellectual significance and its military-political and foreign-economic potential and needs.

This effort was said to be all the more important because other countries are bent on taking Russia down a peg. For this reason, "maximum efforts must be made to elaborate and use means of effectively countering attempts to weaken [Russia's] international positions and prestige."

How kooky is this? Brzezinski argues that it is extremely destructive. These fits of self-glorification allow Russia to ignore how far it has fallen behind economically. Worse, the inevitable emphasis on past greatness, the nostalgia for a time when the Soviet Union could compete on equal terms with the United States—all this implicitly "legitimizes the Communist Party" and postpones "genuine democratization."

Perhaps. But it is worth looking more closely at the "National Security" document just quoted, for taken as a whole it lends all this talk of prestige a different, indeed opposite, meaning. Brzezinski himself could not ask for a blunter description of Russian reality than one finds here—in, of all places, a public document released on the eve of the presidential election. Far from diverting attention from economic backwardness, Yeltsin's national security staff warns that "it will take several generations before we can compare ourselves with the United States, Japan, Germany, Sweden, France, and so forth." Far from pining for lost superpower equality, the document explicitly "renounces the principle of military-strategic parity with the United States." And far from encouraging the confrontational outlook of old, it says something that will surprise those who know of these matters only what the geotherapists tell them: "Russian citizens must mobilize state structures, the public, the family, and schools to mold a non-aggressive type of individual and a secure society and state." Given all the work that has to be done, Russia's foreign policy bottom-line is a very simple one: It needs to be able to direct its resources to the successful completion of massive internal tasks.

Russians have no trouble understanding the fix they're in, because—unlike us—*they're in it*. They can barely think of anything else. In these circumstances, a "policy of prestige" has the function that Hans Morgenthau had in mind when he described it as the effort to impress others with "the power one's own nation actually possesses, or with the power it believes, or wants other nations to believe, it possesses." Strictly speaking, wrote Morgenthau, when your power is not in fact as great as you want others to think, it should be called a "policy of bluff."[9] But the purpose is the same—to discourage them from taking advantage of you in the way that they might if they knew how weak you really were.

Looked at in this light, concerns for prestige should actually seem completely familiar to Americans—and not in the least neurotic. Wasn't the Nixon administration's determination to keep the war in Vietnam from damaging America's international role—the rejection of "peace now" in favor of "peace with honor"—based on exactly the same insight? Certainly anyone who says that the confusion of U.S. policy after South Vietnam's collapse emboldened the Soviet Union is describing the same phenomenon.[10]

Russia's "obsession" with prestige is at bottom an admission of weakness. Recall that Yeltsin's "National Security" document, quoted earlier, speaks of the importance of winning an international role based not on Russia's power, but on its *potential*. The determination to protect the country's prestige is not a demand for "adventures" that will show strength, but a hope to get by without being put to the test. Prestige is not a means of dodging the necessary work of democratization, but—if it works—of dodging unnecessary defeats while this work goes on. (In this sense, the war in Chechnya represents a conspicuous self-inflicted failure of the policy: the Russians have called their own bluff.)

The way Russians talk about NATO expansion supports this view of what they mean by prestige. What is most vexing to them about the Western plan to bring the Atlantic Alliance into Eastern Europe is that it dramatizes Russia's loss of standing. It shows Russia to be isolated, without the ability to affect events, without "standing" in the juridical sense—that is, without the right to have a grievance heard in court. Two prominent Russian specialists on America, Aleksei Bogaturov and Viktor Kremeniuk, wrote recently that NATO expansion shows America's complete "disregard for [Russia's] opinion." Russians may be pained by this, they said, but the truth is that Washington "does not have even a shadow of fear over Moscow's possible reaction."[11]

"Coddling" and Its Consequences

Since the end of the Cold War, American presidents—first Bush and now Clinton—have treated Russian leaders with exceptional personal courtesy, and with the diplomatic hyperbole embodied in the term "strategic partnership." Russians see this. Bogaturov and Kremeniuk acknowledge "a measure of humanism" in U.S. policy toward their country. The West does not want to "unduly hurt Russia," they say, and will even "spare Russia's self-esteem to the extent possible."

Now the geotherapists are not against politeness as such. What bothers them—and this is their fourth proposition—is the thought that the United States might go beyond cordiality, and actually reshape Western policy to take account of Russian objections (or worse yet, Russian excuses about their domestic political situation). Kissinger scorns "the assumption that Yeltsin must be coddled." Treating him "as if he were some tender shoot," he writes, only encourages more assertive nationalism. Brzezinski sees the same risk in the slow pace of NATO expansion. Delay—which he calls a "disgrace"—"has simply encouraged the current Russian rulers to compete with the extrem-

ists."[12] Russia, he insists, is not actually helped by "one-sided deference."
What it needs most is a dose of the reality therapy that we gave the Japanese
and Germans after the Second World War, which obliged them to make a
"clear-cut break" with the past.

This argument is wrong on two separate counts: first, about the course of
Russian policy and, second, about the way in which the United States has
dealt with defeated or declining powers in the past. Far from "competing" with
the Communists in his opposition to NATO expansion, for example, Yeltsin
used the pause that the Clinton administration promised him during his re-
election campaign to explore possible compromises. The new Russian foreign
minister, Yevgeny Primakov, began to say publicly that Russia simply sought
assurances that, if NATO took in new members, there would be no extension
eastward of the alliance's military structures—in particular, no deployment of
its forces or of nuclear weapons. These were precisely the formulas for which
his predecessor, Andrei Kozyrev, was routinely denounced as a traitor. So far,
no one has called for Primakov's head on a pike. Whatever may explain this
latest turn in the story (and the affair is far from over), the one thing that has not
happened, in response to American "indulgence," is the radicalization of Russian policy.

As for the issue that most agitates Kissinger—"whether Russia can be made
to accept [its current, post-Soviet] borders"—the five-year record shows a
huge transformation. When the Soviet Union collapsed at the end of 1991,
both Russian and Western analysts identified a series of possible revisionist
goals that might appear on the Russian policy agenda at some point—and
many people said it would be sooner rather than later. These goals included
recovery of Crimea from Ukraine, detaching and absorbing Russian territories
from northern Kazakhstan or eastern Ukraine, acquiring some sort of protec-
torate over Russian communities in Estonia, and so on. What has happened?
*Every single one of these issues is less charged, and less urgent, than it was
five years ago.* Apart from the occasional Foreign Ministry statement protest-
ing, say, Estonian education policy, it is clearly Russia's aim to downplay all
of them.[13] Yet Kissinger continues to argue that the United States has naively
encouraged more "assertive" Russian policies. His claims have escalated;
Russian policy has not.

A closer look at U.S. policy toward Germany and Japan after 1945 also
takes some of the air out of outraged claims that we must not "coddle" Russia.
Yes, it was American policy to crush Nazism and Japanese militarism and to
prevent their reappearance. But the United States also aimed to build up both
countries as allies, and this goal shaped policy toward each of them from the
very start of the postwar period. Kissinger's insistence, for example, that the
most important test of Russian policy involves acceptance of its borders con-
trasts sharply with U.S. policy toward Germany during most of the Cold War.
West Germany, let us remember, contested the postwar borders of Europe for

decades—and with U.S. support. It was only in 1970, a quarter of a century after the war ended, that German claims to a large part of Polish territory were renounced. Throughout this period, moreover, American leaders were properly indignant at the Soviet suggestion that the only reason West Germany would not waive its claims to Poland was that it had not abandoned its Hitlerian dreams.[14]

U.S. policy toward Japan after the Second World War involved similar choices. Was there a risk in leaving the emperor in place? Clearly. But the possible political—and psychological—impact of toppling him seemed even riskier. Far better, then, to settle for his admission that he was not a demigod.

Fill This Prescription

The geotherapists' case is very, very weak. But, in putting aside their diagnosis, there are good reasons to resurrect their appeal, even if they do not heed it themselves, for a less "psychiatric" way of conducting foreign policy. It is simply not good enough to say that what we don't like, or don't understand, is crazy. Obviously we would all be better off if American diplomacy after the Cold War had been more like American diplomacy after the Second World War. The reason, however, is not that one of them involved too much "coddling" (a concept that barely rises to the level of psychiatry) and the other did not. It is that one of them was based on a far-sighted strategic choice, and the other was not.

After 1945 it was the highest priority of the United States to create an international system in which the defeated powers found a place that they— their leaders and their publics alike—could clearly see served their interests. Doing so served our interests, and decades later we are still benefiting from the choice. Why, this time around, should we choose differently?

Notes

1. Henry Kissinger, "Beware: A Threat Abroad," *Newsweek*, June 17, 1996, pp. 41-43; Zbigniew Brzezinski, "Russia: Neither our partner nor patient," *Washington Times*, December 22, 1995.
2. "Russia's Past, Russia's Future," *Commentary* (June 1996), p. 35.
3. Lukyanov, quoted in the *Financial Times*, May 29, 1996, p. 2.
4. Perhaps the single most astonishing case of such analysis is Kissinger's suggestion that the reason Yeltsin scheduled a visit to China last April, right after Clinton's visit to Moscow, was "to escape the stifling solicitude" of American interest in the Russian reform process ("Moscow and Beijing: A Declaration of Independence," *Washington Post*, May 14, 1996). In this account, post-Cold War diplomacy acquires the interpersonal antics of a Woody Allen movie (Boris Yeltsin to the stiflingly solicitous president of the United States: "Bill, I just need a little space!").
5. A hefty 20 percent said they were influenced by the war in Chechnya, but these were presumably people voting *against* empire (*New York Times*, June 17, 1996.) The poll was conducted jointly by an American and a Russian firm.

6.   The full text is reprinted in *Nezavisimaya Gazeta*, May 23, 1996.
7.   This is not just the preference of the Moscow elite. Anatol Lieven reports the comment of a Russian military officer serving in Chechnya: "These days, who'd be an officer if you could work in a bank?" See his excellent article, "Russia's Military Nadir," *National Interest* (Summer 1996), p. 2.
8.   Kissinger is more tolerant of prideful motives in other cases. He has written understandingly of China's tendency "to react with neuralgia to any perceived slight to its dignity." And he strongly criticized U.S. policy as "insensitive to the psychological problems" of postwar France. Henry Kissinger, *White House Years* (Boston: Little, Brown & Co., 1979), p. 106.
9.   Hans Morgenthau, *Politics Among Nations* (New York: Alfred A. Knopf, 1956), pp. 68, 77.
10.   For an analysis that respects the importance of prestige without using the term, consider the conclusions of the report issued in July 1996 by the "Commission on America's National Interests," co-chaired by Robert Ellsworth, Andrew Goodpaster, and Rita Hauser, and numbering among its members Sam Nunn and Brent Scowcroft. Among "vital national interests" (ones immediately linked to national survival), the report lists "credibility" and the preservation of something it calls "singular U.S. leadership."
11.   "It's the Americans Who Will Never Stop," *Nezavisimaya Gazeta*, June 28, 1996, p. 6.
12.   "Running Out of Illusions," Washington Times, February 4, 1996. See also "A Plan for Europe," *Foreign Affairs* (January/February 1995), p. 27.
13.   Richard Pipes, who, unlike most of the others cited in this article, remains basically optimistic about Russia, nevertheless holds that its adjustment to the loss of empire has been slower and more difficult than for France, Portugal, and other European colonial powers. In fact, this particular comparison makes Russia's adjustment look almost easy: France and Portugal each fought at least two protracted overseas wars after 1945 rather than accept the loss of major colonies.
14.   Because of the importance of preserving West Germany's Western orientation, the United States was prepared to accept the judgment of its leaders about German domestic politics. Adenauer, as Kissinger has written, had taken on the responsibility of "restoring self-respect to his occupied, demoralized and divided society"—and the United States could hardly undercut him. Henry Kissinger, *Diplomacy* (New York: Simon & Schuster, 1994), p. 502.

9

Don't Isolate Us: A Russian View of NATO Expansion

Alexey K. Pushkov*

Russia's arguments against NATO expansion are well known. Moscow warns that NATO enlargement would create new dividing lines in Europe. If NATO military structures were to approach Russian borders and its troops were to appear on the territories of new member-states, Russia would be forced to adjust to these challenges to its security. New tensions caused by enlargement would spoil the post-Cold War political climate in Europe, destroy mutual trust, revive old fears, and throw the relationship between Russia and the West back into the past.

Until recently there was a tendency in the West—mostly in the United States—to downplay the significance of these arguments. Many American observers assumed that Boris Yeltsin and his government voiced opposition to NATO expansion mainly for domestic political reasons and in reaction to pre-election pressures from Communists and nationalists in the Russian Duma. The logic was that if Yeltsin won the summer 1996 presidential elections he would be sufficiently relieved of these pressures and become more receptive to the logic of Western assurances.

This assumption was wrong. There was and is a wide consensus within the Russian political establishment that NATO expansion contradicts basic Russian national interests. The few dissenting voices in the Russian media and academic circles are marginal. Even Anatoly Chubais, a well-known adept of

*Alexei K. Pushkov is director of foreign affairs at Russian Public Television and a member of the board of the Russian Council on Foreign and Defense Policies. Previously he was a speechwriter for General Secretary Mikhail Gorbachev. He is also a member of the editorial board of *The National Interest*. This essay originally appeared in *The National Interest*, no. 47 (Spring 1997).

liberal economic reforms and currently Yeltsin's chief of staff, noted at his February 2 press conference in Davos that opposition to NATO expansion was the only point on which he agreed with Communist leader Gennady Zyuganov and nationalist firebrand Vladimir Zhirinovsky.

Will Compensation Work?

When it became apparent that Russia was serious about opposing the expansion of the alliance, Washington offered to open official consultations that would lead, as President Clinton foreshadowed in his October 1996 speech in Detroit, to a formal agreement—a charter—between Russia and NATO. In December, Russian Foreign Minister Yevgeny Primakov accepted the offer, but stressed that such promises would not change Russia's opposition to the planned expansion. Nor would Moscow sign an agreement or charter unless it was a binding one, containing clear guarantees and obligations.

As a result, the U.S. and Russian positions on this issue are still far apart. It is clear that NATO will formally offer membership to several former Warsaw Pact countries at the alliance summit in Madrid on July 7-8. And the Clinton administration opposes a binding agreement with Russia—a treaty rather than a charter—that would alleviate fully Moscow's concerns. Recent events have confirmed the impasse. Speaking on February 11 before the U.S. House of Representatives International Relations Committee, Secretary of State Madeleine Albright recognized that the United States "must address Russia's legitimate concerns," but said there was little the United States could do to end Russian opposition to an enlarged alliance—themes repeated and broadened during her subsequent visits to Rome, Paris, London, and Moscow.[1] Meanwhile, the Kremlin voiced concern over the possibility of the Baltic states joining NATO, and characterized Secretary-General Javier Solana's visit to four southern former Soviet Republics as being directed against Russia's "special ties" with them.

In this context, the Yeltsin-Clinton summit scheduled for March 20-21 in Helsinki will be of critical importance, though chances for a real solution to the problem do not seem good. A five-power summit to discuss Europe's future security system, proposed recently by French President Jacques Chirac with German backing, could offer another opportunity to establish the broad lines of an agreement between NATO and Russia; but whether it will take place—or succeed—remains to be seen.

A current popular assumption in Washington holds that Russia will finally agree to NATO enlargement and accept a non-binding charter in exchange for compensations in other areas. This was Richard Holbrooke's position in his debate with Michael Mandelbaum at the Council on Foreign Relations in December: Yeltsin and his associates knew that enlargement was going to happen and were deploying a managed reticence in order to get the best bargain possible. These compensations are said to include a favorable revision of the Conventional Forces in Europe Treaty (CFE), the possibility of increased bilateral economic assistance, and a permanent G-7 seat for Moscow, as advocated by France and Germany.

What counts most for Moscow, however, is the nature of the special relationship with NATO itself. While other gestures would alleviate the growing tension between Russia and the West, the compensatory approach misses the point. The new Russia, which parted decisively from the USSR's domestic and foreign policy heritage, strongly believes that it has every right to comprehensive inclusion in modern Europe—economically, politically, and with regard to its security dimensions as well. What Russia seeks is an arrangement that would assure its full participation in European affairs, rather than its isolation from, or marginalization in, Europe. This is the crux of the matter.

Speaking recently on Russia-NATO relations, Deputy Secretary of State Strobe Talbott asserted that the key to a breakthrough is to "really show the Russians that this is not a NATO trick, a grab for a few countries, but really a sincere effort to secure political stability and promote prosperity in Europe for a long time."[2] In Moscow, however, this key must amount to more than verbal assurances—it must mean Russian inclusion in the European security system now under construction. If Russia is to be included in this system, which is in everyone's best interest, the Russia-NATO equation must be defined specifically and not left to the rhetorical vagaries of a non-binding charter.

Preventing New Military Tensions

Until recently Moscow has shown restraint in formulating what specifically it would like to obtain from NATO, and has directed its efforts instead to the larger issue of opposing enlargement as such. The absence of a clear platform concerning direct relations with an enlarged NATO has been the source of a number of contradictory declarations by Russian officials. In this context, on January 6 President Yeltsin convened a top-level meeting on Russia's policy toward NATO, and appointed Mr. Primakov as chief coordinator over the elaboration of this policy. Subsequently, despite vows of confidentiality made between Primakov and Solana when they met in Moscow on January 20, the nature of Russian aspirations has become apparent thanks to the public comments of senior Russian officials.

First, Moscow has suggested that NATO rule out the deployment of nuclear weapons on the territories of the new East European member-states. The Kremlin took careful notice of the "three nos" policy announced by Warren Christopher on December 10—that NATO countries have "no intention, no plan, and no reason" to deploy such weapons on new members' territory. Yet the reluctance of the United States to obligate itself formally on this score creates uneasiness in Moscow. "The American declaration does not remove the issue of nuclear weapons. There should be a formal obligation not to deploy such weapons, and not to engage in preparations for their deployment," says one top Russian diplomat.

The Americans argue that under no condition could NATO possibly offer such a commitment. But in refusing to do so what they overlook is that a binding agreement between NATO and Russia would be relevant only in times of peace. If serious military tension were to develop between the two sides, which is highly unlikely, any standing agreement would become irrelevant. In this case nuclear-capable aircraft and tactical missiles could be quickly transferred to NATO's eastern flank. An agreement on nuclear weapons in Eastern Europe is important not for military reasons, for Russia does not consider NATO a military threat, but because of its political and psychological impact. Nuclear arsenals confronting each other in Europe is a thing of the past. Even the remote possibility of a NATO nuclear missile deployment closer to Russian borders, or in Poland, which has a common border with Russia, would subvert the newly established, fragile sense of mutual trust in Europe. An official refusal to place such weapons in Eastern Europe should not be seen as a concession to Moscow, but as a precondition of any working relationship between Russia and the Atlantic Alliance. It must be codified and confirmed in a Russia-NATO agreement and removed once and for all from the European agenda.

Russia is also opposed to the stationing of NATO troops on the territories of future member-states, and to the spread of NATO military infrastructures to these territories. As in the case of nuclear weapons, Moscow is assured that a forward deployment of NATO troops will not occur. But once again, verbal assurances alone do not suffice. On the eve of the reunification of Germany, Helmut Kohl promised Mikhail Gorbachev that NATO's military infrastructures would not move eastward into the territory of East Germany, a fact since confirmed by the former U.S. Ambassador to Moscow Jack Matlock. Later, as the Warsaw Pact fell apart and new treaties were signed between the Soviet Union and East European states, Moscow was privately assured by their leaders that these states would not seek membership in NATO. All of these promises lay broken three years later.

Clearly, in considering its own security, Russia cannot rely on benign intentions and high-sounding promises alone. Governments change, as do interests. Only a binding agreement—one that addresses the issue of conventional forces, best achieved through a revised CFE Treaty, and that fixes new, reduced ceilings of men and conventional weaponry in Eastern Europe—can remove Russia's concerns as to the military aspects of NATO expansion.

A Real Voice for Russia

Differences over the military aspects of NATO enlargement, however, are not the only ones to be resolved. A Russia-NATO agreement should introduce a mechanism of political cooperation between NATO and Russia. Moscow cannot be satisfied by the present "16+1" formula, or the standing NATO offer of regularized political consultations. The workings of the contact group on Bosnia and the process by which the Dayton Accord was reached taught Russian diplomats that in the loose framework of "consultations" Moscow risks being relegated to outsider status, to be included only occasionally as a sign of courtesy but otherwise having no real role or standing in any significant decision making process.

In order to feel itself an integral part of the evolving European security system, Russia must have a real voice in that process. In early February, on his trip to the United States, Prime Minister Victor Chernomyrdin suggested creating a mechanism, possibly a NATO "Council of 17," which would include Russia and give it an equal say on all issues directly concerning its own security. This is problematic for Brussels, which is clearly unwilling to give Moscow any veto powers, but it would demonstrate that the expansion of the alliance is not directed against Russia, and it could radically improve the relationship between the two sides.

A Russia-NATO agreement should also establish a joint crisis-management mechanism that would facilitate Russia's participation in the decision making process, as well as in the planning and conduct of out-of-area peacekeeping operations. On the American side the experience of Russia-NATO cooperation over Bosnia in this regard is often cited as a promising precedent for future cooperation. The Bosnian experience, however, is not an ideal precedent from the Russian perspective. It is often forgotten that the whole operation was planned in Washington and Brussels, with no Russian participation. It can hardly be a model for future crisis management operations, especially those involving the territories of the former Soviet Union.

Finally, there is the extremely serious and delicate problem raised by the prospect of enlarging NATO to include states that have a protracted border with Russia, namely the Baltics and Ukraine.[3] Moscow has warned Western leaders that the acceptance of those states into NATO, some of which display an open animosity toward Russia, would spark a serious crisis in relations between Russia and the West. Such a move is clearly unacceptable for Moscow, as it would bring NATO military structures to the northern Russian coastline and result in the strategic encirclement of the Kaliningrad region.

A realistic alternative to NATO membership for the Baltic states would be their acceptance into the European Union. It would confirm their European identity and would give them political guarantees of the security they are seeking. As for their eventual membership in NATO, this might well become less of a problem in the future should Russia and NATO reach a comprehensive, binding agreement along the lines sketched above. If NATO accepts Russia as a real partner, it would lead to profound changes in the alliance and in its military doctrine, as well as in Russia's attitude toward the alliance. If

Russia were to approach a status close to that of a NATO member-state, the acceptance of the Baltics would not provoke the kind of response in Moscow that it now does.

The Need for a Binding Agreement

A non-binding charter or declaration of intent that lacks the elements outlined above will accomplish little, and the reason is clear: Anything less will lack the power to put an end to old, mostly bad, habits on both sides.

First, the militaries on both sides would still derive their strategic and operative planning from old assumptions and old doctrines. On the NATO side, moreover, the predisposition to see Russia as a potential enemy would likely be strengthened as new members with strong and fresh anti-Russian feelings join the alliance. The Russian military, meanwhile, would have to plan not on the basis of intentions but on the enhanced military, intelligence, and logistical capabilities of the other side. Worse, Russia's present conventional military disadvantage would incline it to rely more heavily on nuclear weapons in planning its defenses—just as NATO did in similar circumstances starting in the late 1950s.

Second, a charter void of contractual obligations would be impossible to sell to the Russian Federal Assembly and political establishment. That means, in turn, that the State Duma, facing the prospect of a foreign military alliance approaching Russian borders, would not ratify the START-II treaty, and any prospect for a START-III agreement would be nil. Nor would the Chemical Weapons Convention or the Open Skies agreement win Duma support. And ongoing negotiations to revise the 1972 Anti-Ballistic Missile Treaty to mutual satisfaction would stall as well.

These demurrals and setbacks could generate a reciprocal reaction in the U.S. Congress that could lead to the collapse of the whole system of bilateral arms control and reduction agreements reached during the last ten years. As long as Russia's economy remains weak, no extensive new arms race will resume, but by conserving their huge nuclear arsenals Russia and the United States would enter into a gray zone of heightened strategic insecurity. The deterioration of Russia's nuclear command and control systems, of which Russian Defense Minster Igor Rodionov recently warned, would create still additional dangers.

Still other problems might come from an asymmetrical interpretation of a non-binding charter in Russia and in the West. If NATO countries were to consider such a charter a serious declaration while most Russians were to regard it as a meaningless piece of paper, a serious disruption of mutual trust could result. The West might accuse Moscow of violating the spirit of the charter; Moscow would respond by accusing the West of anti-Russian motives in the process of expansion and of holding out the prospect for another round of enlargement ever closer to Russia. Under such circumstances, clearly, there would be no way to escape a revived animosity—even a new Cold War.

Why Take Russia into Account?

It is true that Russia cannot stop NATO expansion or deny the East Europeans their right to join the alliance. That being the case, some ask, why strain so hard in the first place to take Russia into account, let alone to allow Moscow a veto over NATO enlargement? The answer is that the implications of enlargement—if it is not accompanied by a compromise with Russia—are very serious ones.

In addition to the disruption of the present security arrangements between Russia and the United States, the political fallout could include a deterioration of the larger bilateral relationship; a Russian policy toward China, Iran, and Iraq that would disregard American interests and concerns; a more frequent invocation by Russia of its veto in the un Security Council; a more assertive Russia in the former space of the Soviet Union. In short it could mean a Russia that, while not directly challenging the U.S. role in Europe, might become a "loose cannon" of world politics.

A progressive rapprochement with the West is by far the most reasonable and natural path for future Russian diplomacy. Yet this depends not only on Russia's own will, but also on the will of its Western partners. If Russia finds that the door to the West is closed, if it finds itself cut off from Europe, it will have to look for alternatives. Such a development is in neither the Russian, American, or European interest, but this is where the present NATO policy toward Russia, unless seriously reconsidered, will inescapably lead.

Notes

1. "Long Delay Over NATO Is Opposed by Albright," *International Herald Tribune*, February 12, 1997.
2. Joe Fitchett, "Moscow Faces Host of Offers in NATO Talks," *International Herald Tribune*, February 6, 1997; see also Strobe Talbott, "Russia Has Nothing to Fear," *New York Times*, February 18, 1997.
3. See my essay "Russia and NATO: On the Watershed," *Mediterranean Quarterly* (Spring 1996), pp. 26-8.

Part 3

Culture and Society

10

Tainted Transactions: Harvard, the Chubais Clan, and Russia's Ruin

Janine R. Wedel*

Only a few years ago, American policymakers were confidently predicting that a regimen of privatization and market reform would in due course transform Russia into a stable and prosperous democracy. America would smooth this transition and U.S. aid—unselfish and urgent—would serve as a "bridge," enabling representatives from both sides to implement their respective agendas. Pictures of "Bill" and "Boris" embracing and beaming at the camera symbolized the promise of a new era in U.S.-Russia relations, one that bore little resemblance to the preceding decades of Cold War acrimony.

Today all that has passed away. Far from fulfilling their promise of a better life, the U.S.-sponsored "reforms" of the 1990s have left many, if not most, Russians worse off.[1] For this state of affairs many Russians today blame precisely the Western aid and advice they have received.[2] Some, indeed, believe that the United States set out *deliberately* to destroy their economy.

How did the United States, by far the dominant partner in the relationship, allow one of the most promising rapprochements of the last century to founder? Rather than proceeding on the basis of common sense and well-established modes of representation between states, it acted upon an ideology implemented through a most dubious mode of conducting relations between nations. The ideology—that of radical privatization and marketization, applied in this instance in a cold-turkey manner to a society with no recent experience

*Janine R. Wedel, an anthropologist, is author of Collision and Collusion: The Strange Case of Western Aid to Eastern Europe 1989–1998 (St. Martin's Press, 1998). She is associate professor at the Graduate School of Public and International Affairs at the University of Pittsburgh, and director of its research development at the Ridgway Center. This essay first appeared in The National Interest, No. 59 (Spring 2000).

of either—is well known. The way in which advice and aid were given is much less familiar, but it is a vital part of the story.

It is necessary to give this distinctive way of conducting business a name, and, drawing on my experience as an anthropologist, I shall call it "transactorship."[3] By "transactors," then, I shall mean players in a small, informal group who work together for mutual gain, while formally representing different parties. Even though transactors may genuinely share the stated goals of the parties they represent, they have additional goals and ways of operating of their own. These may, advertently or inadvertently, subvert or subordinate the aims of those for whom they ostensibly act. The behavior of members of such groups is marked by extreme flexibility and a readiness to exchange roles, even to the extent of representing parties other than the ones to which they are formally attached.

In what follows, I shall show that during the 1990s the cozy manner in which American advisers and Russian representatives—that is, the transactors—interacted and the outcomes of their activities ran directly counter to the stated aims of the U.S. aid program in Russia. Specifically, those goals were to foster economic development and democratization and to nurture friendly bilateral relations. As a new decade begins, key transactors in this program are under investigation for money laundering, corruption and other criminal activities—the consequences of their undeclared goals.

Transactorship, as it applies in the U.S.-Russia relationship over the last decade, involves individuals, institutions and groups whose official status is difficult to establish. Indeed, nearly everything about transactors is ambiguous. Their sphere of activity is neither fixedly public nor private, neither firmly political nor economic; their activities are neither fully open nor completely hidden and conspiratorial; and the transactors are not exclusively committed to one side or the other. This malleability affords them enormous flexibility, which in turn enhances their influence on all sides. Alas, it is also what has sabotaged the once high hopes for a new era in U.S.-Russia relations.

The Emergence of Transactorship

How in the case of Russia and the United States did the transactors come together to be designated as the bridge builders from their respective sides? As the vast Soviet state was collapsing in late 1991, Harvard professors Jeffrey Sachs, Andrei Shleifer and others participated in meetings at a *dacha* outside Moscow. There, young would-be Russian "reformers" were in the process of devising a blueprint for economic and political change. The key Russians present at the *dacha* were the economists Yegor Gaidar and Anatoly Chubais. These meetings occurred at the time when Boris Yeltsin, then president of what was still Soviet Russia, was putting together his team of economic advisers. Gaidar would become the first "architect" of economic "reform" in post-communist Russia. A long-standing group of associates from St. Petersburg, centered around Chubais, was to figure prominently in Yeltsin's team. Indeed, Chubais would go on to replace Gaidar, and to become an indispensable aide to Yeltsin.

While at the *dacha*, Sachs, his associate Anders Åslund and several other Westerners offered their services to the Russians, including that of facilitating access to Western money—an offer the Russians accepted. In the ensuing months and years the members of the Harvard and Chubais teams saw to it that they became the designated representatives for their respective sides—and transactors in the sense I have described. On the American side, representatives from the Harvard Institute for International Development (HIID) would provide the theory and advice to reinvent the Russian economy.

Maintaining that Russian economic reform was so important, and the "window of opportunity" to effect change so narrow, U.S. policymakers granted the Harvard Institute special treatment. Between 1992 and 1997, the Institute received $40.4 million from the U.S. Agency for International Development (USAID) in non-competitive grants, and—until USAID suspended its funding in May 1997—had been slated to receive another $17.4 million. Harvard-connected officials in the Clinton administration, citing "foreign policy" considerations, largely bypassed the normal public bidding process required for foreign aid contracts. The waivers to competition were backed by friends of the Harvard Institute group, especially in the U.S. Treasury.[4] Approving such a large sum of money mostly as non-competitive amendments to a much smaller award (the Harvard Institute's original award was $2.1 million) was highly unusual, according to U.S. government procurement officers and U.S. General Accounting Office (GAO) officials, including Louis H. Zanardi, who later spearheaded GAO's investigation of HIID activities in Russia and Ukraine. Indeed, the U.S. government delegated virtually its entire Russian economic aid portfolio—more than $350 million—for management by the Harvard Institute. The Institute was also provided the legal authority to manage other contractors (some of whom were its competitors), leaving it in the unique position of recommending U.S. aid policies while being itself a chief recipient of that aid. In 1996 the GAO found that the Harvard Institute had "substantial control of the U.S. assistance program."[5] According to U.S. government procurement officers and GAO officials, delegating so much aid to a private entity was unprecedented.

In Russia, the Harvard representatives worked exclusively with Anatoly Chubais and the circle around him, which came to be known as the Chubais Clan.[6] The interests of the Harvard Institute group and those of the Chubais Clan soon became one and the same. Their members became known for their loyalty to each other and for the unified front they projected to the outside world.[7] By mid-1993, the Harvard-Chubais players had formed an informal and extremely influential transactor group that was shaping the direction and consequences of U.S. economic aid and much Western economic policy toward Russia.

Providing pivotal support to the Harvard-Chubais transactors was Lawrence Summers, earlier a member of the Harvard faculty and at this time chief economist at the World Bank. Summers had strong ties to the Harvard team, including Shleifer, the economist who served as project director of the Harvard Institute's program in Russia.[8] Soon, Summers would play a principal role in designing U.S. and international economic policies at the U.S. Treasury, where he would occupy the posts of undersecretary, then deputy secretary and, finally, secretary.

The Chubais transactors advertised themselves, and were advertised by their promoters, as the "Young Reformers." The Western media promoted their mystique and overlooked other reform-minded groups in Russia.[9] Western donors tended to identify Russians as reformers not on the basis of their commitment to the free market but because they possessed personal attributes to which the Westerners responded favorably: proficiency in the English language; a Western look; an ability to parrot the slogans of "markets," "reform," and "democracy"; and name recognition by well-credentialed fellow Westerners. Members of the Chubais team possessed all of these qualities. By their sponsors in the West, they were depicted as enlightened and uniquely qualified to represent Russia and usher it down the road to capitalism and prosperity. Summers dubbed them a "dream team,"[10] which, given his position and status, was a particularly valuable endorsement.

In Russia, however, the Chubais transactors' primary source of clout was neither ideology nor even reform strategy, but precisely their standing with and their ability to get resources from the West. As the Russian sociologist Olga Kryshtanovskaya explained it,

> Chubais has what no other elite group has, which is the support of the top political quarters in the West, above all the USA, the World Bank and the IMF, and consequently, control over the money flow from the West to Russia. In this way, a small group of young educated reformers led by Anatoly Chubais transformed itself into the most powerful elite clan of Russia in the past five years.[11]

U.S. support proved decisive in this transformation. The administration's "dream team" seal of approval bolstered the Clan's standing as Russia's chief brokers with the West and the international financial institutions, and as the legitimate representative of Russia. It also enabled the Harvard-Chubais transactors to exact hundreds of millions of dollars in Western loans and American aid.

The Modus Operandi

It is time now to look in greater detail at the way in which this extraordinarily effective operation worked—effective, that is, in acquiring standing and funds. There were five basic operating principles.

• *Democracy by Decree*

The transactors' preferred way of proceeding in the Russian context was by means of top-down presidential decree. U.S. officials explicitly encouraged this practice as an efficient means of achieving market reform. As USAID's Walter Coles, a key American official in the privatization aid program, put it, "If we needed a decree, Chubais didn't have to go through the bureaucracy."[12] Rule by decree also allowed the transactors to bypass the democratically elected Supreme Soviet and the Duma. The Harvard Institute's Russia director, Jonathan Hay, and his associates went so far as to draft some of the Kremlin decrees themselves. Needless to say, this did nothing to advance Russia's evolution toward a democratic system, nor was it consistent with the declared American aim of encouraging that evolution.

• *Flex Organizations*

A similar anti-democratic ethos pervaded the network of Harvard-Chubais transactor-run organizations. The transactors established and oversaw a network of aid-funded, aid-created "private" organizations whose ostensible purpose was to conduct economic reform, but which were often used to promote the transactors' parochial agendas. These organizations supplanted or circumvented state institutions. They routinely performed functions that, in modern states, are typically the province of governmental bureaucracies. They served to allow the bypassing of the Duma and other relevant actors, whose input was in the long term crucial to the successful implementation of economic reforms in Russia. Further, the aid-created organizations served as a critical resource for the transactors, a vehicle by which to exploit financial and political opportunities for their own ends. I call these bodies "flex organizations" in recognition of their impressively adaptable, chameleon-like, multipurpose character.

The donors' flagship organization was the Russian Privatization Center, which had close ties to Harvard University. Its founding documents state that Harvard University is both a "founder" and "Full Member of the [Russian Privatization] Center."[13] The center received funds from all major and some minor Western donors and lenders: the United States, the IMF, the World Bank, the European Bank for Reconstruction and Development, the European Union, Germany and Japan.[14] The center's chief executive officer, a Russian from the Chubais Clan, has written that while head of the center he managed some $4 billion in Western funds.[15] The Chamber of Accounts, Russia's rough equivalent of the U.S. General Accounting Office, investigated how that money was spent. An auditor from the Chamber concluded that the "money was not spent as designated. Donors paid . . . for something you can't determine."[16] When I interviewed aid-paid consultants working at the center, I was told that the funds were routinely used for political purposes.

The center was an archetypal flex organization, one that switched its identity and status situationally. Formally and legally, it was nonprofit and nongovernmental. But it was established by Russian presidential decree and received aid because it was run by the Chubais transactors, who also played key roles in the Russian government. In practice, the center played the role of government agency. It negotiated with and received loans from international financial institutions—which typically lend to governments, not private entities—and did so on behalf of the Russian state.

According to documents from Russia's Chamber of Accounts, the center wielded more control over certain privatization documents and directives than did the Russian government agency formally responsible for privatization.[17] Two center officials, its CEO from the Chubais Clan and Harvard's Moscow representative, Hay, were in fact authorized to sign privatization decisions on Russia's behalf. Thus did a Russian and an American, both of them affiliated with a private entity, end up acting as representatives of the Russian Federation.

- *"Transidentity"*

It was not only organizations that could change guises. The flex organization had its individual equivalent in the phenomenon of "transidentity," which refers to the ability of a transactor to change his identity at will, regardless of which side originally designated him as its representative.[18] Key Harvard-Chubais transactors were quintessential chameleons. To suit the transactors' purposes, the same individual could represent the United States in one meeting and Russia in the next—and perhaps himself at a third—regardless of national origin.

Jonathan Hay, who alternatively acted as an American and a Russian, provides a telling example of this phenomenon. In addition to being Harvard's chief representative in Russia, with formal management authority over many other U.S. contractors, Hay was appointed by members of the Chubais Clan to be a Russian. As such, he was empowered to approve or veto high-level privatization decisions of the Russian government. According to a U.S. official investigating Harvard's activities, Hay "played more Russian than American." The financial arena yields many such examples of transidentity, in which Chubais transactors appointed Americans to act as Russians.[19]

It was (and is) difficult to glean exactly who prominent consultants on the international circuit represented, for whom they actually worked, who paid them, and where their loyalties and ambitions lay at any given time. Harvard economist Jeffrey Sachs, who served as director of the Harvard Institute from 1995 to 1999, provides a case in point.[20] According to journalist John Helmer, Sachs and his associates (including David Lipton, vice president of Sachs' consulting firm who later went to Treasury to work for Summers[21]) played both the Russian and the IMF sides of the street. During negotiations in 1992 between the IMF and the Russian government, for example, Sachs and his associates appeared as advisers to the Russian side. But they were at the same time "writing secret memoranda advising the IMF negotiators as well."[22]

Compounding this ambiguity is the question of whether Sachs was an official adviser to the Russian government. Although he maintains that he was,[23] key Russian economists as well as international officials cast doubts on his claim.[24] Jean Foglizzio, the imf's first Moscow resident representative, was also taken aback by Sachs' practice of introducing himself as an adviser to the Russian government. As Foglizzio put it, "[When] the prime minister [Viktor Chernomyrdin], who is the head of government, says 'I never requested Mr. Sachs to advise me'—it triggers an unpleasant feeling, meaning, who is he?"[25]

Sachs also offered his services as an intermediary. According to Andrei Vernikov, a Russian representative to the IMF, and other sources, Sachs presented himself to leading Russians as a powerbroker who could deliver Western aid. In 1992, when Yegor Gaidar (with whom Sachs had been working) was under attack and his future looked precarious, Sachs offered his services to Gaidar's parliamentary opposition. In November 1992 Sachs wrote a memorandum to the chairman of the Supreme Soviet, Ruslan Khasbulatov (whose reputation in the West was that of a retrograde communist), offering advice, Western aid and contacts with the U.S. Congress. Khasbulatov declined Sachs' help after circulating the memo.[26] Sachs also proved adept at lobbying American policymakers.[27]

The most effective and influential transactors are extremely adept at working their multiple roles and identities. One such ubiquitous transactor was Anders Åslund, a former Swedish envoy to Russia who worked with Sachs and Gaidar. Åslund seemed at once to represent and speak on behalf of American, Russian and Swedish governments and authorities. Accordingly, he was understood by some Russian officials in Washington to be Chubais' personal envoy. Though a "private" citizen of Sweden who played a leading role in Swedish policy and aid toward Russia,[28] he nonetheless participated in high-level meetings at the U.S. Treasury and State Departments about U.S. and IMF policies.[29] Åslund was also involved in business activities in Russia[30] and Ukraine.[31] According to the Russian Interior Ministry's Department of Organized Crime, he had "significant" investments in the Russian Federation.[32] In addition to his work for governments, the Harvard-Chubais transactors and the private sector, Åslund was engaged in public relations activities. His assignment in Ukraine, where he was funded by George Soros, explicitly included public relations on behalf of that country, according to other Soros-funded consultants who worked with Åslund there.[33] His effectiveness in this role was no doubt enhanced by his affiliation with Washington think tanks, his frequent contributions to publications such as the *Washington Post* and the London *Financial Times*, and the fact that he always presented himself on these occasions as an objective analyst, despite his many promotional roles.

• *Interchangeability*

The maneuverability for individuals afforded by transidentity was also present at the group level. The Harvard Institute group, though formally representing the United States, also represented the Chubais group.[34] Thus, some U.S. officials and investigators requesting meetings with Russians were instead directed to Americans. In lobbying for aid contracts, the Harvard Institute group continually cited its access to Russian "reformers" as its primary advantage; this was in fact a key component of its public relations effort. In turn, Harvard acted as the Chubais Clan's entrée to the eyes and ears of U.S. policymakers and to American funds. In the United States, the Harvard transactors touted Chubais as the voice of Russia, and he became the quintessential enlightened Russian in the eyes of many U.S. officials and commentators.

Not surprisingly, then, in times of crisis for the Harvard-Chubais nexus— such as the ruble crisis of August 1998 and the Bank of New York money laundering scandals—the transactors and their associates have sought to bolster their colleagues' continued clout and standing in both Russia and the United States. Thus, Summers has frequently rushed to the defense of Chubais and other key transactors. In testimony before the U.S. House of Representatives' Committee on International Relations, for example, Summers stoutly defended Chubais and asked that Chubais' prepared statement ("I Didn't Lie") be placed in the congressional record.[35] Similarly, Åslund serves as a staunch defender of and advocate for Chubais. Of late, he also has been arguing Vladimir Putin's cause.[36]

• *Unaccountability and Self-Perpetuation*

Transactors are largely above formal accountability. The group places its members in various positions to serve its agendas, which may or may not conflict with those of the government or public interest they supposedly serve. The result is a game of musical chairs. For example, a key agency in Russian "reform," the State Property Committee, was headed by a succession of Chubais transactors, among them Chubais himself, Maxim Boycko and Alfred Kokh. Kokh was named chairman of the Committee after Boycko was fired by Yeltsin for accepting a thinly veiled $90,000 bribe from a company that had received preferential treatment in the privatization process. Kokh himself was later removed for accepting a $100,000 payment from the same company. Chubais, Boycko and Kokh also held a variety of key positions in the Harvard-Chubais transactor-run, aid-funded Russian Privatization Center.

The Chubais transactors are unlikely to disappear in Vladimir Putin's Russia. In fact, Putin has long been intertwined with them. An operative in the KGB and briefly head of its successor agency, Putin, like most members of the Chubais Clan, hails from St. Petersburg and was intimately involved in the "reforms" there. After moving to Moscow to work with Chubais, Putin helped to suppress criminal investigations that implicated Yeltsin and members of his family—as well as Chubais himself.[37] Chubais, in addition to running the country's electricity conglomerate, is helping to run Putin's presidential campaign.[38]

Consequences of Transactorship

What, it might be asked, is wrong with the transactorship mode of organizing relations between the United States and Russia in such circumstances? Many U.S. officials have argued that it is the most effective method by which to implement market reform—through a committed group with intimate access to both sides (and to many activities in both countries). In fact, there are several things that are seriously wrong with this argument.

Transactorship has served to undermine democratic processes and the development of transparent, accountable institutions.

Operating by decree is clearly anti-democratic and contrary to the aid community's stated goal of building democracy in Russia. It has weakened the message to the Russians that the United States stands for democracy. Further, the aid-created flex organizations have supplanted the state and often carried out functions that ought to have been the province of governmental bureaucracies.

As well, the flex organizations have likely facilitated the development of what I have called elsewhere the "clan-state," a state captured by unauthorized groups and characterized by pervasive corruption.[39] In such a state, individual clans, each of which controls property and resources, are so closely identified with particular ministries or institutional segments of government that the respective agendas of the state and the clan become indistinguishable. Thus, while the Chubais transactors were closely identified with segments of government concerned with privatization and the economy, competing clans had equivalent ties with other government organizations, such as the ministries of defense and internal affairs and the security services. Generally, where judicial processes are politically motivated, a clan's influence can be checked or constrained only by a rival clan. By systematically bypassing the democratically elected parliament, U.S. aid flouted a crucial feature of democratic governance: namely, parliamentarianism.

Transactorship has frustrated true market reform.

Without public support or understanding, decrees constitute a weak foundation on which to build a market economy. Some reforms, such as lifting price controls, may be achieved by decree. But many others depend on changes in law, public administration or mindsets, and require cooperation among a full spectrum of legislative and market participants, not just a clan.[40]

A case in point was USAID's efforts to reform Russia's tax system, and to establish clearing and settlement organizations (CSOS)—an essential ingredient in a sophisticated financial system. The efforts failed largely because they were placed solely in the hands of one group, which then declined to work with other market participants. In Moscow, for example, despite millions of USAID dollars, many Russian brokers were excluded from the process and consequently declined to use the CSO. Since 1994, when consultants working under USAID contracts totaling $13.9 million set out to design and implement CSOS in five Russian cities, very little evidence of progress has emerged. After an investigation into the Harvard Institute's activities in Russia, the U.S. General Accounting Office issued a report calling the CSO effort "disappointing."[41] Yet, absent support from parties to the reform process, reforms were almost certain to be ignored or even subverted during implementation.

To repeat, transactors, although they may share the overall goals of the sides they represent, may advertently or inadvertently subvert those goals in pursuit of their own private agendas. The Chubais-Harvard transactors were known to block reform efforts on occasion. In particular, they were inclined to obstruct reform initiatives when they originated outside their own group or were perceived to conflict with their own agendas.[42] When a USAID-funded organization run by the Chubais-Harvard transactors failed to receive the additional USAID funds it had expected, its leaders promptly obstructed legal reform activities in the areas of title registration and mortgages—programs that were launched by agencies of the Russian government.[43] In such instances, the transactors' interference put them at cross purposes with their own purported aim of fostering markets.

Lack of transparency, too, became apparent in the manner in which the transactors implemented economic reforms. Secrecy shrouded the privatization process, with numerous, unfortunate consequences for the Russian people. Privatization, which was largely shaped by the Harvard-Chubais transactors and significant parts of which were funded by USAID, was intended to spread the fruits of the free market. Instead, it helped to create a system of "tycoon capitalism" acting in the service of a half dozen corrupt oligarchs. The "reforms" were more about wealth confiscation than wealth creation; and the incentive system encouraged looting, asset stripping and capital flight.[44]

Transactorship has encouraged the maximization of opportunities for personal gain.

The prestige and access of the Harvard-Chubais transactors facilitated their involvement in other areas, including allegedly the Russian securities market, both in Russia and internationally, and may have helped them enrich themselves. In such ways, the private agendas of the Harvard-Chubais transactors helped to subvert the goals of the sides they were supposed to be serving.

Providing a small group of powerbrokers with a blank check inevitably encouraged corruption, precisely at a time when the international community should have been demanding safeguards in Russia such as the development of a legal and regulatory framework, property rights and the sanctity of contracts. Over the years many substantiated reports of the Chubais transactors using public monies for personal enrichment have been published.[45] Today these same persons are among those under investigation for alleged involvement in laundering billions of dollars through the Bank of New York and other banks.[46]

The Harvard Institute has also had its difficulties. In 1996 the GAO found that USAID's management over Harvard was "lax."[47] In 1997 the government cancelled most of the last $14 million earmarked for the Institute, citing evidence that the project's two managers—Hay and Shleifer—had used their positions and inside knowledge to profit from investments in the Russian securities markets and other private enterprises.[48] The two remain under criminal and/or civil investigation by the U.S. Department of Justice.[49] In January 2000 a Harvard task force issued a report alluding to that financial scandal. It recommended that the Harvard Institute for International Development be closed and that selected programs be integrated into other university programs. The Institute was closed shortly thereafter. An inspired Harvard University spokesperson, Joe Wrinn, spun the story thus: "It's a vote of confidence for the study of international development and its permanent integration into Harvard University."[50]

Because the transactors' success is grounded in mutual loyalty and trust, and because of their shared record of activities, some of which have left them vulnerable to allegations of corruption, the transactors have ample incentive to stick together. Any desertions must be well considered, as they could have serious consequences for all involved.

Transactorship has encouraged not only corruption but also the ability to deny it.

Transactorship affords maximum flexibility and influence to the transactors, and minimal accountability to the sides the transactors presumably represent. If the Harvard Institute's manager in Russia were asked by U.S. authorities to account for privatization decisions and monies, he could respond by claiming that he made those decisions as a Russian, not as an American. If USAID came under fire for funding the Russian state, it could claim that it was funding private organizations.

Now that the issue of "Russian" corruption has captured headlines, Treasury Secretary Summers has lately been insisting that the Russian government make amends. "This has been a U.S. demand for years," he claims, as if he had not himself addressed letters to "Dear Anatoly"[51] and met with Chubais as recently as the summer of 1999. This only months after Chubais admitted that he had "conned" from the IMF a $4.8 billion installment in July 1998,[52] the details of that deal having been worked out in Summers' home over brunch—at a meeting that the *New York Times* deemed crucial to obtaining release of the funds.[53]

Transactorship has proved particularly harmful in a setting in which communism until recently prevailed.

The transactorship mode of organizing relations is reminiscent of precisely those features of communism that the international community should be concerned not to reinforce. The informal, but influential, parallel executive established by the Harvard-Chubais transactors recalls the powerful patronage networks that virtually ran the Soviet Union. Political aid disguised as economic aid is only too familiar to Russians raised under a system of political control over economic decisions. As Shleifer acknowledged in a 1995 book funded by Harvard, "Aid helps reform not because it directly helps the economy—it is simply too small for that—but because it helps the reformers in their political battles."[54]

And yet U.S. officials have defended this approach. In a 1997 interview, Ambassador Richard L. Morningstar, U.S. aid coordinator to the former Soviet Union, said, "When you're talking about a few hundred million dollars, you're not going to change the country, but you can provide targeted assistance to help Chubais"[55]—an admission of direct interference in Russia's political life. U.S. assistance to Chubais continued even after he was dismissed by Yeltsin as first deputy prime minister in January 1996: he was placed on the Harvard payroll, a demonstration of solidarity for which senior U.S. officials openly declared their support.

The U.S.-Russian experience of transactorship is interesting and disturbing not only in its own right, but because this mode of operating may well become more frequent as a way of conducting trans-national affairs in the twenty-first century. With the ongoing process of globalization, the nationality of actors is becoming increasingly irrelevant. Already global elites, with ever-closer connections to one another and fewer to the nation-state, see themselves not so much as American, Brazilian, or Italian, but as members of an exclusive and highly mobile multinational club, whose rules and regulations have yet to be written. In many respects, members of what Peter Berger has identified as the overlapping "Davos" and "Faculty Club" cultures have much more in common in terms of lifestyle and taste with each other than they have with their fellow nationals. And as Berger observes, "it may be that commonalties in taste make it easier to find common ground politically"—and, of course, economically.[56]

While all this is true, global elites will continue to operate in a world organized into nation-states. In such a world, assumptions about representation, grounded in national and international law, are based on the idea that an individual can formally represent either one state or another, but not both. The transactor mode of behavior may seem to offer a means of having it both ways, of squaring the circle. But it also raises crucial public policy questions. What are the implications of a state of affairs in which the "choice" of who represents one side is shaped to a significant degree by self-selected representatives of the other? What are the consequences when the same player represents multiple sides? Wherein lies the accountability to electorates and parliaments in a world of growing coziness and joint decision-making among governing elites? Where, if at all, do representation and democracy enter the picture? The U.S.-Russian case in the last decade provides a cautionary lesson in all these respects. But it has been a very expensive lesson.

Notes

1. The Russian "population has suffered increasing hardship" since the ruble devaluation of August 1998. An estimated 38 percent was living in poverty at the close of the first quarter of 1999, as compared with 28 percent one year earlier. Real incomes in June 1999 were 77 percent of their June 1998 level. (*OECD Economic Outlook*, December 1999, p. 132.) Further, Russian citizens became poorer in 1999, even though wage arrears and absolute numbers below the poverty line trended down. "The average level of Russians' real cash income—incomes adjusted to account for inflation—decreased 15 percent," according to the Russian Statistics Agency. (Yevgenia Borisova, "Poverty Still Widespread Despite Modest Growth," *Moscow Times*, January 13, 2000, also in *Johnson's Russia List*, January 13, 2000.) An estimated 70 percent of Russians now live below or just above the poverty line.
2. See United States Information Agency, "Is Economic Reform in Russia Dead?" *Opinion Analysis* (USIA: Office of Research and Media Reaction, March 15, 1999), pp. 3-4. The ratio of Russians who had favorable attitudes toward U.S.-Russia rapprochement versus those who did not declined steeply from 1994 to 1999. In 1994 the ratio was 2.47, as compared with 1.67 in 1999. See Boris Dubin, "Vremia i Lyudi: O Massovom Vospriiatii Social'nykh Peremen," *Russian Public Opinion Monitor* (May-June 1999), pp. 22-3.
3. In coining this usage of "transactor," I purposefully draw on the original meaning of the term: someone who carries through or does business.
4. For further detail, see my "Rigging the U.S.-Russian Relationship: Harvard, Chubais, and the Transidentity Game," *Demokratizatsiya: Journal of Post-Soviet Democratization* (Fall 1999), pp. 478-9.
5. U.S. GAO, Foreign Assistance: *Harvard Institute for International Development's Work in Russia and Ukraine* (Washington, DC: GAO, November 1996), p. 3.
6. A "clan," as Russians use the term, is an informal group whose members promote their mutual political, financial and strategic interests. See Olga Kryshtanovskaya,

"The Real Masters of Russia," *Argumenty i Fakty* (May 1997), also in *Johnson's Russia List.*

7. Although individuals are often thought of as the primary unit to take advantage of economic opportunities, this unit with respect to transactors is often the transactor group. Individual transactors must take the interests of their fellow transactors into account when making choices.

8. The two received at least one foundation grant together (vita of Andrei Shleifer supplied by HIID).

9. For the definitive history of Russian reform efforts, see Lynn D. Nelson and Irina Y. Kuzes, *Property to the People: The Struggle for Radical Economic Reform in Russia* (Armonk, NY: M.E. Sharpe, 1994); and Nelson and Kuzes, *Radical Reform in Yeltsin's Russia: Political, Economic and Social Dimensions* (Armonk, NY: M.E. Sharpe, 1995).

10. *Russia Business Watch* (Spring 1997), p. 19.

11. Kryshtanovskaya, "The Real Masters of Russia."

12. Author's interview with Coles, June 6, 1996.

13. U.S. GAO, *Foreign Assistance*, p. 60.

14. *Russian Privatization Center 1994 Annual Report*, pp. 5, 24.

15. Author's interview with and documents provided by Veniamin Sokolov (auditor at the Chamber of Accounts of the Russian Federation), May 31, 1998.

16. Ibid; Sokolov, talk at American University, June 2, 1998. In 1994 both the Duma and the head of the Russian State Property Committee requested a detailed accounting from the Russian Privatization Center. They got nothing. (Sergei Zavorotnyi, "The Traces of 'Privatization' Go Overseas," *Komsomolskaya Pravda*, April 8, 1997.)

17. Author's interview with and documents provided by Sokolov, May 31, 1998. See State Property Committee order no. 188 (which gave Jonathan Hay veto power over the Committee's projects), October 5, 1992.

18. The concept of "transidentities" draws on Fredrik Barth's work. See his *Ethnic Groups and Boundaries: The Social Organization of Culture Difference* (Boston, MA: Little, Brown & Co., 1969).

19. See my "Rigging the U.S.-Russian Relationship," p. 485; and Anne Williamson, *Contagion. The Betrayal of Liberty: Russia and the United States in the 1990s* (forthcoming), chap. 15.

20. In time, Sachs and Shleifer emerged as rivals and ran largely separate operations in Moscow. Still, they shared the transactorship mode of operating and many contacts in the Chubais Clan.

21. Lipton and Sachs served together on consulting missions in Poland and Russia. "Jeff and David . . . were like an inseparable couple," remarked Andrei Vernikov, a Russian representative at the IMF. (Author's interview with Vernikov, November 22, 1997.) Lipton was named deputy assistant secretary of the treasury for Eastern Europe and the former Soviet Union. After Summers was promoted to deputy treasury secretary in 1995, Lipton moved into Summers' old job and assumed "broad responsibility" for international economic policy development.

22. It was unclear who paid for Sachs and his team. (Helmer, "Russia and the IMF: Who Pays the Piper Calls the Tune," *Johnson's Russia List*, February 17, 1999.)

23. While providing no documentation for his role, Sachs writes, "I was an official advisor of the Russian Government from December 1991 to January 1994. Together with Anders Åslund I directed the Macroeconomics and Finance Unit (MFU) of the Russian Ministry of Finance, housed within Government offices." Sachs further writes that his work in Russia with Åslund "was supported mainly by the Ford Foundation and the Swedish Government. I was not paid by the Russian Government." (Letter to author, March 12, 1998.)

24. Gaidar Institute head Aleksander Bevz told journalist Anne Williamson that, "Sachs was never an official adviser to the government, that's his own illusion." Gaidar, too, described Sachs and Åslund as "insignificant figures." Williamson reports that, "Even Gaidar's archrival, [Grigory] Yavlinsky, insisted, 'What we did was not based on even 10 percent of their [Sachs' and Åslund's] advice. Gaidar was using those people as loudspeakers for the West, but, in fact, Gaidar did as he wished.'" (Williamson, *Contagion*, chap. 7.)

25. Williamson's interview with Foglizzio, February 1, 1994.

26. Memorandum from Sachs to Khasbulatov of November 19, 1992; author's interviews with Stanford University economist Michael Bernstam, August 21, 1997 and October 17, 1997.

27. See, for example, an Action Memorandum of February 4, 1993 from a State Department official to the secretary of state, in which Sachs requests an appointment with the secretary. The memorandum notes that Sachs also had sought appointments with National Security Adviser Anthony Lake, Treasury undersecretary-designate Larry Summers, and ambassador-designate Strobe Talbott.

28. Sources include Dan Josefsson, "The Art of Ruining a Country With Some Professional Help from Sweden," etc English Edition 1 (1999).

29. Author's interviews with U.S. officials in the Departments of Treasury and State.

30. For example, Åslund has long been linked to Brunswick, which began as a Moscow-based brokerage firm and evolved into an investment bank, the Brunswick Group. (See Williamson, *Contagion*, chap. 13.) Two of Åslund's Swedish associates worked for Chubais at the State Property Committee, where they helped to design and implement voucher privatization. (Williamson's interview with Martin Andersson, February 1995.) Later, "with still good relations to Chubais," they started Brunswick Brokerage to participate in voucher privatization and to help sell these and other assets to Western investors. (Sven-Ivan Sundqvist, "Svenska Rad Biter Pa Ryssen: Svenska Finansman i Ledningen for Brunswick Group, Foretaget Som Ska Hjalpa Ryska Staten Att Privatisera Industrin," Dagens Nyheter, June 15, 1997.)

31. Sources for Åslund's business activities in Russia and Ukraine include those specified in the previous endnotes, as well as a number of additional reports and sources in Russia, Ukraine, Sweden and Washington.

32. See Williamson, *Contagion*, chap. 13.

33. Sources include author's conversations with Marek Dabrowski, May 9, 1995 and November 27, 1997. For details of Åslund's Ukraine activities, see my *Collision and Collusion: The Strange Case of Western Aid to Eastern Europe 1989–1998* (New York: St. Martin's Press, 1998), pp. 158-61.

34. Harvard transactors Hay and Shleifer often spoke for key Chubais transactors, notably Maxim Boycko, CEO of the Russian Privatization Center, and Dmitry Vasiliev, head of the Federal Commission, the Russian version of the U.S. Securities and Exchange Commission.

35. "The United States and Russia, Part II: Russia in Crisis," September 17, 1998, Hearing transcript, pp. 29-30.

36. See, for example, Barry Wood, "Russia's Economy," Voice of America, January 3, 2000; also in *Johnson's Russia List*, January 4, 2000; and "The State of the (Former Soviet) Union" (Washington, DC: Carnegie Endowment for International Peace, January 6, 2000), also in *Johnson's Russia List*, January 12, 2000.

37. Putin worked under Pavel Borodin, the Kremlin's property manager, who has been linked to the Mabetex scandal. Swiss prosecutors have alleged that Mabetex Project Engineering, a Kremlin contractor, paid tens of thousands of dollars in credit card

bills for members of the Yeltsin family. In one of his first acts, Putin signed a decree protecting Yeltsin from future prosecution and providing him 1with amenities such as a residence and a pension. See Sharon LaFraniere, *Washington Post*, January 7, 2000; and Paul J. Saunders, *Washington Times*, January 6, 2000.

38. See, for example, Paul Starobin, "The Brain Trust Polishing Putin's Image," *Business Week*, January 31, 2000.
39. See my "Informal Relations and Institutional Change: How Eastern European Cliques and States Mutually Respond," presented at the World Bank, Social Development Group (Washington, DC, April 20, 1998).
40. See my *Collision and Collusion*, pp. 134-7, 145.
41. U.S. GAO, *Foreign Assistance*, p. 8.
42. U.S. GAO sources confirm this observation. (Author's conversations with Zanardi, October 28, 1997 and April 23, 1998.)
43. Author's interviews with USAID-paid contractors and U.S. government sources. A member of the GAO audit team confirms this observation. (Author's conversations with Zanardi, October 28, 1997 and April 23, 1998.)
44. For details, see "Whither Reform" speech by World Bank chief economist Joseph Stiglitz (worldbank.org/ knowledge/chiefecon/); Jonas Bernstein, "Loans for the Sharks," *Moscow Times*, December 19, 1995; and Fritz W. Ermarth, "Seeing Russia Plain: The Russian Crisis and American Intelligence," *National Interest* (Spring 1999).
45. See accounts in *Johnson's Russia List*; my *Collision and Collusion*, pp. 151-5; and Williamson, *Contagion*, especially chaps. 13, 15.
46. In August and September 1999, newspapers reported that billions of dollars had been laundered through the Bank of New York. (See Raymond Bonner with Timothy L. O'Brien, *New York Times*, August 19, 1999.) Anatoly Chubais and other members of Yeltsin's government are alleged to have been involved in money laundering. (See Jack Kelly, *USA Today*, August 26, 1999.)
47. U.S. GAO, *Foreign Assistance*, p. 43.
48. Letter from USAID to HIID director Jeffrey Sachs, May 20, 1997. See also "USAID Suspends Two Harvard Agreements in Russia" (Washington, DC: USAID Press Office, May 20, 1997).
49. Hay has been named in other investigations as well. He, together with Dart Management, Inc., is the subject of a civil action in the U.S. District Court of New Jersey brought by Avisma Titano-Magnesium Kombinat over an alleged fraud and money-laundering scheme.
50. Beth McMurtrie, "Report Advises Harvard to Dismantle its Institute for International Development," *The Chronicle of Higher Education*, January 12, 2000.
51. In a letter of April 1997 (obtained and published by *Nezavisimaya Gazeta*), Summers instructed Chubais on the conduct of Russian foreign and domestic economic policy.
52. *Kommersant Daily*, September 8, 1998; *Los Angeles Times*, September 9, 1998.
53. Michael R. Gordon and David E. Sanger, *New York Times*, July 17, 1998.
54. Maxim Boycko, Andrei Shleifer and Robert Vishny, *Privatizing Russia* (Cambridge, MA: MIT Press, 1995), p. 142.
55. Author's interview with Morningstar, February 11, 1997.
56. Peter L. Berger, "Four Faces of Global Culture," *National Interest* (Fall 1997), pp. 24-5.

11

Tainted Transactions: An Exchange

Jeffrey D. Sachs, Anders Åslund, and others*

Jeffrey D. Sachs:

Janine Wedel, for the umpteenth time, repeats her phony diatribes against me. Please permit me to correct the record.

Despite Dr. Wedel's weird insinuations that I had no advisory role with the Russian government, I was an official adviser to that government, but only for two years and two months, from December 1991 to January 1994. I worked closely with Anders Åslund during this period. President Yeltsin officially designated us as advisers during a meeting with us on December 13, 1991, and we received offices in the Council of Ministers during 1992 and in the Ministry of Finance during 1993. During the period until the end of 1992, Åslund and I mainly advised acting Prime Minister Yegor Gaidar, and in 1993 we led a unit within the Russian Finance Ministry advising Deputy Prime Minister Boris Fedorov. (The most bizarre and entertaining fiction is Dr. Wedel's additional suggestion that I somehow secretly worked with the IMF during 1992.)

During this entire period, there were notoriously heated divisions within the Russian government, and between the Russian government on one side and the Duma and Central Bank on the other. The reformers, led by Gaidar and Fedorov, did what they could to pursue needed reforms, but very often they were blocked. Unlike my experience in many other countries, such as Poland, little of what I recommended was actually enacted. It wasn't pleasant being blamed for high inflation and other ills that resulted from the very opposite of the advice that Åslund and I were giving (such as when the Central Bank ran a

* At the time this symposium appeared, Jeffrey D. Sachs was the director of the Center for International Development, Harvard University and Anders Åslund was a senior associate at the Carnegie Endowment for International Peace. This exchange first appeared in *The National Interest*, No. 60 (Summer 2000).

131

disastrous hyperinflationary monetary policy in 1992 and 1993), but it was still worth the effort of supporting the brave reformers fighting an uphill battle. Åslund and I publicly resigned in January 1994, days after Gaidar and Fedorov left the government. We were concerned about the takeover of the government by the "industrial lobby," with a foreshadowing of the mega-corruption that was to follow, especially in the disgraceful state giveaways of the lucrative natural resource enterprises, mainly during 1994–96. I was also particularly distressed by the lack of appropriate Western advice and assistance, a point that I made repeatedly in writings and speeches at that time and afterward.

Somehow in this maelstrom some people came to assume (or at least claimed to assume) that whatever happened was what I had recommended, even though I was publicly and privately critical of the lawlessness and lack of reform progress. For a few people this has continued despite the fact that I have not advised the Russian government for six years or even been to Russia for five years. Wedel writes in just this nonsensical vein. For many years I have publicly and repeatedly denounced the scandals of privatization such as the "shares for loans" deals, and published articles and books describing and criticizing the lawlessness and corruption in Russia (including *The Rule of Law and Economic Reform in Russia*, 1997).

Dr. Wedel deliberately and systematically mixes personal references to me, the Harvard Institute for International Development (HIID) and other Western advisers, so that she can rope me into her phony conspiracy theories. The HIID projects she refers to were directed by Professor Andrei Shleifer at Harvard, and I had no role in those projects. She seemingly can't understand that I had a completely separate project, and that I resigned from advising the Russian government as of January 1994. One and one half years later, I became director of HIID in July 1995, and Professor Shleifer's project was one of sixty or so ongoing HIID projects around the world. During the period in which I directed HIID (1995–99), I stayed completely away from any personal involvement in any Russian advisory work, consistent with my public resignation in 1994. Moreover, when dubious practices in Professor Shleifer's project came to the attention of the U.S. Agency for International Development (USAID) and myself in the spring of 1997, USAID and I worked together to close the project immediately.

Dr. Wedel writes darkly that "it is unclear who paid Sachs and his team." As I have explained repeatedly to her, and to anyone else that had the slightest interest, I received my academic salary for my work in Russia, with my leave time from Harvard University covered mainly by the United Nations University in Helsinki in early 1992, and thereafter by the advisory project supported by the Ford Foundation and the Swedish government during 1992–93. USAID supported a small amount of my summer academic salary, probably a total of a month or two. Of course, I never invested a penny in Russia, or in any other country in which I have served as an economic adviser. Nor did I engage in any consulting services for private businesses or investors involved with the Russian economy.

Dr. Wedel also accuses me of somehow improperly promoting myself to the Russians as a person "facilitating access to Western money." As any mildly interested observer of the Russian reforms would know from my writings and speeches, I strongly believed and publicly argued in 1992 that the West should provide large-scale assistance to Russia to support the early days of market reforms and stabilization, something the West manifestly declined to do. There was nothing sinister, surreptitious or secretive about any of this: I simply believed (and continue to believe) that timely Western help in 1992 and 1993 could have played an important role in helping real reforms and democratization to take hold, but of course it did not come. The Russian reformers and I knew that the chances for the needed large-scale support were not high, but we felt the effort was worth making anyway.

Wedel's twisting of facts and outright misrepresentations go on and on. What I find hard to understand is how *The National Interest* could publish this nonsense without even doing an iota of fact-checking.

Anders Åslund:

A decade after the collapse of the communist system, history has demonstrated that those post-communist countries that aggressively pursued market economic and democratic reforms are rapidly improving the lives of their citizens. Janine Wedel ignores this reality and seems more intent on denigrating those who have advocated and actively promoted such radical reform. She appears to lack an analytical framework, and her assertion of facts is inaccurate.

The stars among the post-communist countries are Poland and Estonia, which are generally acknowledged as the most radical market reformers. According to the European Bank for Reconstruction and Development, they also have the least corruption. Russia attempted a radical reform, but unfortunately it stumbled. Even so, Russian citizens are better off than Ukrainians, who saw a much later reform and less privatization, not to mention the poor Belarusians, who suffer under a frightful dictatorship in a Soviet theme park. Market reform and democracy go together in the post-communist world. Russia's problem is not too radical reform, but too little reform.

For the past decade, Janine Wedel has been going after leading advocates of radical market economic reform and privatization in former communist countries. Since the shortcomings of her gossip journalism are so obvious, nobody seems to have bothered to answer her as yet, but when a respectable magazine, such as *The National Interest*, publishes an article of hers, this mixture of lies, half-lies, sly allusions and sheer misunderstandings needs to be exposed.

In 1990 she started pursuing Jeffrey Sachs and David Lipton for having destroyed the Polish economy through their "ideology . . . of radical privatization and marketization," which soon turned Poland into a stunning success. Poland's President Alexander Kwasniewski recently bestowed a high Polish order on Sachs and on Lipton in gratitude for their services to Poland.

What is her alternative? In her book, *Collision and Collusion: The Strange Case of Western Aid to Eastern Europe 1989–1998* (1998), she revealed her ideological preferences by repeatedly citing the old-style Soviet communist Leonid Abalkin with sympathy in his criticism of liberal reformers. She seems to advocate U.S. assistance to such communists: "In short, donors, by equating Western-oriented Russians with reform agendas and traditionalist or communist Russians with anti-reform agendas, created stereotypes."

Wedel is patently contradictory. She criticizes Western consultants for their "[l]ack of the understanding of the Russian cultural context," but the particular persons she assails know Russia well. She attacks the major Western economic advisers in Russia for being both ineffective and too influential. You cannot have it both ways.

Similarly, she regrets large amounts of aid to consultants, but she has focused on one institution, namely, the Harvard Institute for International Development, which received less than 1 percent of total USAID assistance to Russia. She ignores the many other general contractors for USAID that received much more money.

The major problem, however, is Wedel's inability to evaluate the accuracy of her sources. She mainly relies on interviews, going around talking to admittedly many people, but she only records vicious and tendentious allegations often made by single individuals. She makes no attempt to check their truthfulness, ulterior motives or even whether her interviewees can know what they say. The Soviet Union was an empire of lies, and systematic lying remains common. Wedel seems unaware of this, revealing her limited understanding of the Russian cultural context.

Sometimes, though, Wedel seems aware of her absence of evidence, but instead of retracting she adds, for instance, ". . . as well as a number of additional reports and sources in Russia, Ukraine, Sweden and Washington."

In a review of *Collision and Collusion* in *Comparative Economic Studies*, Jozef van Brabant, an economist who has persistently opposed radical market reform, concluded: "The book is marred by all too many other inaccuracies some of which are attributable to the author's ignorance."

From a personal perspective, I can say that Wedel's portrayal of my work is simply wrong. She alleges: "Åslund seemed at once to represent and speak on behalf of American, Russian and Swedish governments and authorities." This statement is absurd. I left the Swedish foreign service in 1989. I served as economic adviser to the Russian government from November 1991 until January 1994. I have never been employed by the U.S. government. Although my employments have varied over time, they have never involved conflicts of interest, and I have always made clear what I am doing.

Wedel also complains that "he always presented himself [in op-ed articles] as an objective analyst, despite his many promotional roles." When working with the Russian government and later the Ukrainian government, I always mentioned that. Some may disagree with me, but I have hardly ever been accused of being unclear about what I stand for.

Wedel claims: "Åslund was also involved in business activities in Russia and Ukraine," and in her *Demokratizatsiya* article: "He had 'significant' business investments in Russia." The truth is that while advising any government, I have never been involved in business activities or invested in that country, though I have given lectures and briefings on the state of their economies.

She complains that two of my associates, who worked for Chubais, set up an investment bank *after* having finished their work for Chubais. So what? High U.S. Treasury officials often come from and go to investment banks.

In her *Demokratizatsiya* article, Wedel claimed: "Åslund helped to deliver Swedish government monies to the [Russian Privatization Center]." I would have been happy to do so, but I did not. Wedel writes that I attended a *dacha* in Arkhangelskoe when the Gaidar team prepared its government program there, but I have never visited that *dacha*. Nor is it true that my assignment in Ukraine "explicitly included public relations on behalf of that country."

In public appearances, Wedel has asserted that I have made a huge amount of money on USAID, but USAID has never financed any advisory work of mine. Nor have I worked for HIID, which she also has alleged. My work in Russia was financed by the Swedish government and the Ford Foundation through the Stockholm Institute of East European Economics.

This is a long list of allegations that I know to be wrong because they involve me personally. There is no reason to believe that she is more truthful about anything else, as Wedel's text abounds with inaccuracies. Aleksander Bevz has never headed the Gaidar Institute. Maxim Boycko replaced Alfred Kokh as chairman of the State Property Committee, not the other way around, as Wedel reports. Jeffrey Sachs and David Lipton were rarely in Moscow together, and so on.

Many of these facts can be easily checked. Most of Wedel's claims have been made three or four times in almost identical wording, as she is in the habit of republishing the same article many times, so it is not a matter of typographical errors. In short, Wedel's main shortcoming is that she lacks the faculty to distinguish truth.

Other Responses and Comments

Marek Dabrowski (former first deputy minister of finance of Poland, currently vice chairman of the Center for Social and Economic Research, Warsaw):

I found Janine Wedel's article deeply wrong in its description and interpretation of East European and Russian transition processes, and of the role of foreign aid to this region.

My impression is that the author intentionally and consciously manipulates facts and sources of information in order to support her conspiracy theory and address far-fetched and certainly unfair personal insinuations against key Russian reformers such as Yegor Gaidar and Anatoly Chubais, and leading Western experts trying to help Eastern Europe and Russia such as Jeffrey Sachs, David Lipton and Anders Åslund. Her style of writing and methods of work remind me of the worst instances of Communist Party propaganda, which I had occasion to experience not so long ago as an East European national.

The best example of such practices is footnote 33 of her article where she quotes me as the source of the opinion that ". . . Åslund was engaged in public relations activities. His assignment in Ukraine, where he was funded by George Soros, explicitly included public relations on behalf of that country, according to other Soros-funded consultants who worked with Åslund there."

It is true that I worked with Anders Åslund in Ukraine (and in Russia), but I did not formulate such an opinion, and, what is more important, I never gave Wedel permission to use any fragment of our two conversations as the source of quotation in her publications.

Wedel met me once in 1995 with the purported reason to ask me about a paper I had presented on foreign assistance to transition countries. It seemed a normal academic conversation. Then, she called me on the phone several months later. When she started to put her questions, I quickly realized that she was in the grip of some conspiracy theory, and she tried to provoke me to speak against Jeffrey Sachs and David Lipton. She was not ready to listen to my answers because she knew better what the "truth" was, and she wanted me only to confirm her crazy interpretation of events. At the beginning I tried to convince her that she was wrong, but when I realized that this was a hopeless task, I stopped the conversation. I asked her never to call me again, and not to use any part of our conversation in her work, a request she has not respected.

Peter Reddaway (professor of political science, George Washington University):

Janine Wedel's powerful article focuses mainly on the negative effects of "transactorship" on Russian-Western relations. These contributed to other problems that, taken together, mean that the West has helped to create in Russia a much bigger long-term problem for our foreign policy than most observers have yet grasped.

In my view, the attempted imposition of shock therapy (or "the Washington consensus") on Russia by Boris Yeltsin and the West has been a textbook example of doctrinaire social engineering. It has been based on a mixture of ignorance and arrogance. As I have argued since before the process began in

1991, such an approach was bound—given the legacy of Russian and Soviet history—to be, at the least, premature and dangerous. Russia is not Poland or Estonia. No matter what tricks Yeltsin and his foreign backers used, it was *politically impossible* to fully apply shock therapy in the Russia of the early 1990s. Any government that might have tried to do so would have provoked chaos and fierce opposition—and been thrown out. Governments do not deliberately commit suicide. The repeated complaints of people like Jeffrey Sachs and Anders Åslund that Yeltsin and Yegor Gaidar "lacked the political will to go the whole way" demonstrate, at best, political naivety. At worst, the complaints look like an attempt to divert attention from the incompetence of the advice given by these individuals to the Kremlin, the IMF and Western governments.

The second part of the tragedy is that when, by 1994, it was crystal clear that the "reforms" were not working, the IMF, the G-7, Sachs, Åslund and others continued—for four more long years—to pressure Yeltsin into largely futile efforts to push ahead with them. This compounded failure. For most Russians, such doctrinaire obstinacy put an end to the hopes of better living conditions that had been aroused by the fall of communism.

The pattern was this: the West kept offering loans in return for Kremlin promises to reduce inflation and the budget deficit, privatize industry, appoint Anatoly Chubais to run the economy, circumvent the parliament through presidential decrees, and so on. However, as Dmitri Glinski and I will show in our forthcoming book, *The Tragedy of Russia's Reforms: Market Bolshevism Against Democracy* (2000), not only did these Western recipes fail to stabilize the ruble, halt the steep plunge in investment, and get workers paid on time; they also created a humiliating dependency on the West's aid and foreign policy, promoted crony capitalism, fostered massive crime, corruption, and capital flight, eroded state capacity all around, and destroyed what basis remained for achieving a modicum of social justice.

The devastating effect of all this in terms of values is that the majority of Russians, who a decade ago saw democracy and free markets as beacons of hope, now see before their eyes ugly perversions of these institutions, and wonder if they just won't work in Russia. Opinion polls repeatedly show profound doubt and even despair about Russia's future. They also show that anti-Americanism has permeated the whole society and is probably now deeper than at any time in Russia's history. A substantial majority believe that the United States and the West have weakened Russia deliberately, in order to exploit and humiliate it.

Encouragingly, a few of Dr. Wedel's "transactors"—for example, Pyotr Aven, Konstantin Kagalovsky, and David Lipton—have in varying degrees rethought and recanted the neo-Bolshevik social engineering that is the main cause of this tragic outcome. Others—notably Sachs and Åslund—have not. Åslund, indeed, tries to publicly ridicule people like the former chief economist of the

World Bank, Joseph Stiglitz, who dare to criticize either him or the now exploded "Washington consensus." Also silent as regards rethinking and self-
criticism are the main architects and implementers of U.S. policy toward Russia:
Strobe Talbott, Lawrence Summers, and Al Gore. Their successors will, tragi-
cally, be left with a major, nuclear, long-term "Russia problem."

Igor Aristov (head of the Department for Competition Protection of the Financial Markets, Ministry for Antimonopoly Policy and Entrepreneurship Support, Russia):

It was very useful to learn the details about the Chubais Clan and its illicit
activities from Janine Wedel's article.

It is not possible to overestimate the significance of such an article. For me
personally this information is also very important because Russian tycoons
have used illegal financial inflows for private purposes and against the national interest of Russia. To foresee their future intentions we need to understand the structure of their informal relations. Recent scandals have revealed
the importance of monitoring closely their transactions, property, money and
debts to international organizations.

Wayne Merry (director of the Program on European Societies in Transition,
the Atlantic Council of the United States):

Janine Wedel makes a major contribution to the "Who lost Russia?" debate
by pulling back some of the protective covering on how the U.S. government
sought to impose its economic ideology on post-Soviet Russia. During my
years in the political section of the U.S. embassy in Moscow (1991–94), I also
saw close up the basic flaws of our Russia policy. First came ignorance, as
purveyors of "the Washington consensus" unleashed their dogma on a country they did not understand and, worse, did not wish to understand. Then came
arrogance on many levels: the belief that "the Washington consensus" embodied ultimate economic truth (its manifest failures notwithstanding); responding to any doubts about the dogma with accusations of heresy and disloyalty;
the view of Russia as an economic wasteland (how it had managed to build all
those missiles conveniently ignored) and as a laboratory to refine economic
theory (heedless of the banners carried on the streets of Moscow by some of the
laboratory animals demanding "No More Experiments").

Next came authoritarianism, as Washington encouraged a willing group of
Russian "reformers" to implement our policies by presidential decree rather
than face the compromises of the legislative process, and to create extra-con-
stitutional and clandestine structures of administration to avoid parliamentary oversight or media exposure.

Lastly came hypocrisy, as Washington officials claimed to be "shocked, shocked" when the government-sanctioned corruption and theft of public property in Russia could no longer be hidden. They then piously demanded that Russian governance be all the things the Treasury and IMF had insured it would not be: honest, accountable, transparent, law-based, public-spirited.

Thanks are due to Dr. Wedel for her efforts to document this failed policy process but, sadly, she has so far seen only the tip of the iceberg—what remains "classified" is much worse.

Michael Hudson (president of the Institute for the Study of Long-term Economic Trends):

I would like to give a perspective on Dr. Wedel's theory of transactors as an economist who has worked most of my life for U.S. international banks and money managers, addressed the Duma on numerous occasions, and consulted for U.S. government agencies on U.S.-Russia relations.

I have observed transactorship, and the insider dealings it entails, first-hand. "Average" U.S. investors were not in a good position to profit from the corruption that underlay Russia's stock market boom. One of the leading fund managers (for whom I worked in 1989–90 to help organize the first global sovereign-debt fund) refrained from the outset from riding this roller coaster. The firm's managers didn't trust the visibly corrupt investment climate and, not being insiders, they saw that "arms-length" speculation probably would end in disaster.

Institutional investors from firms that did enter the market explained to me that the safest money to be made was by those who had inside contacts. Money managers who didn't want to invest directly in the risky Russian stock market consigned funds to companies such as Brunswick, which put on promotional shows around the country, in which Anders Åslund and others tried to convince institutional investors that they had an inside track. It was no secret that Russia's market had no legal overseer like our SEC, but that was the very point of investing in Russia!

Based on discussions I had with U.S. global investors during the 1990s, I think I am in a good position to point out why many of them preferred to see major Russian companies pass into just a few corrupt hands. If a few Russian insiders could buy out Russian oil fields and other firms at only 1 or 2 cents on the dollar, they probably would be willing to sell their takings to U.S. and other international investors for 2 to 4 cents. This would enable them to double their money, while providing foreigners with what they wanted: inexpensive ownership of Russia's potentially lucrative mineral wealth and public utilities, as well as its real estate (or, more specifically, its land).

Thus, one reason the U.S. government welcomed the Chubais-HIID mode of "reform" was because of pressure from large investors. If Wall Street investment bankers wanted to take an investment position in Russia, they could do so most easily—and at a much lower price—if only a few "oligarchs" gained ownership of Russia's prize assets. However, if the Russian government or other parties retained control over these assets, they would not be sold as rapidly, and probably would be sold at a higher price.

And so a symbiosis developed between the largest U.S. investors and Russian oligarchs. The largest U.S. investors realized that the kleptocrats for their part wanted to transfer their fortunes abroad. This is what all thieves want to do, for a simple reason: if they keep their money at home, it can be seized by true market reformers. Hence, Russian appropriators sought to move their money to Cyprus, Switzerland and other offshore banking centers, topped by the United States.

To do this, they needed security from Western prosecution. The traditional way to achieve this is to go into partnership with well-placed Westerners. Partnership agreements accordingly were sealed by selling part of their stock ownership to Western investors. Such sales in fact were the only way in which the privatizers were able to realize financial value for their control, for there was no purchasing power within Russia itself to buy their shares. To raise money off the shares they had obtained, Russians needed to sell abroad.

This was well recognized by international investors. It explains why they turned a blind eye to the abuses by Chubais and other insiders, for they knew that they themselves would be the beneficiaries.

Was the subsequent economic devastation directly intended, as a means of "hurting Russia" and thereby disabling it from posing a future threat to the United States and other countries? I believe not. Rather, it was the consequence of the game plan by Western investors (mainly in the United States) to get rich quickly off Russia. The shrinkage of the Russian economy in consequence was a form of "collateral damage," not the intention of the programs themselves. It is the same sort of damage caused by IMF austerity programs imposed on hapless Third World debtors.

My conclusion is that the U.S. government is guilty of gross negligence as to the consequences of the reformers' privatization plans it backed. It didn't mean to kill Russia. It just wanted to take its money and property. Russia's economy got killed in the process. I suppose you might call this second or third-degree murder, not first-degree murder. But that is all that Wedel's article claimed, in my reading.

What is ironic is that the "free-market" strategy that has been followed excludes from the market precisely the arms-length investors that U.S. policy has claimed to attempt to attract as the mainspring in allocating Western capital funds.

David Ellerman (economic adviser to the chief economist, the World Bank):

My only "problem" with Professor Wedel's article is that it attempts to tell the story in such detail that it will allow those who intellectually sponsored what is, in my personal opinion, one of the biggest debacles of the last half of the twentieth century to continue to avoid analyzing the forest by bickering over the details of the bark on the trees.

Steven Rosefielde (professor of economics, University of North Carolina, Chapel Hill):

Janine Wedel's "Tainted Transactions" makes an important contribution to the "Who lost Russia?" saga by investigating the nexus between "radical" economic transition theory and Western foreign assistance. . . . A few facts and comments might prove illuminating.

First and foremost, it needs to be stated bluntly that there is no scientific theory of how to transform a command economy efficiently into a well-functioning competitive market system. Theorists cannot even demonstrate the necessity of general equilibrium with a production sector under perfect competition, so there certainly isn't a shred of justification for suggesting that Yegor Gaidar's and Anatoly Chubais' radical reforms should have produced good results. The policies they adopted, often called "shock therapy," were analogous to removing the control rods from a nuclear reactor, and insisting that the ensuing chain reaction would create a better power system.

The Soviet/Russian basis for this strategy dates to the late eighties when Stanislav Shatalin, Gregory Yavlinsky and others developed their infamous 500 Days program, which promised *perekhod*—transition to competitive free enterprise by the end of 1993. They weren't sincere. Shatalin disclosed his real agenda at Duke University in 1991 when he declared that, "It didn't matter if the transition took 500 days, or 500 hundred years, as long as it destroyed Communism!" The debate between the "shockers" and the "gradualists" was never really about economic "optimality"; it was a rhetorical struggle between a generation of young Turks egged on by Gorbachev, who saw radicalism as a highway to political power, and the old reformist economic guard like academicians Oleg Bogomolov and Yuri Yaremenko, who—like Western Nobel laureates Kenneth Arrow, Paul Samuelson and James Buchanan—understood the necessity of building legal and market structures before leaping into the abyss. The failed putsch in August 1991, and Gorbachev's refusal to allow the military to arrest and execute Yeltsin later that fall when Russia, Belarus and Ukraine seceded from the Soviet Union, enabled the radicals to triumph, as their predecessors had during War Communism and the Stalin era. Their Luddite politics not only instantaneously brought about an economic implosion that has caused 5.4 million premature adult deaths through 1997, but opened the Pandora's box of vicious criminality, just as anyone conversant with the history of Gulag and Soviet mafias would have predicted.

The Western transactors Wedel discusses in her article—the IMF, World Bank, U.S. Treasury, USAID, European Bank for Reconstruction and Development, OECD, EU and the Western private sector—could not have prevented this debacle, even if they hadn't misbehaved in the ways Joseph Stiglitz describes in the April 17 & 24, 2000 issue of the *New Republic*. Only Chubais, Maxim Boycko, and Alfred Kokh—successive chairmen of the Russian State Property Committee and members of the "transactors circle"—could have mitigated the plunder and disorder, had they not been so thoroughly corrupt. From this perspective, it makes little difference whether some Western economic theories were partially or wholly congruent with those of Russia's homegrown radicals. Had Jeffrey Sachs, widely considered an arch advocate of "shock therapy," been a closet conservative, as Joseph Stiglitz now suggests, Yeltsin's vendetta against the Communist Party still would have driven him to recklessly destroy the remnants of central planning and the ministerial system without first preparing the way for a smooth market transition.

The damage caused by Western proponents of "shock therapy" and others who misunderstood the conditions required for empowering Adam Smith's invisible hand was less than that caused by Yeltsin's rash decrees. It is the sum of the tens of billions of dollars that "transitionists" of all stripes coaxed Western leaders into diverting from America's, Europe's and Japan's deserving poor to Kremlin thieves, plus the negative global welfare costs of consolidating Yeltsin's system of anti-productive elite privilege. The new economic model that has emerged is similar to the regime contrived by Hjalmar Schacht for Hitler: a marketized variant of a command economy that allows leaders to utilize a broad array of regulatory instruments, including direct arms procurement contracting, to enrich a narrow clique and rearm, in whatever mix Putin desires. It is precisely in this sense that Russia has been lost, and that those found guilty by the verdict of history of abetting the process through economic myth-making, politicking and moral turpitude should feel profoundly ashamed.

Janine Wedel Responds

Jeffrey Sachs' and Anders Åslund's letters contain a series of unsupported counter-assertions. Both deal in significant part with issues that are not addressed in, or material to, my *National Interest* article. The article presents the theory of transactorship, a mode of organizing relations among nations. Both Sachs and Åslund are stunningly silent on this central issue: neither attempt to refute either the theory or the critical body of facts supporting it. The principal point of the article is that a group of self-interested actors and advocates from both the United States and Russia, supported by Western aid and promoted by high U.S. officials to whom they were closely linked, managed to co-opt U.S.-Russian economic relations and helped to bring about the fiasco that followed. It is not at all "contradictory" to conclude that Western economic advisers in Russia were both "influential" and "ineffective." The Harvard-Chubais transactors, including Sachs and Åslund, were most influential precisely in recommending and implementing policies that turned out to be highly counterproductive. The outcomes of their activities ran directly counter to the stated aims of the U.S. aid program in Russia.

Sachs seems not to understand that the issue is the *multiple* and *conflicting* roles that the transactors assumed (with ambiguous loyalties, ambitions and income sources), not the specific official title they held at any given time. Sachs restates that he advised Yegor Gaidar, which I do not dispute, and does not deny his other roles: his transfer of loyalty from Gaidar to Gaidar's nemesis, Ruslan Khasbulatov, who was seen in the West as a retrograde communist; and his offer of access to Western aid to Khasbulatov, while urging, in his role as an American economist, that vast amounts of such aid be sent to Russia. Sachs seems to deny that he was in correspondence with the IMF while at the same time advising Gaidar. However, one memorandum that I have in my possession was written by Sachs and David Lipton (who became a Treasury undersecretary), dated May 11, 1992, and directed to key Russian decisionmakers at the IMF. It shows that Sachs and Lipton were privy to internal discussion within the Fund and were proffering advice within that context without any mention of their role advising the Russian side.

Åslund and Sachs portray me as a conspiracy theorist "going after leading advocates of radical market reform." On the contrary, I have been trying, as an anthropologist, to understand the roles being played by key actors involved in the aid process and in guiding economic transition. If those studies have resulted in uncovering unseemly activities, that is a consequence of what the actors have done, not of any analytical bias. I have no personal antagonism toward any of the key figures involved, nor did I approach the analysis with any ideological agenda.

As a researcher, I have pieced together the story based on hundreds of documents, U.S. General Accounting Office (GAO) reports and interviews. I have been studying Eastern Europe as the centerpiece of my professional work for more than twenty years. As an anthropologist, I am especially aware that people I interview don't always tell the truth—and not only Eastern Europeans. I always cross-check critical information and confirm key points with multiple sources.

Åslund and Sachs make a number of specific allegations. The facts are as follows:

• Regardless of the percentage of U.S. assistance to Russia flowing directly to the Harvard Institute for International Development, the U.S. government delegated virtually its entire Russian economic aid portfolio—more than $350 million—for management by HIID. Part of this was used to design, implement and promote the disastrous voucher privatization program. In a 1996 report, the GAO found that HIID had "substantial control of the U.S. assistance program." The advisers were also influential under other guises. Project documents submitted by Jeffrey D. Sachs and Associates, Inc. to the Finnish government state: "The [Sachs] team has had an extensive interaction with the [Russian] State Committee on Privatization and has helped in the design of the mass privatization program legislation recently enacted by Parliament."

• Åslund, as I state in the article, *has* been involved in business activities in countries while consulting with their governments. He says he was an adviser to the Russian government beginning in the early 1990s. He continued to advocate on behalf of that government throughout the decade, during which he was also linked to Brunswick. Brunswick began as a Moscow-based brokerage firm and evolved into an investment bank, the Brunswick Group. While Åslund claims that he only gives "lectures and briefings," he attended an April 1997 banking conference in New York sponsored by Brunswick Securities Ltd. *as a representative of Brunswick*. He promoted the Russian stock market to institutional investors and money managers, according to Michael Hudson, who also participated in the conference. Hudson adds that the minimum acceptable investment was between $400,000 and $500,000. As to the significance of Åslund's business ventures in Russia, it was the head of the Interior Ministry's Department of Organized Crime that characterized Åslund's investments in Russia as "significant."

• Åslund appears not to understand that the problem of conflict of interest is no less real where an expert works in serial for conflicting interests rather than at the same time. The American investment bankers he refers to could well end up in jail if they were to use their Treasury Department contacts in violation of conflict-of-interest and revolving door laws and rules that limit the free use of connections. Thus, Åslund sees no problem that the two close associates whom he introduced to privatization minister Chubais, and who helped to design and implement voucher privatization, then started Brunswick Brokerage to help sell vouchers and other assets to Western investors. But there is a problem.

• Nowhere in my article do I say that Sachs has investment activities in Russia.

• Sachs makes much of the distance between his project and that of his Harvard colleague, Andrei Shleifer, who continues to be under investigation by the U.S. Department of Justice. However, Sachs, Lipton *and Shleifer* are listed as the "three senior members" of the Russia advisory project conducted by Jeffrey D. Sachs and Associates, Inc. As I state in the article: "In time, Sachs and Shleifer emerged as rivals and ran largely separate operations in Moscow." However, "they shared the transactorship mode of operating and many contacts in the Chubais Clan," as well as many Western contacts.

• I have never written that Åslund worked for HIID directly. In my book, *Collision and Collusion*, I did point out that Åslund collaborated with Sachs on HIID's unsolicited proposal to advise Ukraine, the details of which are specified in the 1996 GAO report mentioned earlier. I have never said that he has made a huge amount of money on USAID. However, the grants that Sachs and Åslund received from several sources were substantial. Åslund's advisory project was awarded $642,857 in 1991–92 from the Swedish government. Sachs received $322,728 in salary and fees (not including expenses) for a wider Institute-sponsored project billed to Jeffrey D. Sachs and Associates, Inc. The project, the total cost of which was $2,036,122, was funded by the Finnish Ministry of Foreign Affairs and the Sasakawa Foundation.

• Not only do I *not* claim that Åslund was officially on the payroll of the U.S., Swedish and Russian governments simultaneously, but I wrote that he was a "private" citizen who nevertheless "participated in high-level meetings at the U.S. Treasury and State Departments about U.S. and IMF policies." In addition, he "played a leading role in Swedish policy and aid toward Russia" and "was understood by some Russian officials in Washington to be Chubais' personal envoy." (For example, Åslund was highly influential with Sweden's Prime Minister Carl Bildt, who promoted him in Washington and included him in a high-level official delegation to the White House.) I report that Åslund *seemed to speak on behalf* of these governments.

• Åslund suggests that there is nothing wrong with serving as an adviser to a country while presenting himself as a disinterested observer. He denies that his role in Ukraine included public relations. Åslund's team member, Marek Dabrowski, is not my only source on the matter. In my interview with Dabrowski of November 27, 1997, he stated that Åslund's "kind of advertising" and "campaigning" creates a "conflict of interest." Contrary to what Dabrowski now alleges, my conversations with him were friendly and, indeed, *on the record*. I have cited Dabrowski as a source before in print on this subject, and he has never previously disputed its accuracy. I do not know why he has responded now with such a personal attack, but it is a fact that Dabrowski's center has received substantial funding from USAID (and much USAID economic assistance passed through HIID). Both Sachs and Åslund are also listed as members of the advisory council of Dabrowski's center.

• Åslund claims that in writing articles he "always mentioned" his work for the Russian or Ukrainian government. That is simply not the case. For example, in his article "Russia's Success Story" in *Foreign Affairs* (September/October 1994), Åslund presents himself as a senior associate at the Carnegie Endowment and makes no mention of any relationship with the Russian government.

• Åslund characterizes my work as "repeatedly citing the old-style Soviet communist Leonid Abalkin." But I did not cite Abalkin at all in my article and he is cited but twice in my book, *Collision and Collusion*, among some 1,750 interviews.

• Finally, Åslund raises a series of irrelevant and diversionary points. He denies being somewhere—Arkhangelskoe—where I never said he had gone. If he is implying that he was not involved when the Gaidar team prepared its program, then that is contradicted by his own writing (see, for example, his book *How Russia Became a Market Economy*, p. 2). In a similar vein, the order in which Kokh and Boycko chaired the Russian Privatization Center is wholly irrelevant to the issue of their corruption. It was the deputy head of the Gaidar Institute, Dr. Alexei V. Ulyukaev, who said, in a taped interview with Anne Williamson, that "Sachs was never an *official* adviser to the government, that's his own illusion" [my emphasis]. Sachs and David Lipton had a close working relationship, as evidenced in numerous joint publications and in Lipton's position as vice president of Sachs' consulting firm. However, it was a Russian representative at the IMF who said that "Jeff and David always came [to Russia] together," a point that others have made as well.

As to Sachs/Åslund's more general comments, former World Bank Chief Economist Joseph Stiglitz is among a growing number of economists who believe that the policies that Sachs and Åslund advocated were misconceived and harmful to Russia and to most of the other post-communist countries. Russia didn't "stumble," as Åslund characterizes it; it was inundated with counterproductive advice from people like himself.

With regard to Poland, although its economy has grown, this success was achieved not by following a radical transition program, but, as Harvard Professor Marshall Goldman has shown, by rejecting key parts of it. Further, high-level corruption has become so institutionalized that the World Bank has urged Poland to begin fighting it. I have not accused Sachs, as Åslund writes, of "having destroyed the Polish economy." On the contrary, I have pointed out that Sachs' role in the Polish transition was largely promotional, a point confirmed by the Polish government in the *Financial Times* (June 15–16, 1991).

Finally, Åslund manages to cite the only negative review (that I know of) to try to discredit my work. In fact, *Collision and Collusion* has been widely reviewed in places such as the *Wall Street Journal*, the *Washington Post* and *Foreign Affairs*, and the reviews have been overwhelmingly positive. Former National Security Adviser Zbigniew Brzezinski wrote of the book: "Very critical and troubling analysis of the shortcomings of Western aid policy, particularly to Russia. The implications of Wedel's critical assessment need to be seriously taken into account." The other letters printed above share that view, and I thank their authors for their support.

12

The Great Transformation

Zbigniew Brzezinski*

Four years have now passed since the implosion of the communist state in Poland set in train a process that led to the collapse of the other Central European communist states. Two years have now passed since the implosion of the Soviet system itself, following five years of agonizing "perestroika." It is, therefore, not too early to try to draw some lessons from the subsequent attempts to create, on the ruins of the communist systems, politically viable and economically successful democracies.

That on-going transformation poses intellectually challenging questions. When it began, there was no model, no guiding concept, with which to approach the task. Economic theory at least claimed some understanding of the allegedly inevitable transformation of capitalism into socialism. But there was no theoretical body of knowledge pertaining to the transformation of the statist systems into pluralistic democracies based on the free market. In addition to being daunting intellectually, the issue was and remains taxing politically, because the West, surprised by the rapid disintegration of communism, was not properly prepared for participation in the complex task of transforming the former Soviet-type systems. Consequently, it has had to improvise very hastily over the last several years.

It is in this context that I intend to address four important questions. First, what should we have learned by now regarding the processes of post-communist political and economic transformation? Second, what should we have learned regarding Western policies meant to aid and promote that transforma-

**Zbigniew Brzezinski, U.S. national security adviser during 1977-1981, is the author of the recently published *Out of Control: Global Turmoil on the Eve of the 21st Century*. His previous work was titled *The Grand Failure: The Birth and Death of Communism in the Twentieth Century* (1989). This essay first appeared in The National Interest, no. 33 (Fall 1993).*

tion? Third, and in the light of the preceding two, what results can we expect to flow in the foreseeable future—over the next decade or so—from the ongoing efforts at the transformation? Fourth, and more specifically, what else should the United States now be doing in that context?

The Transformation Process

Regarding the broad lessons of the transformation process, the first is that *expectations on both sides—in the old communist states and in the West—were much too high, and rather naive.* The liberated peoples of the former communist countries had truly exaggerated and simplistic notions of the kind of help that they would receive from the West. There was a generalized anticipation of manna from heaven, of some new "Marshall Plan" being applied on a vast scale, notwithstanding the actual historical and intellectual irrelevance to former communist countries of the Marshall Plan experience. And in the West, there was a general underestimation of the systemic complexity of the changes required, of the resistance of established and still-pervasive nomenklaturas, and of the duration of the process itself.

A striking example of the above is that the American aid programs which were initiated immediately after 1989-90 for Poland, and then for the other Central European countries, were based on the assumption that the transition process would last for about five years.[1] We now know that it will be much longer than that—ten years at a minimum for the Central European countries, probably in the range of fifteen to twenty years for the other countries—before it will be possible to say that the transformation has been completed. (One may also add, parenthetically, that the West was also rather overoptimistic as well as simplistic in its assessment of Gorbachev—of his intentions, as well as of his program—and that to some extent we currently display a similar tendency in our reactions to Yeltsin.)

A second and more complicated lesson is that *the transformation process itself is not a continuum, but a sequence of distinct phases.* Moreover, not all of the former communist states are in the same phase of the process of transformation, nor are they traversing the respective stages at the same pace. It is also noteworthy that the rapidity of the shift from phase to phase is heavily conditioned by what transpired politically and economically during the final (pre-implosion but also gestating) stage of the former communist systems.

The above requires some elaboration. The first critical phase, following immediately upon the fall of the communist system, involves a combined effort to achieve both the political transformation of the top structures of political power and the initial stabilization of the economy. The former typically means the imposition of top-down democracy; the latter typically requires stabilization of the currency while undertaking the initial unfreezing of economic controls. This initial stage is extremely difficult because it involves a fundamental change in established political and economic processes. It calls for boldness and toughness, being essentially a plunge into the unknown.

The first phase is also *the* critical one because its success is the necessary launch pad for the second stage, one in which the quest for broader political stabilization has to be combined with efforts at more pervasive economic transformation. The adoption of a new constitution, of a new electoral system, and the penetration of society by democratic processes are designed to institutionalize a functioning democracy. At the same time a broader economic transformation has to be launched, involving, for example, the establishment of a banking sector, de-monopolization, as well as small and middle-scale privatization based on legally defined property rights.

Only when and if that phase has been successfully completed can the next—and third—phase be undertaken, in which comprehensive democratic institutions and processes truly begin to take hold in an enduring fashion, while economic growth becomes sustained as a consequence of the comprehensive unleashing of private initiative. A democratic political culture and an entrepreneurial tradition gradually become reality. This third phase can be described as involving political consolidation and sustained economic take-off. To make all this more concrete, one might hazard the judgment that Poland, the Czech Republic, and Hungary are now on the brink of entering that third phase.

It is also important to note that the ability to embark on, and to traverse, particularly the first critical phase—the most important stage of decision—is heavily conditioned by the degree to which a particular fallen communist regime permitted both political relaxation and economic liberalization in its last years. The important fact to note is that, in effect, the final agony of communism also served simultaneously—at least, in several cases—as a period of political and economic gestation for the emergence of post-communism. The consequences of that gestation in the cases of Hungary (the Kadar regime in the 1970s and 1980s) and of Poland (the Gierek regime of the 1970s and the last five years of Jaruzelski in the second half of the 1980s) are self-evident.

The third lesson to be deduced from what we have seen of the transformation process involves *the primacy of political reform as the basis for effective economic reform. A democratic political consensus and effective political processes are* essential *for the successful initiation and consummation of the first critical stage of change.* One could theoretically postulate the need for an authoritarian system of discipline at this stage, because a great deal of social sacrifice is required—and generated—during its implementation. China obviously comes to mind here. However, in the wake of the collapse of the communist regimes in Central Europe and in the Soviet Union, an authoritarian approach does not seem feasible or desirable.

On the contrary, democratic consensus is imperative. But it must be organized and institutionalized. Initially, that typically calls for the presence of an effective, indeed of a charismatic popular leader—a Havel, Walesa, or perhaps Yeltsin—who can command popular support. It also requires the presence or rapid organization of a political movement that supports the leader in an institutionalized fashion, and is capable of sustaining popular support in the face of the social dislocations and deprivations that typically occur in this phase. But, above all, the initial phase, with its often euphoric postcommunist enthusiasm, must be exploited promptly to build the foundations for legitimate and formal democratic procedures within which longer-term economic reforms are pursued. By the time the second phase is reached, public euphoria tends to have waned while disappointment with the transformation tends to escalate; thus much depends on the resilience and viability of the new democratic processes. Much of Russia's difficulties stem from Gorbachev's and then Yeltsin's failure to focus on the need for comprehensive political reform as an urgent priority.

The foregoing leads to a fourth lesson, which flows from the previous three: *the rapid and comprehensive transformation—the shock therapy of the so-called "big bang" approach—is only possible if both the necessary subjective and objective conditions exist.* The Polish case is a good example of the combination of the two. It involved the existence of a nation-wide counter-political elite, namely the Solidarity movement, which permeated society, was not crushed during the decade of the martial law, and could promptly serve as an effective counter-political elite on the national scale (rather than, as in some other cases, being confined to a few dissidents suddenly installed at the top of the national power hierarchy). That elite, moreover, was buttressed by the presence of a moral authority able to nourish the social will to sacrifice, namely the Catholic Church. In addition, a charismatic leader, who enjoyed special authority within the class likely to suffer the most from the social sacrifices, was able to personalize the political change. A free peasant class and a large underground economy provided economic responsiveness to the workings of the law of supply and demand, upon the lifting of price controls and the termination of subsidies. Finally, Poland benefited from the support given to its surfacing entrepreneurial culture by an engaged diaspora comprised of some ten million Poles who live abroad.

The listing of these factors suggests that while the Polish "Big Bang" approach may be exemplary, it may also be, in many respects, exceptional. In the absence of some combination of political cohesion, commitment, and consensus with economic receptivity and responsiveness, the shock therapy is likely to produce political conflict and economic chaos, with well-positioned monopolies taking advantage of price liberalization simply to increase prices, thereby also stimulating inflation.

The fifth and last general lesson regarding post-communist reconstruction follows from this last point: *One should not rule out transformation strategies that involve slower motion through the needed several stages, and that are also reliant on continued governmental guidance rather than purely on the unleashing of independent and dynamic market forces.* Here the warnings of the very prominent Japanese development economist, the late Suburo Okita, come to mind. He argued cogently in several papers that governmental intervention is needed in countries in which the free market mechanisms lack tradition, experience, and appropriate social culture. He stressed that there are societies in which some combination of market mechanism and governmental planning is necessary for historical reasons, especially as the market mechanism is not always and of itself infallible.

The examples of both Japan and Korea are very pertinent to the case made by Okita. In the summer of 1993, the World Bank was completing an exhaustive analysis of what transpired in the Far East in the last three decades and what lessons may be derived from that experience. According to a preview in the *Financial Times*, one of the Bank's conclusions regarding the Korean experience was that "...from the early 1960s, the government carefully planned and orchestrated the country's development...[It] used the financial sector to steer credits to preferred sectors and promoted individual firms to achieve national objectives...[It] socialized risk, created large conglomerates, created state enterprises when necessary, and moulded a public-private partnership that rivalled Japan's."[2] Much the same could be said about Singapore as an example of successful directed growth. At the very least, such Asian experience should not be disregarded when contemplating the current political, economic and social dilemmas facing both Russia and Ukraine, countries without strong free market traditions and developed entrepreneurial cultures.[3]

The Western Response

Let us now turn to the second of the four major questions posed at the onset: the lessons to be learned concerning Western policy designed to aid and promote post-communist transformation.

First, Western aid is most critical during the first stage of transformation. In fact, significant Western aid is probably essential if that stage is to be traversed successfully. Later, after the first phase, Western aid ceases to be central, whereas access to Western markets and foreign investment become increasingly important. That access becomes the primary source of continued internal change and of export-driven economic dynamism. That is largely the case today in the relationship between post-communist Central Europe and the European Community, with the result that the issue of "access" has become much more controversial than the scale of "aid." In contrast, the former Soviet Union is still in the first phase of the transformation process, when direct Western aid for stabilization and initial political transformation is essential.

Second, and perhaps more controversially, after the critical first phase, the inflow of external capital is not decisive. If Western capital was the key to success, the former East Germany should be flourishing, Hungary should have taken off economically some time ago, followed by the Czech Republic, with Poland trailing behind. Moreover, Russia should be doing much better than China.

The former East Germany (GDR) has received monumental amounts of external capital over the last three years, at a rate of $100 billion per annum, for a population of mere 16 million people. (Just calculate what anything comparable to such a per capita inflow would be required for Central Europe as a whole, or for Russia specifically!) But the crucial point is that the former GDR is still in a massive socio-economic crisis. Similarly, Hungary and Czechoslovakia (prior to its division into two states in early 1993) have been the beneficiaries of much larger capital inflows than Poland. Yet today, Poland has a larger private sector and is the first former communist country to have attained a positive economic growth rate.

China has been the beneficiary of relatively small amounts in terms of grants, loans, credits, and until recently, investments. Over the first twelve years after the start of the reforms in 1979, the total involved for China—a huge country with an enormous population—was less than $60 billion. This is much less than the Soviet Union/Russia has received since 1986—some $86 billion. Yet China has done extremely well in terms of its economic development, growing over the last decade at a rate of 6 percent per annum, last year at 9 percent, this year probably at 13 percent. Russia, in contrast, is still in an economic mess, with a negative growth rate.

In brief, after the conclusion of the first critical phase during which external assistance is central, the nature of domestic policies, social discipline and motivation cumulatively become more important than the inflow of external capital in determining success or failure in the pursuit of economic transformation.

A third lesson with respect to the inflow of external capital is that explicit preconditions and strict supervision of its utilization are imperative. In fact, if a choice is to be made between quite limited but tightly monitored financial assistance and large inflows of external and largely untargeted capital, the former is clearly more beneficial and, therefore, should be favored. This is especially true in the first phase, until trade and foreign investment replace the initial dependence on direct aid. Trade and investment almost automatically tend to be subject to more effective control by the directly interested and personally concerned parties. In the absence of close external supervision, as experience sadly shows, massive diversion and extensive theft of foreign aid is to be expected.

The West should have learned this from its experience with Poland under Gierek. In the 1970s, Poland borrowed about $30 billion, yet it is very difficult to account for what happened to these funds. Today, there are even more serious questions to be raised regarding the $86 billion that has flowed into the former Soviet Union since the second half of the 1980s. Some estimates made in the United States conclude that as much as $17 billion of it has been diverted away from intended purposes and recycled to Western banks. While recently in Moscow, I cited that estimate to Arkady Volskiy, the head of the Russian Union of Industrialists and Entrepreneurs. With a laugh he dismissed the estimate as absolutely wrong, insisting that the total diverted is at least $23 billion.

A recently concluded Japanese study, conducted on the eve of the July G-7 Summit in Tokyo by a private think tank, the Toray Corporate Business Research Inc., also addressed this issue. The study concluded that the Russian government has lost control over the capital flight phenomenon, with the consequence that large amounts of cash, gold, and diamonds have been stashed in Swiss and Hong Kong banks. "The scale of the capital flight has already exceeded 40 billion dollars," the study asserted.[4] Though this estimate may be too high, it is nonetheless clear that the problem of illicit diversion is a very serious one.

Accordingly, precise targeting and close monitoring by donors should be explicitly asserted, even if it offends the national pride of the recipients. Specific conditionality is also essential regarding the fundamentals of reform. Stabilization in the monetary area, depoliticization of the banking system, demonopolization, at least initial small-scale privatization, including in agriculture, and the decentralization of economic decision-making, are the minima that the West has the right to insist upon when granting aid, if the aid is to be helpful.

Fourth, the West ought to encourage the recipient countries to develop some longer-range mobilizing vision, one capable of sustaining domestic support for the needed painful reforms. Even with generous external aid, domestic sacrifices and a great deal of social pain are unavoidable. Therefore, the articulation of a more positive, hopeful, constructive perspective on the future is politically necessary. The public must perceive a sense of direction which justifies their transitional pain and sacrifice.

For the Central Europeans such a vision largely exists already. It involves the notion of united Europe, and of their eventual membership in it. That vision is very meaningful and tangible for an average Czech or a Hungarian or a Pole. It represents something to which they can relate personally. The issue becomes more difficult and elusive when one moves further east. What can provide such a constructive vision today for a Ukrainian who has experienced independence for two years and has found that it has brought mainly socio-economic deprivation? What is that vision for a Russian, who not only experiences similar socio-economic deprivation but also feels acutely humiliated by Russia's loss of the big power status? It is not easy in these circumstances to generate a positive vision of the future.

For the Ukrainians, perhaps it could be the notion of Ukraine eventually becoming, and being accepted by its Western neighbors as a Central European state, and thus part of a community that is already moving closer to the West. That vision certainly would be more tangible to the western Ukrainians than to the eastern Ukrainians, but it might have wider appeal to the Ukrainians who wish to define their nationhood in terms that differentiate Ukraine from Russia.

For the Russians, perhaps, the appropriate vision might be one of becoming a partner of the United States, given the fascination with America that is today so widespread in Russia. But if Russia is to be "a partner" of the United States, America will have to be explicit in insisting that such a Russia be truly a post-imperial Russia, because only such a Russia can become genuinely democratic. The fact is that Russia has still a considerable distance to go in the painful process of adjusting to its new post-imperial reality, a process that was consummated in the case of Britain with the loss of India, in the case of France with the loss of Algeria, in the case of Turkey under Ataturk who defined the concept of a new, would-be modern, would-be European, Turkey. The process of post-imperial self-redefinition is a complicated and difficult one. One can understand why opposition and confusion surround this subject in today's tormented Russia; but the issue must be addressed.

A Differentiated Future

In the light of the responses to the first two questions, what reasonable expectations regarding the post-communist transformation might be entertained in terms of the foreseeable future—say, the next decade or so? It follows from the analysis already offered that the transformation will be differentiated—in kind and time—as well as difficult. But what is likely to be the overall pattern? Are all of the former communist states safely on the way to becoming pluralistic, free market democracies?

Before I hazard some rather arbitrary, personal judgments in response to this question, let me suggest a fourfold predictive framework:

The first category includes countries with essentially positive futures, by which is meant countries in which it would take something altogether unforeseeable and, at the present time, rather improbable for them to be diverted from the process of becoming viable pluralistic democracies.

The second category includes countries whose prospects over the next ten years look somewhat better than even, but in which a reversal, indeed a political and/or economic failure, still cannot be excluded.

The third category involves countries whose political and economic futures, in my judgment, are likely to be still unresolved beyond this decade and into the next century.

Finally a fourth category, essentially an extension of the third, comprises countries whose futures currently, and into the foreseeable future, look distinctly unpromising.

In this classification, as already indicated, Poland, the Czech Republic, and Hungary fall into the first category, as do probably also Slovenia and Estonia. Of these, the first three are likely to be members of the European Community and of NATO within a decade, and even perhaps within this century. Without minimizing their internal difficulties, their futures appear largely predetermined, although Hungary or Estonia could be affected adversely by some external complications (notably, ethnic problems). In any case, the first three can be seen as about to enter, or as entering, Phase 3, while the latter two are in Phase 2.

Even the likely success of the leading three however should not obscure the fact that it will take many years before the gap is significantly narrowed between the standards of living of the richer West and even its most promising post-communist neighbors. If one assumes, for example, that Germany and Austria will grow at 2 percent per annum, while Poland, Hungary, and the former Czechoslovakia will grow twice as fast, at 4 percent p/a, it would still take 30 years in the case of Czechoslovakia, 46 years of Hungary, and 63 years of Poland for the gap in the respective GNP per capita to be closed.[5] Even if the rates of growth were 2 percent and 8 percent respectively, the years required would still be 12, 17, and 23 for the respective Central European populations. Obviously the prospects are much dimmer still for the countries listed below in the second, third, and fourth categories.

The second category—countries whose futures are generally positive but which are politically and economically still vulnerable—includes Slovakia, Croatia (if it does not get entangled in a new war with Serbia), Bulgaria, perhaps Romania, Lithuania, Latvia, Kyrgyzstan, and Turkmenistan (the latter two because of indigenous economic potential). Some of them—e.g., Latvia or Bulgaria—may be nearing Phase 2 but the others are still navigating through Phase 1.

The countries which fall into the third category—those whose political and economic futures are likely to be still unresolved for a decade or more—are, first and foremost Russia—and then Ukraine, Belarus, Georgia, Armenia, Azerbaijan, Kazakhstan, and Uzbekistan. Finally, those in the fourth category, whose futures for a variety of reasons look rather grim, are: Serbia, Albania, Macedonia, Bosnia, Moldova, and Tajikistan. None of the above can be said to be very advanced (or successful) in traversing Phase 1; some may not even have entered it; and most of them are, in fact, still governed by their former communist elites who masquerade under new labels, but whose commitment to a pluralist democracy and sensitivity to its nuances is still questionable.

Of those in the uncertain (third) category, Russia is, of course, the most important. One has to recognize some positive trends in ongoing Russian developments. The process of drafting the constitution has been moving forward, albeit with many difficulties. One can expect at least an initial formula regarding a new constitutional order to emerge from this exercise, and that in itself will be a step forward in the institutionalization of a democratic system. There has certainly been general democratization, particularly of the upper-metropolitan levels of Russian society. In a number of the large cities, democracy is an operational reality, though it lacks genuinely pervasive institutionalization. There has also been some privatization of the economy, and initial steps toward its stabilization. Also, at the top political levels, both President Boris Yeltsin and Foreign Minister Andrei Kozyrev have been willing to denounce—at least rhetorically—traditional imperial aspirations, thereby breaking with a past that would otherwise certainly inhibit genuine democratization.

But there are also contradictory trends: economic chaos is a reality; there is no effective monetary policy, inflation is still extraordinarily high, unemployment is rising; the writ of the government is effectively limited to a few metropolitan centers and does not run throughout the country; there is a lack of policy cohesion and consistency; the much hallowed privatization accounts for only about 50,000 of Russia's approximately 300,000 small shops, with most of those privatized located in Moscow, St. Petersburg, and Nizhny Novgorod6 ; there is massive diversion of Western funds and aid by the remnants of well-positioned nomenklatura and by the new class of middlemen; and many, probably most, of the new capitalists represent parasitic wealth, channeled mainly into consumption and not into productive investment.

Also complicating the economic picture is the evident renewal of imperial aspirations, which increases the likelihood of intensifying tensions with Ukraine and also generates problems with some of the other neighboring states. Most noteworthy here is the use of economic leverage and of military pressure to preserve informally the essential elements of the Kremlin's former imperial status. Quite symptomatic of Moscow's continued reluctance to accept Kiev's independence as an enduring fact was the contemptuous dismissal of it (in the words spoken to me in 1993 by a senior Russian policymaker) as "that conditional entity called Ukraine."

All of this justifies—and generates—some uncertainties regarding the future. One can expect, most probably, continued democratization, but in a context of inconsistent reforms that run the risk of producing periodic phases of intensifying anarchy—and thus the temptation to resort eventually to more authoritarian solutions. As a result, Russia does not fit either category one or category two, but has to be placed—reluctantly and regrettably—in category three. The same is true of Ukraine, whose independence is still in jeopardy and whose internal transformation has been lagging even more badly.

The foregoing cumulatively suggests that history is still open-ended as far as the final outcome of the post-communist transformation is concerned. *As of now, politically and economically successful liberal democracy is not a fore-ordained outcome, except perhaps for five out of the twenty-seven post-com-munist states.*

What Else Should the West Do?

It is time to turn to the last of the four questions posed at the onset; namely, what should be the posture of the West, and of the United States in particular? *The first need is still for a long-term and comprehensive strategy that integrates geopolitical and economic objectives.* As yet, it simply does not exist. The needed strategy should be neither Russo-centric nor Russo-phobic. It must deal with the post-communist area as a whole, but recognize the significantly different stages of change within it. To develop and sustain such a comprehensive policy, the United States should press for the creation of a standing G-7 strategic planning board, one capable of monitoring changes and of advocating the needed division of labor among the principal Western powers, perhaps on a geographical basis. For example, Japan with its hesitations about aiding Russia, could be encouraged to be helpful by concentrating on some other formerly Soviet regions, such as Ukraine. Such a standing strategic board should also interact with pertinent representatives of the affected countries.

In addition, a more comprehensive strategy might involve, for example, Western credits for Central European exports of food and consumer goods to Russia. This would facilitate the Central European transformation while increasing the likelihood that aid for the Russian people will reach the designated recipients rather than being diverted into the black market by middlemen—as sadly has often been the case. In any case, some restoration of trade between Central Europe and the former Soviet Union is clearly in the interest of all of the parties concerned.

Second, the G-7 should now develop an aid package for Ukraine, parallel-ing the one adopted for Russia. Geopolitical pluralism in the space of the former Soviet Union should be viewed by the West as an objective of co-equal importance with systemic transformation. This point deserves repetition: geo-political pluralism is as important as systemic transformation. The United States is beginning in a hesitant fashion to move in that direction, but its policy in this respect has been slow, marred by historical ignorance, beset by bureaucratic stalemates, and instinctively Russo-centric. An aid package for Ukraine, conditioned quite explicitly and specifically on a Ukrainian reform program, is justified on humanitarian and economic, as well as geopolitical, grounds.

Early in 1992, the head of the IMF, Michel Camdessus, publicly stated that Russia would need about $24 billion in external assistance, and that the other former Soviet republics would need an additional $20 billion.[7] A little over a year later, that total sum has been allocated for Russia but little or nothing has been designated for Ukraine and the other non-Russian republics. Yet chaos around Russia will either undermine Russia's own reforms or stimulate a revival of Russia's imperial ambitions, or both—with all of these outcomes being very detrimental to the cause of postcommunist transformation.

Third, facilitating access to Western markets and increased investment should now be the major focus of G-7 initiatives, especially as the EC has been slow in this regard. Some concessions were made by the EC at its June 1993 Copenhagen meeting, but they involved only a partial liberalization of the existing quota-based system limiting Central European access to Western markets. West European economic lobbies—for example, the European Chemical Industry Council or the European Largest Textile and Apparel Companies— as well as some key national ones—for example, the German Steel Association—have teamed up with European agricultural interests in agitating for continued discrimination against competitive Central European products.

The United States should press its allies on this score, because it has been somewhat more open than the EC, but it should also further liberalize its own policies, which have also been unduly restrictive toward Central European and Russian exports. The economies of Central Europe and Russia badly need trade-driven stimuli.

Fourth, the United States should de-emphasize some of the dogmatic elements in the advice that it offers to the former communist states. There has been a tendency in the West, and particularly in the United States, to make shibboleths of the free market and of the elimination of the role of the government in guiding economic development. Indeed, even advice on democracy should be offered with the historically humbling appreciation of the prolonged stages that were required to nurture and consolidate democracy in the West. Cultural conditioning and specific circumstances should be taken into account to a far greater degree than they have been in the rather dogmatic advice that has often been proffered.

Finally, it is not too early to start deliberations about the needed new security arrangements, designed progressively to encompass the former communist states. Geopolitical insecurity is rising in the former communist world and it is becoming as severe a political problem as socio-economic anxiety. There needs to be a response to it, developed and applied in stages, pointing toward the progressive acceptance into NATO of former communist states. Inclusion by stages of some of the former communist states will be more acceptable to Russia and to Ukraine if it is presented as part of a process, the end result of which should be the emergence of a broad Euro-Atlantic system of security that someday might also include Moscow and Kiev. In any case, as a practical matter, some former communist states should be able to enter NATO sooner than others, since it makes no sense to wait until all are ready to enter before letting the first one in. Accordingly, the admission of one (probably

Poland) or more Central European states into NATO, roughly by 1996, should be a major goal of Western policy.

All of this represents a manageable agenda, provided the West has the needed political will and strategic direction. But will America address these issues? Will the West respond? Probably not quite as deliberately and as strategically as one might wish. The West is currently in a phase of internal preoccupation, with cultural hedonism dominating its value system. Cultural hedonism does not lend itself to an activist policy which entails commitment and also requires some measure of sacrifice. While it may be unfair to accuse the United States of embracing isolationism—for America is certainly not disengaging from its formal global obligations—it does appear that Washington is currently pursuing an essentially minimalist foreign policy. Though not deliberately isolating itself from the rest of the world, the United States at this stage seems inclined to define its obligations in the most narrow fashion, exercising its leadership responsibilities only in exceptional circumstances, when the necessity for action becomes overriding.

Hopefully, Western hedonism in general and American minimalism represent but a passing phase of what might be called "post-victory blues"—the inevitable let down after the sustained historical effort of the Cold War. One must hope so because if this phase does not end soon, the post-communist transformation will not only be much more painful and prolonged, but its outcome will be even more uncertain.

Notes

1. See, for example, the U.S. General Accounting Office Report, "Poland and Hungary—Economic Transition and U.S. Assistance," May, 1992, pp.18-26, 30.
2. See Michael Prowse, "Miracles Beyond the Free Market," *Financial Times*, April 26, 1993.
3. A useful compendium of Saburo Okita's writings on this subject is contained in "Steps to the 21st Century," *Japan Times*, 1993. In addition to Saburo Okita's numerous writings, see also D.W. Nam (a former prime minister), "Korea's Economic Take-off in Retrospect," a paper presented at the Second Washington Conference of the Korean-American Association, Washington, DC, Sept. 28-29, 1992; and N. Yonemura and H. Tsukamoto (both of MITI), "Japan's Postwar Experience: Its Meaning and Implications for the Economic Transformation of the former Soviet Republics," March 1992.
4. As reported by KYODO, May 24, 1993. Further shocking details regarding the diversion of Western aid for illicit purposes are contained in Grigory Yavlinsky's op-ed article "Western Aid is No Help" in the July 28, 1993 *New York Times*.
5. Based on the CIA World Fact Book 1991, with the per capita GNP for Germany being $14,600; for Austria $14,500; for CSFR $7,700; for Hungary $5,800; for Poland $4,200.
6. See also "Measuring Russia's Emerging Private Sector," Intelligence Research Paper, CIA, Washington, DC, November, 1992.
7. *New York Times*, April 16, 1992.

13

A Skeptical Look at Aid to Russia

Nicholas Eberstadt*

If Western leaders press forward with their present plans, the principal focus for international development assistance in the 1990s promises to be the former Soviet Union. Indeed, the scale of aid now being contemplated could easily make the CIS the largest single recipient of development assistance transfers. At the Munich economic summit in July, the leaders of the seven major industrial democracies ratified a $24 billion aid program—a one-year package, and for Russia alone. "Never before," noted analysts at Germany's Deutsche Bank, "has a comparable amount been made available to one single country."

Yet the initiative for Russia is merely meant to be a beginning. The managing director of the International Monetary Fund, for example, stated last April that the fifteen countries from the former Soviet Union will require an average of at least $25 billion a year in economic aid for at least the next four years—and by implication very possibly longer. Such a sum would substantially exceed the present volume of aid for all of sub-Saharan Africa or for all of low-income Asia. In fact, a program of that size would absorb nearly half of all Western "official development assistance"(ODA) disbursements at current levels of giving.

Whether such an ambitious international aid program can actually be arranged and approved, of course, remains to be seen. But the ultimate magnitude of the West's pending bequest is by no means the only question that arises in reviewing the many plans and packages for CIS aid now under discussion. One major question can be posed bluntly: Apart from the immediate symbol-

---

*Nicholas Eberstadt is a researcher with the Harvard Center for Population and Development Studies and the American Enterprise Institute. His books include *The Poverty of Communism* and *Foreign Aid and American Purpose*. This essay originally appeared in *The National Interest*, no. 29 (Fall 1992).

ism of the gesture, just what is Western "development assistance" to the former Soviet Union supposed to accomplish, and exactly how is it expected to achieve these results?

Obvious as the question may appear, it is not easily answered, for this particular aspect of the various aid initiatives in question seems to have received remarkably little consideration from prospective donor governments. The oversight in itself is revealing. And unfortunately, it is consistent with a pattern that is all too familiar.

To a disturbing degree, Western bilateral and multilateral aid agencies treat objectives and strategy as peripheral to the real business at hand. Throughout the so-called "donor community" there is a pervasive tendency to equate performance with "moving money": to judge aid not by the effectiveness with which it is spent, but simply by the *fact* that it is spent. Needless to say, this does not augur well for the impact of development assistance on recipient economies.

Examined in its particulars, the actual record of bilateral and multilateral development assistance should not inspire confidence among potential new "beneficiary" populations. In recent decades the international aid community has subsidized wasteful or even positively destructive economic policies in many countries; it has underwritten a transition to self-sustaining economic growth in very few. By comparison with most developing economies, moreover, the task of restoring economic health to the CIS states looks truly imposing. Why the "donor community" should be expected to succeed in this challenge when it has conspicuously failed in many easier tests is far from obvious.

Does It Work?

Any realistic assessment of the likely impact of economic aid on the former Soviet Union must take a measure of the performance of Western bilateral and multilateral aid in the developing regions over the past few decades. Though the self-evident diversity of the Third World and the limited reliability and availability of data for these countries must temper any generalization about overall performance, several distinct tendencies nevertheless stand out.

First, the donor community has succeeded in transferring vast amounts of potentially productive capital to the various governments of Africa, Latin America, and low-income Asia. According to estimates by the Organization for Economic Cooperation and Development (OECD), net disbursements of ODA, at 1989 prices and exchange rates, totalled nearly $600 billion for the period 1980-1990 alone. (If one needs a concrete image to put that figure in perspective, think of two-thirds of the entire U.S. farm system.)

Second, the economies of ODA-receiving countries are today characterized by severe structural distortions—distortions which have become steadily more pronounced over the past generation. To be sure, the developing regions as a whole witnessed considerable improvements in both per capita output and life expectancy during the past quarter century. Yet paradoxically, despite this progress, Third World economies seem ever less capable of maintaining self-sustained economic growth. "Investment without growth" and "industrialization without prosperity" are today widespread phenomena among aid-receiving countries. According to the World Bank, for example, Jamaica's investment ratio over the past generation was much higher than the average for OECD countries—yet per capita growth in Jamaica over the 1965-1990 period was *negative*. By the same token, despite its manifest poverty, Peru's industry reportedly accounts for a greater share of its national output than does Sweden's, and sub-Saharan Africa now appears to be more "industrialized" by this measure than Denmark. During the era of massive aid flows, many Third World economies have evolved in directions that neither generate high rates of return on their scarce capital nor satisfy the demands and needs of their consumers.

Finally, the performance of development assistance programs over the past generation may be judged by the very nature of the continuing resource transfers to Third World countries. According to the OECD, despite four decades of economic assistance premised on "helping countries help themselves," concessional ODA still accounts for over half the net flow of funds from the West to the developing regions. Moreover, the share of direct private investment within this overall flow actually declined between the mid-1960s and the late 1980s. If many recipient states seem incapable of, or unwilling to, attract voluntary private investment from abroad, they seem correspondingly reluctant to embrace financial self-reliance. The roster of governments accepting American development assistance, for example, is virtually the same today as twenty years ago. According to one report by the U.S. Agency for International Development, "Only a handful of countries that started receiving U.S. assistance in the 1950s and 1960s has ever graduated from dependent status." What is true of the U.S. program also obtains for other bilateral and multilateral efforts.

The unavoidable fact about development assistance—indeed, its defining characteristic—is that it is a bequest transmitted not to a population at large but to a presiding government. Some governments choose to use aid funds in economically productive ways; others do not. More than a few Third World states have used their aid funds to finance wasteful policies, or even obviously injurious ones. The donor community, for its part, has continued to finance otherwise unsustainable policies and practices by numerous "beneficiary" governments.

The economies of today's long-term ODA recipients are typically distinguished by a variety of features: external debt obligations they cannot or will not repay, chronic budget deficits and price inflation, nonconvertible currencies and restrictive trade regimes, abnormally swollen investment and industrial sectors, far-reaching economic planning apparatuses, and pervasive state ownership of capital assets. These same features, of course, are characteristic of the economies of the former Soviet Union. The variants in the former Soviet Union, of course, are generally more extreme than those found in most developing countries. This being the case, one may well wonder: If aid policies have financed milder versions of the CIS' current afflictions among so many of its current long-term recipients, why should these transfers be expected to restore the CIS itself to economic health?

The Stabilization Myth

To the extent that the Western economic aid packages now being fashioned for the former Soviet Union have been publicly explained, they are apparently meant to underwrite two major efforts: "stabilization" and "policy reform." Let us examine these in turn.

Russia and the other former Soviet republics are today wandering in a no-man's land between Leninist central planning and the market order. As a system, these current arrangements are inherently unstable; it is far from obvious why one should wish to stabilize them. In its IMF and World Bank usage, however, stabilization has a more limited focus: it refers to the objective of restoring balance or reducing volatility in specific macroeconomic indicators, such as aggregate output, price levels, and external accounts. Traditionally, the IMF has underwritten stabilization programs that move recipients toward economic health through austerity measures (such as budget cuts, elimination of subsidies, and devaluation). Traditional stabilization policies, unfortunately, are fundamentally miscast for economies like those of the CIS. The reason is simple: economic activity in these countries is dominated by state-owned enterprises which do not behave like firms in a competitive market setting. In these post-communist societies, the macro-response to stabilization policies will be different from those evinced in a market-oriented society precisely because their macro-environments are so very different.

Poland already offers an example of what can be expected from "stabilization without privatization" in a post-communist economy. Two-and-a-half years ago, the Polish government embarked upon a bold program of "shock therapy." Prices were decontrolled, the budget was very nearly balanced, and a trade surplus was achieved. Despite strenuous stabilization efforts, however, the Polish economy has not yet been stabilized. By the IMF's reckoning, inflation in Poland in early 1992 was running at over 60 percent a year—a much more rapid pace than in Mexico or Venezuela. Though technically convertible (for transactions within Poland), the zloty has weakened almost continuously against all the major currencies, and a balance of trade deficit has emerged. Official data suggest that Poland's GNP continues its decline, and that industrial production may have fallen by nearly half since 1989.

Why has this shock therapy ushered in such disappointing results in Poland? In the main, it is because the country's vast and predominant network of state-owned enterprises was neither constrained nor motivated by the rules of the market. Accountable essentially only to themselves, the enterprises could grant themselves credit as they saw fit, thus thwarting the government's monetary policies. Similarly, they could refuse to pay their bills with impunity, thereby adding to the budgetary burden. Producing for themselves rather than their customers, they proved to be largely indifferent to the incentives and signals evoked by price decontrol. And by continuing to suck capital into money-losing activities, they effectively strangled much of the supply-response that would have been expected from Poland's competitive private sector.

Prospects for stabilization are hardly more auspicious for the CIS states than they were for Poland. To the contrary: the economic situation in the former Soviet Union is, if anything, even more thoroughly distorted. Unlike Poland, the CIS states own the farms as well as the factories. And an arrangement linking (at this writing) fourteen separate central banks and fourteen separate budgets to a single currency creates a situation in which the temptations of "beggar thy neighbor" policies may prove overwhelming. Even the comparatively modest objective of moving the ruble to the status of technical convertibility within Russia may prove elusive in the absence of a far-reaching privatization and genuine economic reform.

To be sure, under current conditions Western stabilization aid (or other sorts of balance-of-payments support) could have an immediate impact on the economies of Russia and the other CIS states. It could pay for imports from abroad. It could subsidize local consumption. It might even provide the illusion of price stability and ruble convertibility until the stabilization funds or balance-of-payments supports run out. But until and unless there is domestic and international confidence in the governments—and the economic arrangements—*behind the ruble*, neither convertibility nor stabilization can be feasible propositions. Without the sorts of measures that would lend credibility to Russia's money and her economy, stabilization aid, no matter how generously it is provided, can only postpone the ultimate hour of reckoning.

The Policy Reform Myth

The other concrete suggestions for economic aid to Russia concern subventions for policy reform. By offering the CIS governments assistance as they privatize state assets, eliminate expensive subsidies, and veer toward more liberal economic arrangements, it is argued, Western governments can help speed the transition to a market economy and reduce the attendant social pains.

In the abstract, one may wonder why it should be necessary to reward governments for desisting from demonstrably unwise economic practices, or for embracing policies that stand to improve the well being of their citizens. Such philosophical issues notwithstanding, it is far from obvious that policy reform aid for the former Soviet Union is capable of achieving its desired results.

Unlike dams, irrigation networks, or even family-planning programs, policy reform aid is not associated with a tangible "product." When such aid is extended in the form of subsidized loans—as is the common practice at the World Bank and some other institutions—these loans are contracted without identifiable collateral. In return for immediate infusions of cash into their treasuries, recipient governments simply promise to amend their current practices.

Since policy reform aid is by design untied to any specific project, it is virtually impossible to evaluate. Indeed, judged by its own terms of reference, it is impossible to demonstrate failure for any policy reform loan or grant. After all, if conditions improve after a government accepts policy reform aid, lenders can take credit for the changes; if conditions deteriorate, lenders can argue that things would have been still worse but for their intervention. (This fact may not have escaped prospective recipients, and may help to explain why this particular type of aid is in such demand today.) But if a policy reform loan cannot be shown to fail, it is correspondingly impossible to demonstrate success.

Yet there is one indirect indicator of the efficacy of policy reforms by governments that have accepted money for this undertaking. This is the price of their debt on the "secondary market"—i.e., the amount that private purchasers are willing to pay for a given dollar of outstanding commercial debt obligations contracted by a sovereign government. The price of a government's debt on this secondary market speaks to the credibility of its policies in the eyes of those who are not directly involved in accepting or dispensing policy reform aid.

Almost all of the governments whose bonds are traded in this secondary debt market have been recipients of structural adjustment loans or other types of policy reform aid at some point during the past decade. Despite these agreements, and infusions, the overall price of secondary sovereign debt dropped drastically during the 1980s. By 1989, the unweighted average for these issues was down to barely a third of their nominal face value. (Prices have improved a bit over the past three years; some portion of this improvement, however, may be due to the stimulating effects of lower international interest rates on *all* bond markets, including this one.)

Despite the generally poor performance of sovereign debt in the secondary market, certain issues have witnessed a vigorous recovery in recent years. Mexican debt's secondary price, for example, has risen steadily since early 1989, after having fallen for years. The date of the turnaround is significant: it coincided with the assumption of power by a new president. Under the previous president, Mexico had attempted to muddle through its economic crisis with a series of pseudo-reforms. Confidence in Mexican debt issues grew only as the international business community gradually concluded that his successor was both intent on, and capable of, leading his country to economic health.

Is Boris Yeltsin willing and able to do for Russia what Carlos Salinas de Gortari has been doing for Mexico? The question is central to the efficacy of the policy reform aid pending for the CIS. What is equally apparent, unfortunately, is that the former Soviet Union suffers by comparison with contemporary Mexico in a number of significant respects.

For one thing, the road to economic health is vastly longer for Russia and the other CIS states than it was for Mexico in 1989. Their economies are far more distorted, and they lack the civil-legal infrastructure which even Mexico could take for granted. For another, it is not yet clear that Russia's leadership is ready to confront the enormity of the effort that will be required to establish a competitive market economy.

To date, Russia's "privatization" program has been almost entirely talk; there has been almost no action. Despite its huge burden on society, the military industries continue their activities, the civilian government's determination to decommission or convert them notwithstanding. A host of restrictions continues to discourage international trade. High taxes and a hostile regulatory atmosphere discourage foreign entrepreneurs from risking investment in the Russian market. Enormous subsidies are still being granted to money-losing state-owned enterprises.

Nor do the forensics of the reform process inspire confidence that the Russian regime is ready to take the steps necessary to make its economy viable. In the spring of this year, when it finally seemed clear that the West would soon be granting the CIS a major aid package, the Yeltsin government did not redouble its efforts at transformation. Quite the contrary, it restricted the portfolio of the adviser perhaps most closely associated with radical reform, Yegor Gaidar; it backtracked on price decontrols; and it granted further subsidies to money-losing state ventures. Moreover, as the *New York Times* (July 13, 1992) put it, "Russia let its budget deficit and inflation rate soar in the second quarter [April-June 1992] after having slashed them in the first quarter [January-March 1992]." At this writing, Western observers guess Russia's budget is now running at about 17 percent of GNP—back up, in other words, to the level that characterized the economy in the last days of the Gorbachev era. As for monetary policy, the only firm program to date has been raising the denomination of the country's currency: a new 5,000 ruble note has just been introduced, and the word is out that a 10,000 ruble note is already being planned.

Ultimately, this reversal may prove to be akin to Lenin's *peredyshka*: a tactical retreat for "breathing space" while the government gathers strength to push its true program forward. So we may certainly hope. Yet however events may unfold, such temporizing only underscores a simple but basic fact about aid for policy reform: depending on the disposition of the government in question, such funds may be used either for financing the reform process, or for postponing it.

Any Aid at All?

The preceding review should not be taken to suggest that *all* forms of state aid to Russia and the other CIS republics would be wasteful or unwise. Humanitarian aid—temporary relief during famines or after natural disasters—has an impressive record of saving endangered lives. If a catastrophe were to strike within the CIS, Western aid could certainly help to contain its human toll and suffering.

Political aid or security assistance could also serve useful purposes. At the moment, for example, the United States is providing a program of limited aid to help dismantle outmoded Soviet nuclear warheads. And at the July economic summit in Munich, the G-7 leaders agreed to assist (both technically and financially) in the clean-up of nuclear and toxic chemical sites in the former Soviet Union.

Further aid and cooperation of this general nature is easy to imagine. Japan, for example, might wish to offer an aid package to the Russian government in explicit exchange for the return of the Northern Territories that Moscow has forcibly occupied since 1945. South Korea might premise future grants or loans to the CIS upon a full disclosure of past cooperation in, and current knowledge about, Pyongyang's nuclear program. Western states might also consider extending aid to the CIS states in return for the removal of atomic, biological, and chemical weapons from their territories.

But humanitarian aid and security assistance, we must remember, are motivated by very different considerations—and evaluated by very different criteria—than development assistance. Humanitarian aid reflects the Western view that life is precious and that it be protected. Political and security aid, for their part, are meant to further the international policy, and enhance the safety, of the states and citizens dispensing it. Neither form of aid needs to be justified by its prospective impact on the economic health or the pace of material advance in the recipient state.

Unlike humanitarian aid and security assistance, development assistance *must* be justified on economic grounds. Until Russia's business climate is favorable, rates of return cannot be high on physical or human capital—or for that matter, on official development assistance offered by well-meaning foreign friends. Barring changes in legal and commercial arrangements which only the Russians—and other CIS populations—can make, the economic assistance programs now under consideration in the West may not only prove to be wasteful, but may even ultimately retard reform worthy of the name.

14

Has Democracy Failed Russia?

Peter Rutland*

The sudden collapse of the Soviet Union was immediately taken as vindi-
cation of Western values and proof of the superiority of both market economics and a democratic system of government. America had won the Cold War,
and "market democracy" (to use President Clinton's concise term) would spread
from Belgrade to Bishkek. No one stopped to question the teleological assumption that events in Russia could be understood in terms of a transition
from point "A" (a state-socialist political system with a command economy) to
point "B" (a democratic polity with a market economy).

Few were inclined to ponder the special problems that the concepts "democracy" and "market" might encounter in the post-socialist landscape. On
the contrary, building democracy and a market economy were assumed to be
compatible and complementary processes which could be introduced to any
country on the planet. This left Yeltsin playing the double role of George
Washington and Adam Smith—either of which on its own would have strained
even his considerable thespian skills to the limit.

This article challenges the Panglossian complacency of the "market democracy" paradigm, on three fronts. First, it will question the model of democracy which is being propagated by Russia's Western advisers and well-wishers.
Second, it will consider democratization in the context of unresolved problems of state- and nation-building in Russia, challenges which most other
countries in political transition do not have to face. Third, it will probe the
linkages between flawed democratization and market reform.

The key point to bear in mind is that Russia is still on the downward path of
disintegration rather than the upward march of transition. The abrupt collapse

*Peter Ruland is associate professor of government at Wesleyan University, and author
of *The Politics of Economic Stagnation in the Soviet Union* (Cambridge University Press,
1993). This essay originally appeared in *The National Interest*, no. 38 (Winter 1994/95).

of the Soviet state unleashed turbulent centripetal processes which are still coursing through the political, economic, and social fabric of Russia. Yeltsin and the democratic movement managed to mobilize sufficient political force to destroy the old system, but have not been able to agree among themselves on the shape of the new order.

The democratic opening of 1988-90 created two new political actors: a broad but shallow democratic movement, geared to election campaigns and mass protests; and a ramshackle parliament with minimal legislative power, which was temporarily graced with legitimacy as the symbol of democracy. Alongside these two new players were the serried ranks of the old elite: the military, the bureaucrats, the managers, the secret police, the ex-communists. This transitory political regime has been dominated by *presidentialism* and *regionalism*. Presidentialism refers to the pivotal role played by Boris Yeltsin in mediating between the old and new political groups. It may be something of a misnomer, since the authority wielded by Yeltsin adheres more to his person than to the office he holds, and for the most part it is neither defined by law nor checked by institutional structures. Regionalism surfaced because the loss of control of the old bureaucracies led to a shift from functional to territorial representation of political interests. This is good for democracy in the long run, but makes the national leadership's task much more difficult in the short term.

The Working Model Applied

Most discussions of the spread of democracy to Russia share similar assumptions about the elements that constitute a democratic political system. The checklist includes:

1. free and fair elections;
2. separation of powers;
3. a fair and independent judicial system;
4. a free and inquisitive press;
5. the widespread sharing of democratic
   values in society at large;
6. respect for human rights: at least
   individual rights, and possibly collective
   rights (e.g., for ethnic minorities); and
7. the presence of civil society, i.e., a
   plurality of social organizations.

Each of the elements in the liberal democratic canon has been introduced in Russia, but in a curiously distorted form. To paraphrase Trotsky, it is democracy reflected in a samovar. Its faltering steps down the road to democracy have been accompanied by economic disintegration, rampant crime, the collapse of public morals, rising death rates, loss of international influence, and the continuation in power of much of the old communist-era elite. Rather than question the applicability and appropriateness of their own model of democracy, Western liberals typically blame these problems on Russia's political culture or the personal qualities of its leaders. We are told that Russia has failed democracy, and not that democracy has failed Russia.

In fact, the checklist approach is extraordinarily naive in reducing democracy to a set of values and institutions. What is absent is any consideration of *politics*: the struggle for resources and clash of ideas between different social and political groups. The assumption is that once democratic values and institutions are in place, parties will emerge to compete for the popular vote, and sound policies and good government will follow. Democracy is seen as a source of political legitimation rather than a forum for policy resolution. After all, the market democracy paradigm assumes that the new Russian government had no choice but to introduce market liberalization. When one thinks about it, it is a curious sort of democracy which begins by telling people that they have no alternatives.

Let us look at the seven items on the West's democratic list and consider how they relate to Russian realities.

1. Free and Fair Elections

Partially free elections were held in the USSR in 1989 and 1990, and in June 1991 Boris Yeltsin was elected President of the Russian Republic. Gorbachev refused to submit himself for popular election, and Yeltsin came to be seen as the legitimate voice of the Russian people. This experience showed how dangerous it can be for authoritarian regimes to toy with elections, no matter how unfair the electoral process or how pusillanimous the powers of the legislature. Gorbachev's experiment set in train a dynamic of democratization which swiftly undermined the authority of the Communist Party.

So far, so good for the liberal democratic model. However, after the failed coup of August 1991 Yeltsin proved strangely reluctant to pursue the electoral path. In Eastern Europe, free elections were held within months of the cracking of the socialist regime. Yeltsin found he could not agree with his democratic allies on the key issues of the day—market reform and the creation of a post-Soviet federation. Thus he chose to go it alone, and delayed calling new elections until December 1993. If elections had taken place in late 1991 the democrats would probably have won handsomely. After the price liberalization of January 1992, however, the economic collapse accelerated, and in the eyes of the public the democrats had to share some of the blame for that.

The crucial problem is that even by the end of 1994 no credible political parties worthy of the name have emerged in Russia. Political parties come from one of two sources: they either grow upwards from social movements or downwards from parliamentary factions. During the elections of 1989 and 1990 a loose coalition of voters' clubs emerged, which came together as the Democratic Russia movement. They showed they could win elections and bring thousands of followers into the streets. The sole issue on which they agreed, however, was the need to dislodge the Communist Party from power. Given the postponement of elections, there was no opportunity for the fledgling parties to develop through campaigning. Instead, their leaders had to engineer crises and confrontations around which to mobilize their followers, which added to the polarized climate in Russian politics.

The top-down route of party formation was also weak. The Interregional Deputies Group, which democratic deputies formed in the USSR Supreme Soviet in 1989, never coalesced into a coherent political party. It was riven by personal jealousies and divided over the national question (i.e., the viability of the USSR). All decision-making power rested in the presidential apparatus, which left nothing of substance to bargain over in parliament and provided no incentive to forge lasting political coalitions. Instead, there was an endless succession of small parties—"taxicab parties"—which were used as launching pads for politicians seeking entry into government. Communists and nationalists aside, it was hard to differentiate between the various parties on the policy spectrum.

The key distinguishing characteristic of politicians was whether or not they were part of Boris Yeltsin's patronage network ("Ours or theirs?"). The political map of Russia did not consist of a left-right policy spectrum, but a series of concentric circles of diminishing access, radiating outwards from the Kremlin. To the annoyance of the democrats, Yeltsin refused to take over the leadership of Democratic Russia, arguing that the president should be "above politics." He instead chose to forge a new ruling elite out of old and new politicians by doling out individual jobs and favors.

When fresh elections were finally held in December 1993, in the wake of Yeltsin's crushing of the old parliament, there was a frantic scramble among the democrats to come up with viable parties. The campaign turned into an American-style media blitz, with the three leading democratic parties spending $85 million on their media campaign, and Vladimir Zhirinovsky's Liberal Democrats $14 million. The U.S. National Democratic Institute issued a handbook on the art of campaigning, with detailed instructions on handling the press and the role of the *sked'yuler* in managing the candidate's time.[1]

It was hard to tell the parties apart on policy grounds. Everybody was in favor of stopping inflation, ending subsidies to the other republics, and so on. Dissatisfaction with Yeltsin's use of force against the parliament and the ongoing economic crisis meant that the four democratic parties only polled 35 percent of the vote. The Communists and their Agrarian allies won 20 percent from their traditional constituencies. The Liberal Democrats topped the party list with 23 percent, thanks to the nationalist rhetoric of their charismatic leader.

Thus Russia's first free election produced a propaganda victory for an eccentric neo-fascist whose campaign pledges included irradiating Lithuania and seizing Alaska. The Democrats had little choice but to cooperate with the Communists and Agrarians in order to keep Zhirinovsky well away from power. Because of Yeltsin's reluctance, the election had come two years too late. By the end of 1993 the voters had lost their faith in all politicians. Ironically, while free elections had been vital in destroying the old communist system, they came to be seen as an awkward obstacle in the path of building the new market democracy.

2. Separation of Powers

Yeltsin's second crucial political error after August 1991 was procrastination in drawing up a new constitution. His advisers urged him to model the Russian political system around a U.S.-style presidency, with a Constitutional Court policing the separation of powers between president and legislature. There were several problems with this approach:

First, Yeltsin was in no rush to create a strong legislature which could rival his power. Despite the fact that it was the Russian Congress that had propelled him into power, Yeltsin felt himself to be an independent political actor after his election in June 1991 and his pivotal role in facing down the August coup.

Second, while the idea of a strong executive had plenty of parallels in Russia's past, the other elements of the American model—an independent constitutional court and a powerful legislature—were totally absent from Russian history.

Third, there are grounds for arguing that the U.S.-style separation of powers is less universally applicable than is often assumed. (The Founding Fathers themselves were all too aware of the uniqueness of the model they were devising.) The U.S. system assumes civilian control over the military and a reasonably wide dispersion of economic power in society—neither of which pertain in Russia or in countries like Brazil. Presidentialism in Latin America has typically resulted in deadlock with a hostile congress.2   One can argue that Russian democracy would have been better served by a parliamentary system, in which the executive and legislative branches of government are joined rather than separated.

After the coup of August 1991, Yeltsin persuaded Congress to grant him emergency power to rule by decree for one year. He then appointed a team of young technocrats, led by Deputy Prime Minister Egor Gaidar, to implement radical economic reform along Polish lines. The stage was thus set for two years of increasingly tense political confrontation between a truculent Congress and a president determined to pursue his own political and economic agenda. The rivalry between Yeltsin and Congress was not driven by alternate conceptions of Russia's future, or even by the interests of different social groups. It was not a dispute over policy, but simply a struggle for power. Yeltsin tried to rule the country directly, with scant regard for the opinions of Congress.

The presidential apparatus grew to more than twenty thousand officials, and took over the former Central Committee building in addition to the Kremlin. This hastily assembled bureaucratic leviathan operated in a very inefficient manner. Yeltsin's own chief of staff, Yuri Petrov, admitted that he was unable to keep track of the thousands of decrees the president was signing.

There followed two years of political trench warfare between Yeltsin and Congress. Yeltsin used television addresses and calls for referenda to appeal directly to the people. He continued to play the anti-communist card—accusing the parliamentarians of seeking the restoration of Soviet socialism. He lured parliamentary deputies into jobs in his administration. Each side accused the other of corruption on a lavish scale. Yeltsin's half-hearted efforts to forge a coalition with centrist forces fell apart at the Seventh Congress in December 1992. He challenged Congress by holding a referendum on presidential power in April 1993. While voters expressed their confidence in Yeltsin's rule and in his economic policies, the questions calling for new elections for President and Congress in 1993 failed to win the required majority. When Yeltsin summoned a Constitutional Assembly to discuss his draft constitution in June, Congress blocked its approval.

Yeltsin decided to lance the boil by disbanding the parliament on September 21 and calling for fresh elections. Neither of these actions was within his legal powers. Parliamentary deputies occupied the White House, and were ousted by troops on October 4. The striking television images of tanks shelling the White House would cost Yeltsin dearly in the December election.

In the wake of the October events, Yeltsin disbanded all the regional councils, suspended the Constitutional Court (whose members he himself had selected), and banned eight political parties and their newspapers (although these bans were subsequently lifted). Yeltsin also dropped his pledge to hold early presidential elections (not due until 1996).

The hastily written draft constitution was weighed heavily in favor of presidential rule. For example, the president nominates the prime minister, and can dismiss parliament after three refusals of his candidate. The constitution was approved in a referendum on the same day as the congressional elections. Despite initial reports that 51 percent of voters endorsed the constitution, it was later revealed that the actual figure was 46 percent. Technically, this meant that the constitution was invalid, but in Russia people had long since stopped paying attention to technicalities.

3. An Independent Judicial System

The non-emergence of an independent judiciary has been one of the weakest spots in Russia's attempted transition to democracy. The old system of political controls collapsed with the banning of the Communist Party after the August coup. But politicians, Yeltsin included, continue to ignore or manipulate the judicial system as they see fit. This has been evident in his reliance on rule by decree, his reluctance to recognize the authority of the Constitutional Court, and his centralization of control over the judiciary.

Liberals hope that marketization will promote the rule of law, by creating a new class of property owners with a strong incentive to have their rights respected. In Russia's free-for-all economy, however, businessmen turn to private enforcement regimes (i.e., the mafia) and not the courts to ensure contract compliance.

4. A Free Press

Russia's democratization began with glasnost, and over the past decade the country has acquired a combative and broadly independent press staffed by a core of dedicated journalists. A broad spectrum of opinion is available, from the far right and far left to a clutch of pro-government newspapers. But it is still premature to talk of a completely free press. Financial constraints have caused a catastrophic decline in circulation, and only the tabloids have been able to remain profitable. The others all depend on business sponsorship and/or government assistance (through the allocation of subsidized newsprint).

President Yeltsin and his advisor Gennady Burbulis have proved all too willing to use their financial and political leverage over the press to serve their own partisan agenda—an issue which dominated Yeltsin's clashes with Congress. The television networks are particularly subservient to Yeltsin, and in some respects are less objective than they were back in 1991. In the provinces, liberal national newspapers are often hard to obtain, and most of the local press remains under the control of provincial political bosses.

5. Popular Support for Democratic Values

The presence or absence of a civic culture in Russia has been a topic of controversy among Western political scientists. Most of the research money allocated by bodies such as the National Science Foundation has gone into opinion surveys, whose findings appear to show that democratic norms such as free speech are widely respected in Russian society.3 Many Sovietologists have challenged these findings. In most cases the questions were taken straight from U.S. surveys, where the political context is quite different. It is well known that respondents tend to give what they suppose to be the "right" answer, and this is even more likely to apply in Russia, where citizens are unused to opinion polls. The surveys typically test attitudes in the abstract, without exploring the trade-offs between different values. The surveys have also shown a preference for strong political leadership. The results of the

December 1993 elections did little to bolster the case of those who argue that democratic values have taken root in Russia.

6. Respect for Human Rights

Human rights at least have seen dramatic progress. Just about all the political prisoners inherited from the communist era have been released, although some people remain in prison for "economic crimes" which would not feature on Western statute books. Freedom to travel and emigrate is enjoyed by all. Although the lack of due process is worrying, measured in terms of human rights Russia has moved decisively towards democracy.

Ironically, the use of human rights as a political tool has switched sides. It is now the Russian government which is invoking the Helsinki Accords, to protest the denial of citizenship and language rights to Russians living in Estonia, Latvia and elsewhere. And Western governments are worried not about the denial of the right to emigrate, but about the prospect of a flood of impoverished migrants heading West.

7. The Growth of Civil Society

De Tocqueville argued that the strength of democracy in the United States lay in the dense network of social organizations characteristic of American society. Reflecting this belief, U.S. aid for democratization in Russia has focused on the promotion of associative behavior, from independent trade unions to environmental action groups, in the belief that this is the best long-run foundation for democracy.

In the 1980s some academics began to argue that elements of a civil society were sprouting up under the surface of Brezhnevite stagnation. This Tocquevillian vision seemed to be coming true during the Gorbachev era, when there was an explosion of informal groups, ranging from Buddhists to body-builders, anti-Semites to amateur theatricals. The informals played an important role, chiseling away at the mortar holding together the communist monolith.

Once glasnost gave way to democratization, however, these groups proved unable to make the transition from the social to the political sphere. In the Baltic republics and Armenia they helped generate mass political movements, but no such pattern appeared in Russia. As political and economic disintegration accelerated, the informals were left behind. Many of their leaders were elected to legislatures, and there was no longer a Communist Party to protest against, nor ministries to lobby. In the Russia of 1994 it is still hard to find voluntary associations which could be cited as incubators of democratic values and experience. The hypothesis that a nascent civil society was maturing within Soviet society has not been vindicated by events.

Indeed, there seems to have been a conceptual error at the heart of the civil society approach. While Marx followed Hegel in portraying civil society as arising in opposition to the state, Adam Smith saw it as superior to and inclusive of the state. For Smith the essence of civil society was private property and the rule of law, both of which served to limit the state. If one accepts the Scottish Enlightenment approach, it is premature to talk of civil society in Russia, since private property and the rule of law are still essentially absent.

The Antinomies of Russian Nationalism

In Russia, the democratic transition involves the break-up of a multinational empire. This raises profound questions about the existential nature of the state which most other nascent democracies have not had to face (though the cases of South Africa, India, Czechoslovakia and Yugoslavia are in some ways comparable). Democracy presupposes agreement on the boundaries of the demos (the people) that is to rule. Liberal political theory has little to say on the subject of where nation-states come from and the principles upon which they should be constituted. The Western experience with nation-building is a long and painful one, extending over several centuries and invariably involving warfare. In Russia there is still no agreement on the shape of the political community which will enjoy self-determination. Russia must choose not merely what sort of political system it desires, but also *what* Russia is as a cultural entity, and *where* it is in terms of physical borders. Young American democracy faced similar challenges—and came up with some answers (such as Manifest Destiny) which the international community would obviously not accept in Russia today.

Russia had never been constituted as a nation-state in the conventional sense. Less than half the population of the Russian Empire were ethnic Russians, and 350 years of expansion across contiguous territory made it difficult for Russians to perceive where Russia ended and foreign land began. Although ethnic Russians dominated the Soviet state, many aspects of Russian culture were suppressed and Russians had to rule in the name of multinational socialism.

Nationalism emerged as the crucial factor in the demise of the USSR. Gorbachev's political reforms opened up a Pandora's box of ethnic claims, suppressed for decades, which Gorbachev himself was unable to resolve. One can however argue that it was Russian nationalism, rather than the nationalism of the non-Russian peoples, which was ultimately responsible for the destruction of the USSR. Gorbachev's commitment to the Soviet state created an opening for Yeltsin's political comeback (after his dismissal from the Politburo in 1987). Yeltsin was able to turn the institutions of the Russian Federation into a power-base to rival that of Gorbachev in the federal Communist Party and government. In August 1991, the core institutions of the Soviet state—the army and the KGB—switched their loyalty to Yeltsin's Russia.

Having freed itself from the Soviet Union, however, Russia's problems in defining itself as a nation-state are far from resolved, and its cohesion is threatened from within and without.

The internal challenge stems from the fact that 19 percent of Russia's population are non-Russians, most of them living in twenty-one autonomous republics within the border of the federation. Secession is not an option for these republics, since most are surrounded by Russian territory, and in many cases the titular nationality is outnumbered by Russian inhabitants. (The exception is Chechnya in the north Caucasus, which has achieved de facto independence.)

The external challenge to Russia's identity and cohesion involves Russia's relations with the newly independent states. Twenty-five million Russians live outside the Russian Federation, and Moscow feels obliged to look out for their interests. The economies of the ex-Soviet republics remain heavily dependent on Russia—and many Russian factories are still tied to their old customers in the "near abroad." They form a powerful lobby within Russia and argue for maintaining the subsidized trade with the CIS.

The security dimension also remains unresolved. What military policy should a democratic Russia adopt towards its neighbors? Should it stand by while Tajikistan is torn apart by civil war? Should it intervene to try to stop the six-year long conflict between Armenia and Azerbaijan? Should Russia do nothing if Ukraine uses force to prevent the secession of Crimea (75 percent Russian, and a part of the Russian Federation until 1954)? Democratization does not provide an answer to any of these questions—yet these are the very questions at the forefront of Russian politics, around which battle lines are being drawn.

The European empires, which had the benefit of an ocean between their homeland and their colonies, all suffered political identity crises of various severity after the end of empire. The Russian post-imperial dilemma is far more wrenching and will overshadow the democratization process for years to come.

Moscow and the Regions

Even taking the national boundaries of Russia as given, the crucial issue in Russian domestic politics is state-building rather than democratization. Russia remains an unwieldy giant of a country, spread over seven thousand miles with atrocious means of communication between its component parts. The collapse of the Soviet state apparatus severely weakened Moscow's ability to manage the country, and it is a misnomer to describe the resulting decentralized, unstable political system as "democratized." Rather, it reminds one of the periods of confusion—such as the "Time of Troubles" (1598-1613)—which have interrupted Russian history.

As a student of Russian history, Yeltsin is no doubt well aware of the dangers of anarchy. But in 1990-91 he had to make concessions to provincial elites in order to overcome his political opponents in Moscow. In October 1991 he persuaded Congress to suspend regional elections for one year, during which he would directly appoint regional governors. He also set up a network of presidential envoys in the provinces (for which he had no legal authority).

Within each of Russia's twenty-one ethnic republics and sixty-seven regions, new and old political elites battled for power as the old order collapsed. At the same time, these regional elites maneuvered for allies in Moscow. Some came under Yeltsin's patronage, others lined up with Congress. Thus in Nizhni Novgorod, for example, the old and new elites were initially able to forge a compromise, and established good relations with Yeltsin's apparatus. In the tradition of the Potemkin village, "Nizhni" became the model city for the transition to capitalism, and the favorite destination for the army of Western consultants who descended on Russia. The compromise in Nizhni Novgorod subsequently broke down.

The ethnic republics were exempted from Yeltsin's direct rule and were allowed to select their own leaders. Following the lead of Tatarstan and Chechenya, they forced Yeltsin to sign a new Federation Treaty in March 1992, which seemed to recognize their sovereign authority over everything except military affairs. Yeltsin poured subsidies into the republics in 1992 to wean them away from supporting Khasbulatov and Congress. The balance shifted in 1993, as Yeltsin tried to rein in the regions. Provincial leaders blocked his efforts to establish presidential rule, and some regions began electing their own administrators. In several cases these elected leaders were thrown out of office by the police, with Yeltsin's connivance. The original draft constitution of July 1993 recognized the sovereignty of the ethnic republics, and granted each republic and region two seats in the upper chamber of parliament. After the October events, however, Yeltsin dismissed all the regional councils, and the final version of the constitution revoked many of the republics' special rights.

The Russian Federation is not about to go the way of the Soviet Union, and break up into independent states. Russians share a strong sense of cultural homogeneity, and have four centuries' experience of life in a common state. Central and northern Russia are totally dependent upon European Russia for access to the outside world, while the Russian Far East needs Moscow's support to safeguard against its potential vulnerability to China and Japan. But in the short term the political struggles between the center and the regions have derailed the process of democratization. Yeltsin's success in establishing his grip in Moscow rests in no small measure on his manipulation of these disintegrative tendencies.

Democracy and Economic Development

The economics of transition is typically discussed in terms of a trade-off between social justice and economic growth, or even between democracy and economic development. Russia has not yet faced the luxury of such a trade-off. Social inequality has been increasing and economic output has plummeted, while the struggle to build a viable democracy is still far from over.

Talk about building a market economy is premature, since Russia is still experiencing the death throes of central planning. The command economy was not built in a day and it cannot be got rid of overnight. The 40 percent decline in industrial output is a consequence of the collapse of the old system, not of the decisions taken by politicians since 1991. The "shock" did not come from the government's decision to liberalize prices—in 1991 inflation was already out of control. Rather, it came from lifting the stone on seventy years of gross misallocation of resources and violation of the laws of market economics.

The January 1992 price liberalization simply delivered the *coup de grâce* to an economic system that was already in its final agony. That said, Gaidar can be properly criticized for being too optimistic in believing that freeing prices and foreign trade would sweep away the inherited inefficiencies of the past. Price liberalization without the presence of competing producers was a recipe for sustained inflation. Liberalizing foreign trade led to a fire sale of natural resources, with much of the earnings staying outside the country. Since 1992 capital flight from Russia has been $12-15 billion a year—while the government reneges on its debt repayments and pleads for Western loans.

In its enthusiasm to apply shock therapy, the Gaidar team overlooked the state's inability to provide the minimum public goods necessary for the functioning of a market economy (freedom from crime, a stable currency, the rule of law). In a travesty of Hayekian logic, it was assumed that such market institutions would be self-generating. Rebuilding an effective Russian state would require political compromise with key political elites inherited from the Soviet past—the parliament, the industrial managers, and so on. The Gaidar team eschewed such efforts, preferring a "technocratic fix:" the swift implementation of economic reforms before an opposition coalition could be assembled. Economic reform came to be seen as a substitute for political reform. In the event, however, Congress forced Yeltsin to delay key elements of the program, and the shock therapy—dubious in the best of circumstances—was stillborn.

The reformers hoped that Yeltsin's political prestige would carry through the economic reforms. In practice, the polarity was reversed, and Yeltsin's political authority came to hinge on his controversial economic program. There was a mass distribution of privatization vouchers in July 1992, in the hope that this would build popular support for economic reform—as in the Czech Republic. The Supreme Soviet was persuaded to adopt the privatization law by including a provision allowing workers and managers to buy 51 percent of the shares. Privatization thus became a vehicle for the consolidation of managerial control over the old state enterprises, even as it was trumpeted by the government to be the most successful element in the reform program.

The traditional industrialists still control most of the country's resources out in the provinces, although they have not been able to articulate a collective interest at the national level. While the old lobbies have lost much of their political base, the new businessmen have failed to create one. Russia's new capitalism revolves around short-term, rent-seeking behavior. There is no money to be made in manufacturing, whereas rich profits can be had speculating in foreign currency, exporting raw materials and importing consumer durables. The old and new elites compete for access to the political decision-makers who can allocate export quotas or bank credits.

It is hard to see how this raw, predatory capitalism can be justified to a democratic electorate. On the other hand, this is just what many Russians, raised on Upton Sinclair, expected a market economy to look like. Given the lack of real democratization there is little chance of this popular discontent being translated into an effective political movement. For most long-suffering Russians the "market" is a political abstraction, a symbol of change which must be accepted as inevitable.

In their haste to embrace capitalism, the reformers did not dwell on the fact that there is no standard Western model. The emphasis on trade liberalization is particularly puzzling. Most capitalist countries saw their economies grow behind protective barriers for decades, and only introduced convertible currencies in the 1970s. China has enjoyed spectacular economic growth without implementing almost any of the prescriptions of the Russian reform program. Chinese exports have boomed—but exchange controls are still in place, and barriers keep out foreign imports. The existence of a range of options within the capitalist path did not deter the Russian reformers from presenting their program as the only alternative that could save Russia. This accords well with the ideological mindset inherited from the past, in which politics is reduced to a choice between right and wrong, between obedience and dissent.

Unlike most of Eastern Europe, Russia has not experienced a more or less clean break with the old system. Instead of a wholesale turnover of the political elite, there has been a protracted battle between the executive and legislative branches of government, each claiming to be the true guardian of democracy. Unlike the other countries in transition, Russia is a former empire that has still not defined its relations with its neighbors and its character as a federal state. Very few countries with a living standard of less than $5,000 per capita a year have been able to operate as a democracy. Russia is less than half way to this target, and has few of the cultural traditions (such as a history of British colonialism) which have enabled countries like India and Botswana to buck the trend. Thus the prognosis for the future of democracy in Russia must be rather grim.

None of this is to suggest that Russia would be better off with some sort of authoritarian regime. For all its flaws, the haphazard democratization of Russia was the only way to rid the country of the Soviet system and set it on course towards a more civilized society. But the adoption of the American separation of powers model has exacerbated political feuding at national level and encouraged the fragmentation of central authority. Russia has not been and will not be served by hasty efforts to transplant models of democracy and the market economy, as if local circumstances and conditions count for nothing. Still less does it need the "propaganda of success" which has often accompanied the exercise, usually at American taxpayers' expense.

Notes

1.   U.S. National Democratic Institute, *Kak pobedit' na vyborakh*, Moscow, 1993.
2.   A. Valenzuela, "The Crisis of Presidentialism," *Journal of Democracy*, October 4, 1993, pp. 3-16.
3.   J.L.Gibson and R.M. Duch, "Democratic Values and the Transformation of the Soviet Union," *Journal of Politics*, 54 (May 1992), pp. 329-71.

15

The Russian Aid Mess

Charles Flickner*

The well-intentioned effort to use United States tax dollars to influence significantly the course of events in Russia and Ukraine died a quiet death over the past few months. Born in 1991 as a $400 million bipartisan congressional initiative to reduce the threat from excess Soviet weapons of mass destruction, by 1993 aid to Russia and Ukraine had become a $3 billion hobby shop. When Presidents Clinton and Yeltsin met in September 1994, with few concrete results to show for the time and money invested in aid, the two frustrated leaders quietly agreed to focus on trade and investment. The Russians, badly cast as supplicants, were relieved.

This is not to say that the winding up of grant aid programs will end claims by the former Soviet Union on the United States Treasury. The disturbing Russian and Ukrainian habit of ignoring bills due could result in future claims against federal export credit and investment agencies that far exceed the $4 billion already disbursed in grant aid between 1991 and 1994. This year alone, $900 million in agricultural loans have been rescheduled. Moreover, massive disbursements from the International Monetary Fund and the World Bank could lead to future losses by their largest shareholder, the United States. No doubt pundits will seek again to attribute setbacks in Moscow to a lack of support from Washington. It may therefore be useful to provide a brief draft history, before it is revised, of recent American aid to Russia and Ukraine.

In particular, during the hectic transition following the November 1994 mid-term elections, it may be useful to recall that Senators Bob Dole and Jesse Helms joined Sam Nunn and Richard Lugar in backing the original 1991

---

* At the time this essay was written, Charles Flickner was a professional staff member of the Senate Committee on the Budget, of twenty years standing. The views expressed are his own and do not necessarily represent those of the U.S. government. This essay originally appeared in *The National Interest*, no. 38 (Winter 1994/95).

legislation to fund cooperative efforts with what was still the Soviet Union. The goal of the Nunn-Lugar law was to dismantle Soviet nuclear weapons and safeguard nuclear know-how, and especially to prevent Soviet nuclear scientists from seeking employment in rogue states. A month before the 1992 presidential election, another bipartisan coalition secured passage of the Freedom Support Act, authorizing $425 million in assistance to the former Soviet Union. The bill also created a precedent by largely exempting such aid from the restrictions applied to other aid programs. With all three major presidential candidates publicly backing them, these measures reflected wide support for helping the Russians. This broad-based, bilateral support continued, and even grew, after the election.

The desire to aid the Russians has overcome normal differences in Congress. In the Senate, for example, deficit-hawk Pete Domenici and long-time opponent of foreign aid Robert Byrd joined together in September 1993 to bend rigid budget rules, in order to enable President Clinton to meet his rash commitments to find more than $2.5 billion for Russia and Ukraine. And in the House, even as late as the spring of 1994, Minority Leader Newt Gingrich and Majority Leader Dick Gephardt agreed in a confidential report on their joint delegation to Russia that, despite problems, the aid effort should continue.

Following the Vancouver and Tokyo summit meetings in the spring of 1993, the aid effort reached its peak: $1.7 billion in civilian aid and $1.3 billion in defense funds were appropriated later that year. Though the amounts of aid have since fallen, they remain substantial. In the current fiscal year, President Clinton's overall request of $1.3 billion was finally funded at $1.25 billion. Increases up to $1.6 billion have been considered within the administration for next year, but the final appropriation may not reach half that amount. And much of what is eventually appropriated will be directed toward support for private American trade and investment in Russia and Ukraine.

Original Intent, Original Sins

What was the intent of those undertaking this short-lived effort? Although advocates of helping Russia and Ukraine have consistently maintained that external assistance could merely supplement internal changes, they also believed that supporting aid might secure them a small but favorable place in history. Most public officials could empathize with the new leaders of Russia and Ukraine as they faced the daunting task of encouraging democracy and implementing effective reform, and most preferred to risk wasting several billion dollars rather than see them fail and have that failure attributed to lack of American support. In retrospect, it is apparent that few Washington officials had a clear or deep understanding of the situation in Russia and Ukraine, and many were influenced by academic experts who promoted simplistic solutions with the enthusiasm of door-to-door salesmen.

There were reasons for Americans of all political persuasions to be support-ive. Conservatives had already established personal contacts with Russian leaders during the last years of the Soviet Union. Dole, for example, met Boris Yeltsin at the airport on his first visit to Washington, at a time when Yeltsin was being demonized by the Bush Administration. The Heritage Foundation pro-vided a hospitable refuge for Russian officials while the executive branch clung to the Soviet illusion. Moderates such as Librarian of Congress James Billington and Senator Bill Bradley saw the key to successful transformation to be vastly expanded exchange programs that would expose young Russians and Ukrainians to the American way. At times there would be more visitors than qualified hosts. Many liberals believed that beyond transforming Russia, investments in the former Soviet Union would be more than offset by defense cuts. Indeed the success of those investments would justify even greater reduc-tions in Pentagon spending. Some estimated a peace dividend of $230 billion, and urged that the savings go toward domestic programs. This effort faltered in the face of federal budget deficits and a more realistic appraisal of defense reductions, as well as costly new missions assigned the Pentagon.

Between the hopes of Washington and the reality of Russia and Ukraine lay a huge gulf. From the perspective of Moscow and Kiev, the main local benefi-ciaries of American aid were luxury hotels billing an endless stream of visiting delegations at the rate of $300 per night. By deliberate intent, Russia and Ukraine didn't see a single dollar—the money went to foreign consultants and contractors. From ordinary citizens of Russia and Ukraine, questions about aid from the United States most often elicited the resigned shrug of those used to unmet promises. Some former Soviet officials in the defense and energy sec-tors came to view the effort as a conspiracy to undermine them, and to cause their defense and nuclear industries to degenerate. Technocrat managers in both countries asked why so many of their American counterparts appeared to lack the stature and competence to bring efforts to closure.

Nonetheless, the aid effort has contributed to some real progress. The cen-tral focus of the civilian program has been support for market reform in Russia. According to data compiled by the Agency for International Development, American-assisted privatization in Russia has put about eighty thousand small enterprises and fourteen thousand medium and large industrial enterprises in private hands. Over 40 percent of the industrial labor force now works in the private sector. On the other hand, while assertions that many of these privatized companies are controlled by criminal elements cannot be verified, many Rus-sians believe that private managers are stripping company assets and removing corporate capital to foreign bank accounts, rather than paying salaries.

Perhaps because reform in Ukraine didn't begin in earnest until late 1994, Americans have been slow to react to the situation in that country. During his November 1994 state visit to Washington, Ukraine President Leonid Kuchma obtained from President Clinton a precedent-making balance of payments grant of $72 million to help guarantee supplies of natural gas from Russia as he undertakes a drastic reform effort. Together with the January 1994 Trilateral Agreement, under which Russia will provide nuclear fuel rods to civilian reactors in Ukraine, there is at last some evidence that the United States is turning its attention to the particular problems of Ukraine.

The record of defense-related aid is dismal. The Nunn-Lugar program has departed from its original objectives: Not a single nuclear warhead nor a single chemical weapon has been dismantled in Russia under the American aid program. Little if any increase in control over weapons-grade fissile material has resulted from American aid. There is reluctance in Russia to move on these matters until the United States is ready to follow suit.

Some secondary objectives are being met. Delivery systems for weapons of mass destruction, such as strategic missiles and bombers, are beginning to be scrapped with funds from the Nunn-Lugar program. Nearly fifteen hundred nuclear warheads from Soviet missiles remaining in Ukraine, Kazakhstan, and Belarus have been deactivated, and American aid has been instrumental in moving these countries towards compliance with the Non-Proliferation Treaty. But the resulting concentration of nuclear warheads and fissile material in Russia has been ignored, and the joint effort to phase out plutonium production in reactors capable of making weapons-grade material faces an uncertain future.

Finally, and as a result of both Russian and American delays, the original plans to secure Soviet nuclear weapons expertise and to prevent it from going to dangerous locations matured slowly, and may in any case have been misdirected. Since 1991, it has become evident that covert exports of weapons-grade fissile material may prove a greater proliferation danger than nuclear scientists emigrating to rogue states. Indeed, several hundred Russian scientists and engineers formerly associated with nuclear and chemical weapons are now working on peaceful, civilian projects under bilateral and multilateral programs, thanks to $60 million of American taxpayers' money. Efforts to commercialize civilian technologies developed by nuclear weapons institutes in Ukraine and Russia are hampered by lack of funding and agency sponsorship in Washington.

Bureaucracy is Destiny

Why have Washington's lofty goals yielded such mixed results in Russia? Despite a genuine desire to streamline and reform the aid process, the bureaucracy continued to assert its traditional prerogatives and institutional biases. While harassed and overworked mid-level officials in the executive branch might initially have welcomed the absence of Congress' customary micromanagement, they soon found that they were unable to get prompt, effective guidance from their own senior managers. Then, when congressional appropriations committees reviewed the results, they often balked at the proposed projects, further delaying the program. Throughout, turf fights among agencies, weak mediation by the president's staff, and interventions and visits to Russia by senior officials in other agencies distracted the action officers.

No agency has been immune. Like President Bush before him, President Clinton hesitated to offend his secretary of state by designating a single individual responsible to him for the coordination and management of all federal efforts to assist Russia and Ukraine. Strobe Talbott's promotion to deputy secretary of state in early 1994 left a vacuum—though if the truth be told and contrary to widespread impression, he never filled such a role effectively. While from time to time he has intervened to support reform and denuclearization in Ukraine, Talbott's appetite for the details of management has been limited.

The Agency for International Development (AID), relegated to the background during the Bush-Baker era, maneuvered during the first year of the Clinton administration to seize operational control of the aid effort in Russia and Ukraine. Predictably, the impact of AID, an agency more accustomed to promoting development in Rwanda than to creating democracy and capitalism in a superpower has been stifling, as it has attempted to impose its Byzantine practices on often-bewildered Russian officials. Some of them however, have adjusted readily to AID procedures; Russian privatization minister Anatoliy Chubays quickly found ways to attract almost $200 million to support his voucher privatization program. In an effort to deal with the problem, AID has imported one of Washington's most skilled foreign policy operatives, Tom Dine, to energize and focus its program. Surrounded by AID careerists, and charged with management of programs in Central Europe, the Caucasus, and Central Asia, as well as Ukraine and Russia, his energy was sapped by extensive travel, and the promised new focus didn't begin to emerge until late 1994. Outside Foggy Bottom, a joint U.S.-Russian commission under Vice President Gore and Prime Minister Chernomyrdin has tried to coordinate policy and negotiations between the two countries; but Gore has never allocated funds, which remains the prerogative of the state and defense departments.

The Department of Defense, unable to move beyond providing air transportation for humanitarian emergency aid during the Bush Administration, received authority to spend up to $400 million for the Nunn-Lugar program each fiscal year between 1992 and 1995, although its deliveries and disbursements have not yet totaled $100 million. Dr. William Perry, first as deputy secretary and then as secretary of defense, brought knowledge and enthusiasm to the task of helping Russia. Prior to his going to the Pentagon, Perry held a professorship at Stanford University, where his special interest was defense conversion. This has now come to supersede the original narrow objectives of nuclear dismantlement and non-proliferation called for in the Nunn-Lugar legislation. Ashton Carter, a Harvard professor who had helped Nunn sell the bill to skeptical colleagues in 1991, was appointed by Perry to head the policymaking element of the Nunn-Lugar program. Carter and Perry recruited a number of young associates without Pentagon experience to run the program.

By the time in early 1994 that the new policy team secured the bilateral agreements needed to undertake actual work in Russia and Ukraine, they had managed to lose $318 million of the initial $800 million provided for 1992-93. The lost authority technically expired after two years, to the surprise of top officials who were unaware of the problem because Carter and his policy team had neglected to establish close relations with other parts of the executive branch and the defense committees of Congress. As a result, quiet opposition from other elements of the defense establishment frequently delayed the effort. The appointment of an experienced official to oversee the Defense Nuclear Agency's implementation of the program did not come until the summer of 1994; his effectiveness in implementing the Nunn-Lugar program has been restricted by the continuing influence the now discredited policy shop has on Perry.

Until recently, few probing questions have been raised about the aid programs within the executive branch or by Congress. With responsible officials struggling to show results without breaking any of the complex federal procurement laws, few staff members undertook rigorous oversight of a program backed by the president and the bipartisan congressional leadership. Little was heard from the General Accounting Office or the Office of Management and Budget. Hearings before the congressional appropriations committees identified a number of problems, but received little further attention. More time was devoted by the Senate to the allocation of funds between Russia and Ukraine than to program content. In the House, however, objections have been raised to the Pentagon's move away from nuclear issues toward broader defense conversion efforts, and to rapid expansion of semi-private enterprise funds to promote joint investments.

In retrospect, it is evident that all American leaders simply assumed that conditions in Russia and Ukraine were ripe for peaceful intervention by the United States. They also assumed that somewhere in the vast federal complex there were men and women who knew with some precision what to do and how to do it. Although schemes to help the former Soviet Union were based on massive amounts of direct financial assistance, both the Nunn-Lugar programs and the AID technical assistance efforts largely excluded qualified Russian and Ukrainian institutions and firms from contracting and procurement efforts. The resulting "Made in America" effort to import everything (except housing) unnecessarily antagonized some of the Russians and Ukrainians who were most ready and able to work with American counterparts.

Recently, the aid effort has begun enlisting the for-profit private sector, often on a cost-share basis. The five enterprise funds[1], and the transfers of funds to government agencies that support foreign trade and investment (the Export-Import Bank, Overseas Private Investment Corporation, and the Trade and Development Agency), show some possibility of greater positive impact on Russia and Ukraine than does the massive influx of technical assistance consultants. While the latter may help, Haid. already recognizes the negative impact of continuing to contract for the bulk of its technical assistance though a small group of international consulting firms whose annual cost per advisor (including housing, travel, security and corporate overhead) can exceed $400,000, and is moving to attract bids from a more diverse group.

The Clinton administration's decision to cut back on grant aid to Russia as it begins to engage seriously with Ukraine's new reformers demonstrates more skill and realism than the administration has shown in other regions. The Nunn-Lugar Threat Reduction program needs to be placed under effective policy management and returned to its original narrow focus on nuclear proliferation concerns, and failure to do so will alienate defense appropriators. Too few details are presently known about the much larger technical assistance effort and exchange programs to characterize them as a success or failure, but the ongoing reduction in their size and scope will almost certainly continue, if only because fewer and fewer senior officials in the countries involved are willing to make the effort to sustain them. The perception exists that aid to Russia and Ukraine has not met expectations. Looking back, it is increasingly evident that there was no way the program could have done so.

Although future United States economic cooperation with Russia and Ukraine will depend mostly on the extent of commercial trade and investment links, a smaller (less than $1 billion per annum) grant aid program could serve the national interests of all three countries for the rest of the decade. For such a proposal to survive in Washington's radically changed environment, it would need to meet three criteria. First, it would have to meet shorter-term, *concrete* objectives identified by the assisted country (such as assuring energy supplies during Ukraine's adjustment to reform). Second, it would have to meet high priority American national security interests (such as returning the Nunn-Lugar program to its original narrow focus on the actual dismantlement of Russian nuclear and chemical weapons, as well as prudent disposition of their contents). And third, it would have to offer solid value for the money invested (which means no more American development and nuclear tourists whose U.S.-funded expenses amount to more per week than members of the Russian Academy of Sciences make in a year).

Note

1.   These include: Russian-American Enterprise Fund (RAEF) focusing on small and medium-scale businesses; Fund for Large Enterprises in Russia (FLER) focusing on medium to large-sized enterprises emerging from the Russian mass privatization

program; the U.S./European Regional Venture Fund (RVP) focusing on medium-sized private enterprises in the lower Volga region; the Defense Demilitarization Enterprise Fund, involving joint ventures with industries previously involved with the production of weapons of mass destruction and their delivery systems; and the Western New Independent States Enterprise Fund (WNISEF).

16

Russia's Crisis, America's Complicity

*Dimitri K. Simes**

The appointment of the Primakov government in September represents more than a change in personalities or a shift in Russian economic policy. It reflects profound changes in Russian politics, some of which have serious implications for the United States.

Since its first days in office the Clinton administration has made "strategic partnership" with Russia a focal point of its foreign policy. But the administration's interpretation of strategic partnership has gone far beyond what is conventional in state-to-state relations. It has included de facto intervention in Russia's domestic politics on behalf of President Boris Yeltsin and the so-called "radical reformers," particularly former acting Prime Minister Yegor Gaidar and former First Deputy Prime Minister Anatoly Chubais.

Of course, as long as Boris Yeltsin remains Russia's president, he deserves to be treated with appropriate respect and attention. And it was only natural that Gaidar's and Chubais' enthusiasm for the economic prescriptions of the U.S. Treasury Department and the International Monetary Fund should be appreciated in Washington. But the Clinton administration has not merely favored Yeltsin and the radical reformers; it has acted as if their success would, almost by definition, be good not only for Russia but for the United States as well. As a result, President Clinton and his advisers have gone well beyond whitewashing Yeltsin's personal transgressions—including his excessive drinking and his propensity for grandstanding—and have consistently urged him to stay on course with radical reform at almost any cost.

No truly democratic government would ever have dared impose on its citizens measures as harsh as those implemented by Yeltsin. Despite this, and

---

*Dimitri K. Simes is president of The Nixon Center. This essay originally appeared in *The National Interest*, no. 54 (Winter 1998/99).

after the predictable backlash, the administration endorsed Yeltsin's unconstitutional dissolution of the Congress of People's Deputies in 1993, his shelling of the Russian White House (where the parliament was located), and his virtual imposition of a new constitution granting the Russian president almost dictatorial powers. The administration clearly gave priority to its notion of economic reform over democracy, and to Yeltsin's personal fortunes over respect for Russia's constitution—and over the obvious U.S. interest in the establishment of political checks and balances that would discourage a future Russian autocracy from returning to an aggressive foreign policy.

Later, in 1996, the administration deployed IMF loans in such a way as to help Yeltsin win re-election, and then portrayed his victory as a triumph of democracy. This proclamation came despite the fact that Yeltsin's campaign team rendered legal spending limits meaningless through massive violations; used the federal treasury as a campaign war chest; exploited its de facto control over the media to undermine not only the Communists but all of Yeltsin's rivals (even Grigory Yavlinsky, the leader of the impeccably pro-reform Yabloko Party); pressed local officials to deliver the vote to Yeltsin, even through fraud; and concealed his heart attack on the eve of the election from Russia's voters.

As a result of its unstinting support of Boris Yeltsin, the administration developed an enormous stake in his success and the success of his radical reformer protégés. The appointment of the Primakov government thus came as a double blow: it came about at the initiative of opposition politicians in the Duma; and, for the first time since the collapse of the USSR, the Russian government did not include any of the administration's favorites.

Not on the Shoulders of Titans

Yevgeny Primakov was appointed prime minister after the humiliating failures of his two predecessors, Sergey Kiriyenko and Victor Chernomyrdin. Kiriyenko, dismissed in August, had announced Russia's de facto devaluation of the ruble, its ninety-day moratorium on the repayment of debts to foreign creditors (the equivalent of a default), and its unilateral restructuring of short-term state bonds (known as GKOs). He replaced Chernomyrdin, who was fired in March to allow for "new blood."

Despite Yeltsin's claim, however, Chernomyrdin's original dismissal had little to do with a sense that the Russian government needed new energy and momentum. While there certainly was such a need, politics rather than policies played the decisive role. By now it is clear that Yeltsin and his entourage had become resentful of Chernomyrdin, who seemed increasingly to be a real second-in-command with an independent power base and ever more obvious presidential aspirations. But the Russian prime minister fatally miscalculated Yeltsin's willingness to tolerate his growing prominence. Whoever became too visible under the aging and insecure president was bound to activate his self-protective instincts. With little or no warning, Chernomyrdin was dismissed in March less than one month after his return from high-profile meetings with Vice President Al Gore in Washington.

In retrospect, Yeltsin's decision to fire his prime minister of five years appears to have been largely spontaneous. This is demonstrated by the Russian president's initial announcement that he himself would temporarily assume the duties of prime minister, followed only hours later by the appointment of the relatively unknown thirty-five year-old energy minister, Sergey Kiriyenko, as acting prime minister. Although there have been numerous attempts at after-the-fact rationalization of Kiriyenko's appointment—highlighting his youth, competence, commitment to reform, and pragmatic approach to politics—the mechanics of his arrival make clear that its principal purpose was to unseat the powerful Chernomyrdin. Kiriyenko, a former Komsomol leader and then business executive in Nizhniy Novgorod brought to Moscow by Boris Nemtsov in 1997, had served only a few months as a minister and was a virtual unknown to Yeltsin.

Kiriyenko's eventual confirmation by the State Duma was predictable. After two strong but nevertheless pro forma rejections, the deputies overwhelmingly approved Kiriyenko's candidacy in the face of threats to force new elections with revised rules unfavorable to the opposition. Transparent suggestions by the president himself that he would "take care of the deputies' needs" if only they would cooperate also helped.

Ultimately, though, the Russian constitution, narrowly approved in a questionable referendum held after Yeltsin's 1993 assault on the Supreme Soviet, was the decisive factor. It allowed Kiriyenko to assume office in an acting capacity prior to his confirmation, and also ensured that if the parliament rejected Kiriyenko in a third vote, the Duma would face dissolution. The new Duma, too, would still have to vote on Kiriyenko, if not a less palatable presidential appointee. Although the opposition would perhaps have won additional parliamentary seats if it had forced new elections, the Duma has so little power that the opposition's strength is of little relevance if Yeltsin feels confident enough to ignore the legislature. Yeltsin had also put opposition leaders on notice that he might abolish by decree the current system of proportional representation in any new parliamentary elections. This would significantly damage the smaller parties, particularly Yabloko, which has a substantial nationwide electoral base but could win few races in single-mandate districts outside Moscow, St. Petersburg, and a few other major cities. Because the Duma would be unlikely to vote for such a change, Yeltsin could probably not have introduced it constitutionally—but with his record of acting outside the constitution, his threat had enough credibility to sober the opposition into submission.

Kiriyenko won almost instant endorsements from the Clinton administration and the IMF. Their quick support for the new prime minister could hardly have been based on his reformist record—he had served as a cabinet minister only since the previous November, when he replaced his political mentor, Boris Nemtsov, as energy minister. Nor was Washington's satisfaction based on any displeasure with Chernomyrdin, with whom the administration had worked amicably for years. Instead, the fulsome praise for the new Russian government seemed to reflect the Clinton administration's predisposition to find something positive in almost any move taken by Yeltsin on one hand and, on the other, its trust in assurances from Nemtsov and former First Deputy Prime Minister Chubais, whom Yeltsin had just appointed to head Russia's electricity monopoly, United Energy Systems of Russia. The fact that another radical reformer—Yegor Gaidar—was a key unofficial adviser to the Kiriyenko team also reassured the administration and its proxy international financial institutions.

The near euphoria in Washington was, however, totally divorced from realities in Russia. Once Kiriyenko was confirmed, Yeltsin lost his leverage over the Duma, which by then was deeply resentful at having been railroaded into approving the young appointee. It was thus very unlikely that the Duma would cooperate with the new radical reform government and, without crucial legislation, the government was unable to implement significant new policies. The new government, even more than previous ones, was forced to turn to reform by decree. But this failed to assuage the concerns of skeptical foreign investors, undermined the legitimacy of the political system still further, and did little to improve Russia's economic condition.

Thus, despite their monetarist rhetoric—which fell on enthusiastic ears in the U.S. Treasury Department and the IMF—Sergey Kiriyenko and his team had no realistic economic program. The government could not simultaneously rationalize Russia's tax system and respond to IMF pressure to improve tax collection, even though the latter was objectively necessary. This was especially true as the drive to save money by whatever means possible, including forced cuts in the country's social safety net and the non-payment of wages and pensions for months, further strained the government's relations with the State Duma. That in turn made the necessary tax legislation even less likely, because many deputies, including those committed to reform, perceived tax collection efforts—such as widely publicized raids by hooded tax inspectors armed with automatic weapons—as either arbitrary or politically motivated attacks on opponents of the government and its allies. Pressure to increase tax receipts also stifled the development of Russia's cash-starved businesses and scared off foreign investors, whom Moscow often saw as an easy source of additional revenue. But in an economy in which about 60 percent of cash turnover occurs beyond the reach of tax authorities in the shadow economy, and in which 75 percent of transactions take place through barter[1]—a new tax system was of much more fundamental importance than an improvised, one-time improvement in tax gathering. As in the case of Gaidar's government, the Kiriyenko government (which Gaidar advised) proceeded in a cavalier fashion with hastily conceived radical measures implemented in an authoritarian style. It never developed a systematic approach to what is, after all, a very complex problem.

Chaos and Collapse

Russia's financial collapse was a logical result of the policies of the Chernomyrdin and especially the Kiriyenko governments, which had relied heavily upon foreign borrowing to sustain federal budget expenditures. As oil prices continued to fall and Western investors simultaneously began to pull money out of Russia to cover their losses in the Asian financial crisis of 1997, the Russian government was forced into greater borrowing at escalating interest rates. GKOs were offered at such high rates of interest—up to 150 percent when inflation was still at a relatively low level—that there was little incentive for Russia's banks, or investors in general, to put money into production. Without that investment, however, there could be no growth in income to allow for the repayment of Russia's mounting debts. At the same time, it became increasingly expensive for the government to support the overvalued ruble. The result was a typical pyramid scheme. When the Kiriyenko government was finally forced to devalue the ruble, it found that it—and Russia's banks—could no longer meet their international obligations.

Key radical reformers, including Chubais, have admitted to understanding what was happening and what the likely consequences of Russia's economic policy manipulations would be.[2] Nevertheless, in the best Russian tradition, they hoped against hope that somehow, something would happen to resolve the crisis—or that the Clinton administration and the IMF would again step in to offer a way out. But it was too late. The resulting chaos and collapse of the ruble led quickly to the further decline of Russia's GDP, a new wave of inflation, consumer hoarding and shortages, unemployment, and accelerated capital flight. The fact that a reformist government that enjoyed particular confidence in the West took such drastic measures and produced such dire results compounded the damage to Russia's international credibility. Chubais' admission that he and the Russian cabinet deliberately deceived the IMF and foreign investors alike about the weakness of the Russian economy delivered a further blow.

Chubais later maintained that while he and his colleagues in the Kiriyenko government misled foreign investors, they did not deliberately lie to the IMF. This Clintonesque denial is not without a certain element of credibility. IMF and particularly World Bank officials in Moscow were quite skeptical of Russian assurances. After having my own conversations with then Central Bank

Chairman Sergey Dubinin and Deputy Prime Minister Boris Nemtsov, I was convinced that devaluation was inevitable and that only Russians' traditional faith in miracles gave the Kiriyenko government hope that it could be avoided. It appeared that senior Russian officials felt that they had no alternative but to delay devaluation until after the announcement of the July IMF credit package in order to fulfill the expectations of the Clinton administration's top decision-makers on Russia policy, Deputy Secretary of State Strobe Talbott and Deputy Secretary of the Treasury Larry Summers, who were eager to maintain the façade of Russian economic progress. This was more a mutually agreed pretense (undertaken to avoid alarming the U.S. Congress) than it was a unilateral deception.

The bubble predictably burst, but not until the first $4.8 of the $22.6 billion IMF-led bailout announced in July had been wasted supporting the value of the ruble and protecting Russia's top banks, which were controlled by the country's new oligarchy. There was much finger-pointing; many, including the IMF and President Yeltsin, claimed to be "shocked, shocked" at the collapse.

When Kiriyenko was fired, most in Moscow seemed to assume that the candidacy of Victor Chernomyrdin would sail through the Duma. Chernomyrdin had the support of most of Russia's oligarchs—including Boris Berezovsky, who took public credit for the appointment—and, in addition to being on fairly good terms with Communist leader Gennady Zyuganov, he was generally acceptable to the country's regional leaders. Two regional governors with presidential ambitions of their own—Moscow Mayor Yuri Luzhkov and Krasnoyarsk Governor Alexander Lebed—also offered important early support.

According to Moscow political analysts, another strength of the former prime minister's candidacy was that despite having been fired by Yeltsin, he could be counted on to protect the president's interests. This triggered speculation that Yeltsin's declining physical and mental health might lead him to cede some power to the prime minister and possibly even to the parliament. Yeltsin's entourage signaled as much in preliminary discussions with Duma officials. Soon, however, the Russian president demonstrated—as he had many times before—that unless pushed into a corner he would not compromise his personal power, and that no redistribution of authority could take place until he stepped down or was incapacitated. The Duma was thus being asked to confirm Chernomyrdin in a situation in which—given his strong presidential ambitions—he could first protect Yeltsin and then inherit his broad powers. Not surprisingly, the Communists and a number of other factions quickly backed away from supporting Chernomyrdin on those terms, and his prospects for confirmation collapsed.

Yevgeny Primakov's appointment as prime minister after the Duma's rejection of Chernomyrdin avoided a new sharp confrontation between the president and the parliament. Had Chernomyrdin been rejected a third time, Yeltsin would have been bound by the constitution to dissolve the Duma. However, because the Duma was planning to initiate impeachment proceedings against Yeltsin—which, according to the constitution, would prevent its dissolution—the situation could have resulted in a constitutional crisis. Such a crisis would have been much worse than that of October 1993, as no one would have been sure what the demoralized, divided, and underpaid Russian military—or Russia's increasingly assertive regional governors—would have done during such a standoff. Moreover, Yeltsin's options were severely limited by his unprecedented unpopularity after the August financial collapse.

This was a part of the rationale for the suggestion of Primakov as a compromise candidate by pro-reform economist and Yabloko faction leader Grigory Yavlinsky. He and others in the Duma were also delighted to demonstrate that the legislature could no longer be ignored. But Yavlinsky refused to join in the government once it became clear that it would be an eclectic coalition representing a variety of approaches. Included in it were Gorbachev-era officials such as Yuri Maslyukov, a former head of the Soviet planning agency Gosplan, and Victor Gerashchenko, a former Soviet banking official who served as the first chairman of Russia's Central Bank.[3] Embarrassingly, two members of the pro-Chernomyrdin Our Home is Russia party also refused to serve after being appointed publicly by Yeltsin: Duma Deputy Speaker Vladimir Ryzhkov and the faction's leader in the Duma, Alexander Shokhin, who joined the government only to resign after a few days. This made it more difficult to assume that the Primakov government could rely upon the support of reformers in the parliament.

Since Primakov came into office without a program or a background in practical economics, his disjointed cabinet has had considerable difficulty developing a coherent economic package while the Russian economy continues to decline. The good news, though, is that since Primakov was appointed through a compromise, there has been no immediate strong opposition to him. Fearing a further unraveling of the situation, most major political figures, including Mayor Luzhkov and Governor Lebed, have offered the new prime minister their support. At the same time, the Duma's role in Primakov's selection has given the new prime minister greater freedom from Yeltsin's destabilizing meddling than any of his predecessors enjoyed.

Simultaneously, the Russian people—tired, confused, and preoccupied with their own survival—appear to be in no mood to start a new revolutionary uprising. But Russian revolutions have often started in spontaneous and unpredictable revolts. In a nation with a constitutionally powerful but personally weak president and a disaffected, disillusioned population, even a fairly limited rebellion could start a chain reaction, especially if the fragmented Primakov government cannot find a way to halt skyrocketing inflation and limit shortages.

To their credit, no important Russian political party—including the Communist Party and Vladimir Zhirinovsky's Liberal Democratic Party—has adopted the Bolshevik slogan of 1916-17, "the worse, the better," and bet on victory through social upheaval. Curiously, the radical reformers have come the closest to adopting this position, through Chubais' apparently calculated admission of hoodwinking the IMF and Boris Fyodorov's call for no further IMF assistance to Russia immediately after the failure of his own attempt to remain in the cabinet.

In many countries, certainly most democratic countries, a crisis of the magnitude of the August-September 1998 events in Russia would have resulted in a comprehensive change of leadership. But in Russia, where Yeltsin is a declining czar rather than a hands-on chief executive, a change of government may do if Primakov and his aides are able to avoid completely alienating foreign investors and cutting off Russia from most international assistance. It is also possible if the situation continues to deteriorate that Primakov may be able to reshuffle the government and include responsible reformers in key positions.

The good news about the Primakov cabinet, as Secretary of State Madeleine Albright has observed, is that "Russia now has a government with a mandate from both the parliament and the president."[4] While the inclusion of ministers associated with the Communist and Agrarian factions in the government makes it more difficult for the cabinet to develop a coherent pro-reform program, to the extent that it is possible to do so such a program may garner more support in the Duma than any previous government initiative. At the same time, because the Duma can no longer excuse its obstructionism by pointing to the contempt with which the executive treats it, it finds itself under pressure to cooperate constructively with the cabinet. This creates an opening for economic change to be implemented through legislation rather than less credible presidential and government decrees—if the Primakov team manages to get its act together.

In the long run, the success of this dialogue is important to establishing a viable democratic system in Russia. More immediately, it may be essential in avoiding a social explosion. Much is at stake here for both Russia and the world; while new turmoil is possible but still not probable, its consequences could be so profound that trying to avoid—or at least not to facilitate—such upheaval should be a priority for the United States in dealing with a Russia on the brink.

The American Stake

In this context, it was appropriate for Secretary Albright to advise against "taking a census of reformers in the Kremlin." Still, the secretary of state could not resist the temptation to do precisely that by expressing doubts about the

Primakov government, saying, "We can only wonder if some members of Primakov's team understand the basic arithmetic of the global economy." She was similarly unable to conceal her disappointment that America's radical reformer protégés were no longer in government.

As the secretary also said, though, Primakov is "a forceful, straight-talking advocate of a major power's national interests." The new Russian prime minister has a long record of dealing with the United States as an adversary during the Soviet period as well. But attempts by some to demonize him as an anti-Western Arabist or a KGB agent are an oversimplification. First, even if he had worked for the old KGB, he would have been employed in a foreign intelligence capacity—not as a political policeman. Given that Yeltsin himself is a former party apparatchik, it is hypocritical to become exercised over the new prime minister's old KGB contacts.

Second, and more to the point, it is clear that while a person with Primakov's illustrious career had to have close ties to the KGB, it is very unlikely that he was ever a staff officer. If there were any firm institutional rules in the post-Stalin Soviet Union, one was that the party was above the security services and, therefore, that party personnel could not work for the KGB. As a correspondent for *Pravda*, the official party newspaper, in Cairo in the 1960s, Primakov was a part of the Central Committee *nomenklatura*. Because he was directly supervised by the International Department of the Central Committee, it would have been highly unusual for him simultaneously to take orders from the KGB. Lieutenant General Vadim Kirpichenko, a retired first deputy chief of foreign intelligence for the KGB, confirmed this in a recent book, where he wrote that *Pravda* correspondents such as Primakov maintained "close professional contacts" with KGB station chiefs but "could not be engaged for cooperation."[5]

Primakov's appointment, like so much else, seems to have taken the Clinton administration off guard. In all likelihood this was not a result of dark suspicions about Primakov personally; after all, Secretary Albright and others in the administration know him well and, despite obvious disagreements, feel that they can do business with him. The real problem for the administration is that because the Primakov government came into power as a result of a compromise between Yeltsin and the parliament, it has enjoyed greater autonomy than any previous Russian cabinet and has been much more representative of opinion in the Duma and in Russia in general. As a result, it is less interested in guidance from Washington than were Yeltsin's protégés among the radical reformers.

For years the Clinton administration has paid lip service to the importance of promoting democratic reform in Russia. Its policies of promoting strict monetarism and crony privatization, however, have actually frequently worked in the opposite direction by limiting economic growth and the development of a legal framework for a free but regulated market. Almost since its inception in late 1991, radical economic reform has triggered a strong popular backlash in Russia. Sensing public opinion, sizeable majorities in both the old Congress of People's Deputies and the Duma have consistently opposed radical reform.

Despite this opposition, Yeltsin was in a position to ignore the legislature and appoint governments of his own choosing responsible only to himself. This was particularly true after the adoption of the December 1993 constitution, which provided him with enormous powers. However, the Russian president was able to ignore parliament only at the double cost of further polarizing Russian society and encouraging obstructionist behavior by the Duma.

Nevertheless, the Clinton administration consistently urged Yeltsin to follow U.S. Treasury and IMF recommendations no matter the social and political consequences. This encouragement—backed by detailed conditions established for IMF credits—often went beyond policy advice to include not-so-subtle suggestions about which specific individuals should occupy key positions in the Russian cabinet and even on Yeltsin's personal staff. According to knowledgeable Russian sources, President Clinton himself coached Yeltsin on several occasions about the importance of retaining such administration favorites as Chubais and former Foreign Minister Andrei Kozyrev in the government. The administration thus put its desire to influence the Russian president's policies above the development of democracy in Russia. At the same time, the administration's strict adherence to its own somewhat arbitrary vision of what constituted reform in Russia actually undermined the economy's prospects for growth. The continuing lack of legislation became a serious obstacle to foreign, and even domestic, investment; few investors were willing to commit their money in the absence of a reliable legal framework. The deadlock between the government and the Duma was similarly an obstacle to tax reform—another problem that must fall to solution if Russia is ever to put its financial house in order.

The failure to attract investment and to raise tax revenues made Yeltsin uniquely dependent upon the good will of the outside world, particularly the United States, which was rightly seen as having a decisive influence over IMF lending decisions. As a result, there are now strong suspicions in Russia that Washington deliberately sought to keep it on its knees by forcing it to accept destructive economic policies. While there is no evidence that the Clinton administration was either capable or desirous of so Machiavellian a policy, senior administration officials certainly must be aware that, notwithstanding the rhetoric of partnership advanced by both sides, there could be no genuine equality in the relationship between a powerful donor and a beleaguered recipient.

Primakov's Prospects

In contrast to its rhetoric, deep down the administration has also acted as though it shared Henry Kissinger's observation that, "In Russia, democratization and a restrained foreign policy may not necessarily go hand in hand."[6] In fact, President Clinton and his advisers supported Yeltsin not only because of naive romanticism, but also because of a perfectly pragmatic—if shortsighted—calculation that he was prepared to subordinate Russian foreign policy interests to Western, and especially American, preferences to a much greater extent than the parliament or the Russian public at large. For example, it is hard to imagine that a Russian government responsive to popular sentiment would have sent military units to serve under NATO command in Bosnia, as Yeltsin did, when NATO launched air strikes solely against Orthodox Serbs despite strong Russian claims that each of the parties in the conflict had committed excesses. Similarly, it is unlikely that such a government would express willingness to participate in the international monitoring effort in Kosovo essentially on NATO terms.

The underdevelopment of democracy in Russia and the resulting broad autonomy of the Russian president have thus helped the Clinton administration to win Moscow's acquiescence to U.S. foreign policy actions that it may otherwise have strongly opposed. From this standpoint, the emergence of the Primakov government, which relies on parliamentary support from the Communists (among others), was bound to make the administration think twice. Administration officials were forced to ask how the new Russian cabinet would respond if the United States were to take the lead in organizing a NATO air campaign against Serbia in response to Slobodan Milosevic's brutalities in Kosovo. Use of the Russian UN Security Council veto became a real possibility for the first time in years. It was by definition much easier and more predictable to make arrangements with only Yeltsin and his lieutenants.

Similarly, the Primakov government is likely to be less open to U.S. Treasury and IMF guidance on how to manage Russia's economy. Taking into account how deeply flawed that advice has been thus far, this may to some extent be a blessing. It has also already become clear that the Primakov government has had great difficulty putting together an economic program; the new prime minister has emphasized several times that he is not a magician. His is not a cabinet looking for bold new approaches—whether toward or away from the free market through large-scale re-nationalization. Muddling through is the best one can realistically expect from his cabinet—and even that will not be easy.

Russia's new government has inherited a banking system near collapse, spiraling inflation, negative economic growth (a 5-6 percent decline in Russia's GDP is projected by the Russian Central Bank for 1998), and severely undermined investor confidence. Some $17 billion in debt is due in 1999 and there is no chance that Russia will be able to raise sufficient revenue to avoid—to put it delicately—restructuring its obligations. It is clear that difficult economic times are still ahead and that conditions will become worse before they get better.

Nevertheless, on the positive side, key members of Primakov's economic team, including Central Bank Chairman Victor Gerashchenko, First Deputy Prime Minister Yuri Maslyukov, and Finance Minister Mikhail Zadornov, are all pragmatic and competent professionals. They are capable of heading off disaster or, at a minimum, of adjusting their policies if disastrous consequences become evident. Moreover, the government's relationship with the Duma may allow the passage of long overdue legislation on property rights, bankruptcy, tax reform, and other key issues. Like the Primakov cabinet itself, that legislation is bound to be imperfect, contradictory, and disappointing to many. But it would still be a modest step in the direction of rebuilding sagging investor confidence.

As the relatively mild demonstrations on October 7 suggest, the government's ties to the Duma will also be helpful in avoiding social upheaval. Given that one of the most essential—if not *the* most essential—U.S. interests in Russia is the avoidance of anarchy or civil war in a nation with thousands of nuclear warheads, whatever contribution the new government makes to reducing that likelihood should be welcome.

Relatedly, it is important to recognize that the Primakov government may smooth the transition to the post-Yeltsin era as well. Yevgeny Primakov has several advantages in this respect. First, he is on good terms with both Yeltsin and the opposition. Second, he is a master of political maneuver and a skillful survivor. Third, and perhaps most important, because he has no constituency of his own—and no known presidential ambitions—he is generally viewed as a caretaker. This perception helps significantly to calm tensions in a period when Yeltsin—while maintaining both his enormous constitutional powers and his strong attachment to them—is increasingly unable to exercise effective leadership.

Solutions to Russia's broader problems will have to await new elections to the State Duma in 1999 and for the presidency in 2000. But, for the first time, the Communists and their allies may be forced to bear some of the responsibility for the Russian government's policies. Should the government go too far in implementing retrograde policies under pressure from the Communists, pro-democracy and pro-reform parties in the parliament, such as Yabloko, may have an important opportunity to increase their electoral appeal and exercise greater influence on the government (or even join it).

Still, even assuming that Russia can muddle through until the post-Yeltsin era, the United States will have to accept that Moscow's willingness to walk in lock step with it on foreign policy matters is increasingly a thing of the past. Russia's limited resources and continuing dependence on the West will of course discourage any responsible government from confronting America over issues that are not vital to Russia, including Kosovo and Iraq. But if a perception of hostile American intentions begins to guide Russian foreign policy, attempts to counteract U.S. policy would likely follow even before Russia regains its feet economically.

It is not easy for Americans, particularly in our current triumphalist mood—which has been only slightly dented by the impact of the global economic crisis—to appreciate the perceptions that U.S. conduct is generating in Russia. American actions such as NATO enlargement, resistance to Russian influence over pipeline routes out of the Caspian Basin, efforts to discourage Russia from sharing weapons and high-technology with those who do not play by the rules internationally, and the imposition of strict conditionality on international economic assistance to Russia make sense individually on their merits. But collectively these policies contribute to a widespread impression that the United States is deliberately exploiting Russia's historic vulnerability. These steps have been seen by some as the aggressive expansion of a hostile military alliance, an attempt to restrict Russian access to key oil resources and lucrative investments, an effort to monopolize the international arms and technology markets, the hypocritical use of military force against Russia's Serbian friends, and, through offering assistance on conditions that prevent economic growth in Russia, a policy intended to keep the country weak and dependent upon the West.

This is certainly not a fair picture of U.S. intentions or, for that matter, Clinton administration policy. But that is beside the point. What matters is whether Russian public opinion sees U.S. policy as an effort to bring Russia to its knees—and increasingly it does. Also, while the administration cannot be accused of deliberately undermining Russian reform, it was not above taking advantage of Moscow's continuing weakness—to which its policies contributed—to marginalize it on a variety of international issues. With regard to NATO air strikes against Yugoslavia, for example, Secretary Albright said, "If force is required, then we will not be deterred by the fact that the Russians do not agree with that." Such an attitude, and the behavior resulting from it, only contributes to the development of a "Weimar Russia" psychological syndrome, the avoidance of which must be a priority for U.S. policymakers.

That syndrome will only be enhanced if the administration opts for pre-emptive abandonment of Russia, out of a combination of fear and self-righteousness not dissimilar to that with which some of its members once advocated pre-emptive appeasement of the Soviet Union during the days of Moscow's imperial glory. Despite the rhetoric of continued engagement, Strobe Talbott suggested recently that Washington might wash its hands of Russia unless the Primakov government agrees to follow IMF guidance.[7] Strikingly, Talbott's remarks lacked any reflection about the U.S. role—and his personal complicity—in Russia's predicament. Moreover, he knows that Primakov could not deliver on this demand without provoking a major conflict with the Duma; that a large part of a second IMF loan installment would be used to repay previous ill-conceived IMF loans (for which the administration cannot escape responsibility); and that the consequences of a collapse in Russia far surpass the danger of wasting $4.3 billion. Talbott's remarks appear to be either a reflection of indignation at Russia's refusal to follow his advice, an attempt to create an alibi in the event that the administration finds itself in a "Who lost Russia?" debate, or possibly both.

It may be difficult to focus on Russia's long-term potential to assume a major role in the international system when the country is seemingly trapped in an almost catastrophic economic crisis. Russia today is in a uniquely weak international position; its military is not ready for combat and its economic ordeal clearly reduces its options in foreign policy significantly, and Russians recognize this. A Russian proverb describes their understanding of the current situation: *ne do zhiru, byt' by zhivu* (do not worry about getting fat when you are struggling to stay alive).

But it would be a mistake for the United States to interpret Russia's current weakness as endorsement of America's effort to shape a new international system around itself. Russia is biding its time until it is able not only to express its preferences but also to do something about them. While it may be some time before Russia can significantly constrain American foreign policy, approaching the country realistically means recognizing that it may have a much more serious impact on the world a few years hence.

In this context, National Security Adviser Samuel R. Berger was wrong to claim that NATO air strikes against Serbia would not "affect [America's] fundamental relationship with Russia."[8] At the present time, when Russia is exceptionally weak and is desperate for foreign assistance (ranging from the next tranche of the July 1998 IMF credit package to food aid from Europe and the United States), Moscow does have limited options in responding to whatever NATO does in Yugoslavia. But there will be a reaction sometime, somewhere— and perhaps on a matter of greater importance to America than events in Kosovo. Accumulated scar tissue on the Russian side from such perceived indignities will hardly add to the strength of what the administration has called one of America's most important bilateral relationships.

Nevertheless, it is true that under even the most optimistic scenarios for Russia's economic recovery, Moscow cannot regain its lost superpower status in the foreseeable future. And most serious presidential contenders—including Yavlinsky, Luzhkov, Lebed, and even Zyuganov—appreciate the unique role of the United States in today's world and understand that needlessly alienating Washington could have devastating consequences for their country. Thus, a great deal will depend on American policy toward Russia and, more generally, on U.S. global strategy in the twenty-first century. Russia alone is not likely to be able or willing to mount a serious challenge to American predominance. Likewise, there is no potential for Russia to become the focal point of a new coalition against the United States—although it could facilitate such an effort by others.

Thus, Russia could become a serious problem for the United States if the Clinton administration continues to try indiscriminately to run the world according to American preferences while still failing to take tough stands when it really counts. Such irritation without intimidation is very likely to generate a Russian backlash against U.S. global leadership, and this could be the case regardless of who replaces Boris Yeltsin.

Notes

1. Grigory Yavlinsky, "Whither Russian Reform?," remarks at The Nixon Center, September 25, 1997.
2. Yevgeniya Albats, interview with Anatoly Chubais, "Anatoly Chubais: We Should Expect One and a Half to Two Very Difficult Years," *Kommersant-daily*, September 8, 1998.
3. Mikhail Rybyanov, "Grigory Yavlinsky: 'In Russia, of Two Evils, We Chose Both'," *Komsomolskaya pravda*, September 18, 1998.
4. "Address by Secretary of State Madeleine K. Albright to the U.S.-Russia Business Council," October 2, 1998, *usis Washington File*, www.usia.gov.
5. Sergei Maslov, "Lieutenant General Vadim Kirpichenko Says in His Book: Primakov is Not at All Characterized by an Idiotic Standing on Principle," *Komsomolskaya pravda*, September 12, 1998.
6. Henry Kissinger, *Diplomacy* (New York: Simon & Schuster, 1994), p. 221.
7. "Talbott Urges Strategic Patience Toward Russia," speech at Stanford University, November 6, 1998, *usis Washington File*, www.usia.gov.
8. Berger quoted in Philip Smucker, "Serbs Seen Rallying Around Milosevic," *Washington Times*, October 12, 1998.

Part 4

Russia Under Putin

17

Realism about Russia

William E. Odom*

Reacting to the Bush administration's promise of "realism" in dealing with Russia, a former Clinton administration official observed that "the issue is what is reality."[1] Indeed it is.

Clinton administration officials had their reality: Russia was on the path to liberal democracy, albeit stumbling occasionally; it was building the institutions for an effective market economy, although suffering periodic setbacks; its large arsenal of nuclear weapons entitled it to major power status, but at the same time the United States could help to reduce significantly the number of operational Russian warheads and to improve the security of Russian nuclear weapons and materials. This assessment prompted the Clinton administration to believe that Russia could be induced to play a constructive role in the Balkans, with NATO, in Iran, and elsewhere.

The Clinton reality also implied alternative futures, partly depending on U.S. policy choices. Although never voiced as an official view, defenders of the Clinton policy outside the administration emphasized that Russia's progress toward liberal democracy and economic recovery required constant U.S. support, both with technical assistance and by encouraging generous IMF and World Bank loans on relatively easy terms. If such support were not provided, it was intimated, a "red-brown" Russian dictatorship would emerge, analogous to Weimar Germany's transformation into Hitler's Third Reich. The assumption in either case was that Russia would soon return to the ranks of the great powers, and prudence dictated making an effort to avoid getting on Moscow's future enemy list. If one accepts this line of reasoning, then it can be

*William E. Odom is a senior fellow at the Hudson Institute and an adjunct professor of political science at Yale University. Lt. General Odom (USA, ret.) served as director of the National Security Agency from 1985 to 1988. This essay first appeared in *The National Interest*, No. 65 (Fall 2001).

claimed that the Clinton administration's assistance programs to Russia made political sense despite their questionable economic results.

What different reality might the Bush administration see if it takes an un-varnished view of contemporary Russian realities? It will see a Russia that has indeed become a "normal country," which is to say a member of that large majority of states in the world that are weak, poor, and ambling along their own paths headed nowhere in particular—certainly not to liberal democracy or effective market economies. It will also see that the security of Russia's nuclear arsenal is beyond significant U.S. influence but, nonetheless, that nuclear weapons do not make Russia a great power. It will see that Russia can engage in trouble-making diplomacy in the former Soviet republics along its periphery, but that it is not capable of major military operations.

More broadly, it will also see that Russia cannot be expected to act con-structively in international affairs because most of its elite class angrily blames the West for Russia's drop to third rank status—although the real culprit is the legacy of seven decades of Soviet rule. Western magnanimity cannot change Russia's foreign policy behavior for the better; it is far more likely to make it worse. Moreover, Russia as a "normal country" in this special sense of the term may remain in a sharply reduced condition for a very long time. It is liable to become, in Jeffrey Tayler's colorful phrase, "Zaire with permafrost."[2]

What if we were reasonably certain that Russia will not soon return to great power status, either as a liberal democracy or a dictatorship? What if we knew that no amount of aid and assistance will produce a dynamic and effective Russian economy? What if, in other words, Russia simply cannot "make it," with Western help or without it? What is the evidence for this possibility, and what would be the implications for U.S. policy?

Russia's Institutional Deficit

Formally speaking, of course, Russia is "making it" to democracy in the sense that it holds periodic elections in which opposition parties participate—as long as their chances of winning are scant. Russia has not yet, however, seen an incumbent president voted out of office. If "making it" means achieving "liberal" democracy, then evidence accumulates that Russia is not making it and may not do so for many decades.

Its formal democracy notwithstanding, Russia lacks genuine constitution-alism. A true constitutional system requires a durable elite consensus on: rules for making rules; rules for deciding who rules; and individual rights that no ruler can violate or abridge. Russia is developing no such consensus. Presi-dent Vladimir Putin's carefully managed succession to President Boris Yeltsin made clear to all but the most obtuse observers that a genuine breakthrough for constitutionalism in Russia is not about to happen. Most of Putin's key programs—taking all effective political power away from the Federation Council (the upper chamber of the parliament); imposing a new administrative level over the regional governments; conducting a genocidal war in Chechnya; and methodically reducing media freedoms—appear to violate the Yeltsin constitution of 1993, calling to mind the Russian proverb that "paper will put up with anything written on it."

The unreconstructed optimist will object, insisting that all this signifies merely a temporary setback on a difficult road, a claim frequently made by Clinton Administration officials as well as numerous analysts and scholars in think tanks and universities. In truth, however, Russia is on some other road altogether, and this truth really should not surprise us.

If in 1992 one had taken the best theories available on how liberal democracies come to be, and what kind of state institutions are required for effective economic performance, one would have known that Russia's chances of taking the liberal path were poor. After a decade of post-Soviet experience, one should now conclude that the chances are trivial to none, barring a major dislocating shock such as a major war or revolution, or the very improbable emergence of the kind of elite consensus that produced the Meiji restoration in Japan. Russia is now locked into a mix of old and new institutions that daily becomes more costly for the Russian elite to escape than to perpetuate. This predicament is neither unusual nor abnormal; most countries are trapped in the "weak state" syndrome and locked into economically ineffective institutions. *Abnormal* countries are the wealthy liberal democracies located almost exclusively in North America, Western Europe, and a few rim-land states in Northeast Asia.

Political theory, and not just Russia's experience, supports these observations. It does so by clarifying the link between political institutions and economic performance.

Clearly, all liberal democracies have market economies where, despite sometimes large welfare programs, prices are set largely by supply and demand. But the reverse is not true; not all market economies exist within a liberal democracy. Indeed, the rim-land economies in Asia, some of their leaders have insisted, perform well precisely because they do *not* have liberal democratic governments. Thus, the connection between good economic performance and liberal political institutions has been a disputed one, and the mixed empirical evidence allows disparate views their day.

Mainstream Western economists have shed little empirical light on these disputes, preferring instead the many simplifying theoretical assumptions of neoclassical economics. This is why individual Western advisors to the Russian government in 1992–93, including officials of the IMF and World Bank, ignored such complications. Ironically, the winner of the Nobel Prize for economics in 1993, Douglass C. North, who had published the last of several books in 1990, confronted directly the question of the connection between political institutions and economic performance.[3] In his 1993 acceptance speech, he called attention to the relevance of his work for the Russian case—evidently in vain.

A few of this Nobel laureate's central ideas should have given pause to U.S. policymakers as well as to those economists advising Russia. First, North observed that if neo-classical economics could explain economic development, then all countries, whatever their level of development, would be moving on converging axes toward a common efficiency level. But, as North's research shows, they do not converge. The reason, he suggests, is that they have different institutions, and institutions greatly affect economic performance. Looking at the historical record, those institutions arising from the Glorious Revolution in seventeenth-century England—especially stable property rights and a judiciary largely independent of royal power—work best because they greatly lower transaction costs, facilitating profitable commerce and investment.

North stresses that effective "third-party enforcement" is critical for achieving sustained, long-term economic growth. In his words, "third-party enforcement means the development of the state as a coercive force able to monitor property rights and enforce contracts effectively, but no one at this stage in our knowledge knows how to create such an entity."[4] This should have been a chastening observation for those Western advisors and policymakers who marched with such confidence to help Russia. Did they "know how to create such an entity"? These economists clearly did not, and as U.S. policymakers funded hundreds of technical assistance programs for implementing the rule of law, privatization, accounting methods, and so on, it soon became clear that neither did they.

Even as the importance of institutional reform began to dawn on many observers, certain critics of the Clinton administration's policies insisted that there was a "better" or a "right" way to help Russia.[5] But they, too, failed to show how one can induce the Russian state to perform an effective "third-party enforcement" role. It is difficult to see how the key Western governments, even had they pursued some wiser set of aid policies, could have overcome Russia's political and economic development problems without an extremely intrusive overhaul of virtually the entire institutional structure of the Russian state.

This is not to say that there are no examples of U.S. policy producing effective "third-party enforcement" in other countries; there are, specifically, in Germany and Japan after World War II. The Marshall Plan itself did not cause this development in Germany. Rather, the U.S. military occupation government did. True enough, roots for an autonomous judiciary existed there and, to a lesser degree, in Japan, but it was the conscious use of a military occupation to sponsor precisely the institutional developments called for that explains the success. An effective Marshall Plan for Moscow, then, would have required a military occupation as well as hundreds of billions of dollars—and might still have failed, for Russia has no heritage of inchoate liberal institutional development toward effective constitutionalism that both Germany and Japan had achieved by the turn of the twentieth century (or that the Baltic states and the countries of central Europe have today to one degree or another).

In the absence of a compelling refutation of North's interpretation of the historical evidence, we should recognize that no available U.S. policy can put Russia on the path to a liberal political system. Nor is North alone in suggesting such a conclusion. Political scientists have long noted the powerful role of political culture, a concept that embraces, among other things, what North calls "informal institutions" in a society. Robert Putnam has exposed centuries-old continuities of political culture that block the effective use of public funds in parts of Italy today.[6] Notwithstanding the "third wave" of new democracies since World War II, the number of truly liberal democracies—that is, those that have fully instituted a constitutional breakthrough, or have become what Robert Dahl calls "mature polyarchies"—has not grown much since 1945. By Dahl's count in 1989, Germany, Japan, and Austria were the only new ones, solidly rooted through more than two decades of existence. Today he would add Spain and Portugal as third-decade democracies, and perhaps South Korea and Taiwan as second-decade candidates.[7] The special conditions that favor the emergence of liberal democracies exist in few places, meaning that the prospects for additional ones are not promising. Judged against Dahl's prerequisites, Russia would appear to have dismal prospects.

Russia's Path Dependence and the Weak State Syndrome

Those poor prospects can be best described with the aid of North's concept of "path dependence." At its most basic, path dependence means that once a country has put in place a set of institutions—formal and informal—they are difficult to change. The origins of the "path dependence" idea are varied and old. Historians as well as political scientists have long noted the propensity of social and political arrangements to persist in countries, devising in some cases theories of historical continuities. Samuel Huntington's "clash of civilizations" thesis is a recent example of such an approach. In technology, the idea has acquired more specificity, of which the typewriter keyboard is one example. The "QWERTY" key layout was designed to slow down fast typists so that the keys did not pile up on early models. As mechanical designs improved and typewriters became capable of handling very high-speed typing, the less efficient keyboard layout was retained because the costs of retraining typists and buying replacement keyboards were judged too high. We are thus still "locked in" to the "QWERTY" layout, and similar "lock-ins" can be observed in other technologies.

North applies this concept to institutional development. When England broke out of its old institutional pattern based on absolute monarchy, it established a far more effective economic path, one that also took hold in Holland at about the same time. Meanwhile, France, Spain, and other European countries remained on their old paths, chained to absolutist institutional arrangements that yielded far less effective economic performance. They remained locked in for a long time, trailing the booming English and Dutch economies for the next three centuries.

If we view Russia today through the "path dependence" concept, what do we see? First, the legacies of Soviet institutions—e.g., informal rules on property rights, on the place and purpose of courts and legal practices, taxation, accounting systems and others—remain strong. Second, in the absence of an effective "third-party enforcement" role by the state, alternative methods of enforcement have begun to take root. Contract disputes are more often settled informally despite the fact that new laws and legal remedies are formally available in the courts. Private security firms will readily handle such disputes, resorting to rough measures and even murder if necessary. Much of the old Soviet bureaucracy remains in place, allowing poorly paid civil servants to supplement their incomes through "rent seeking" and the misappropriation of state property and funds. Regional governors and mayors have many means for extracting wealth from their citizens, not as legitimate taxes but for lining their own pockets.

With every month that passes, the mix of Soviet and post-Soviet institutions becomes more costly to reverse. Several studies of the business "oligarchs" who gained enormous wealth during the Russian privatization process have noted that although the oligarchs initially supported reform, they began blocking further reform once they themselves got rich.[8] They prefer the murky arrangements that made them wealthy to an environment of effective "third-party enforcement" by reasonably honest state officials. Thus they persist in asset stripping, moving capital abroad, and tax evasion, although such practices yield terrible economic consequences for the country as a whole.

Boris Yeltsin and many of his close supporters in the government came to share an interest in the status quo as they themselves learned to profit from it. Putin claims to be committed to reining in the oligarchs in order to break these perverse institutions, but will he create better institutions or merely displace the first generation of post-Soviet oligarchs with his own supporters? His primary bases of political support—the military and the intelligence services—would lose their strong claims on the state's resources if more effective institutions existed. This and other evidence has persuaded the Swedish economist, Stefan Hedlund, that a post-Soviet equilibrium has already been reached, signaling the virtual permanency of these institutions; i.e., a path-dependence lock-in has already occurred in Russia that promises very poor future economic performance.[9] To escape from it, Russia would have to experience powerful changes in the pay-off matrix that now exists for businessmen and state officials. A few top leaders alone are not likely to be able to change it, even if they wished to do so.

Two aspects of Russia's reality should now be clear. First, the country will not become a liberal democracy within the next several decades, maybe much longer. Second and concomitantly, the Russian economy will perform poorly for the indefinite future. Taken together, these judgments support a third one: Russia is now locked in the "weak state" syndrome.[10]

Weak states are best identified by the ineffectiveness of their tax systems. The cost of effective modern government is somewhere in the range of 20-30 percent of GDP, and most tax revenue must come from direct taxes. Direct taxes, however, are the most difficult to collect, requiring strong local government, communications, reliable local police and courts, and so on. An effective tax system is normally good evidence that the appropriate state structures and institutions exist and operate reasonably well. Because indirect taxes require less administrative capacity, and export-import taxes very little indeed beyond control of airports and seaports, they are less compelling measures of state strength. Finally, weak states tend to be directly in business; that is, they are "statist" states.

The clear majority of states in the world belong to the weak state category and, once in it, escape is the exception, not the rule. Military dictatorship is no salvation; on the contrary, praetorian regimes are almost always manifestations of the weak state syndrome. Many of President Putin's policies—"statism" in some parts of the economy, arbitrary use of violence and intimidation, as in Chechnya and against the media and the oligarchs, and changes in state organization by unconstitutional processes—stand as illustrations of Russia's status as a weak state. Worse, such policies will perpetuate Russia's "weak state" condition and perhaps weaken the country further.

Russian Reality and Russian International Behavior

A congenitally weak Russia is very unlikely to play a constructive role in international affairs. The Western goal of integrating Russia into the international economic and political mainstream is laudable, but will prove exceedingly difficult to achieve. The wounded pride of Russia's elite cannot be assuaged by restraint, such as no more NATO enlargement, or by inclusion in organizations like the G-7 or in peacekeeping operations in the Balkans. Moscow is more likely to use such opportunities to cause trouble rather than to cooperate. Under the new code word for anti-Americanism, "multipolarity," Putin has focused most of his diplomatic attention on China, India, Iran, Iraq, Libya, North Korea, Cuba, and Vietnam. In other words, Moscow apparently seeks to lead those countries with poor economic performances and repressive social and political institutions, and at the same time to participate as a great power in Western international organizations. This is obviously a losing strategy. It cannot in this manner aggregate sufficient power to counterbalance the United States—its ostensible aim—but will certainly irritate Washington and most capitals in Europe.

Moreover, Russia simply does not have the political or military power to act constructively on a global scale. It is strong enough, however, to menace its weak and newly independent neighbors, and it manifests an increasing appetite for doing so. Some will object to this evaluation, citing Russia's nuclear weapons as the key to its strength. But that objection is both perverse in the kind of Russian behavior it encourages and dubious in the measure of power it imputes to nuclear weapons.

The perversity is that expressions of Western fear about nuclear weapons tempt Russian leaders to exaggerate their value and to charge a higher price for their own good behavior. The Nunn-Lugar monies have achieved some modest results, but they probably have also lined the pockets of military leaders, nuclear power officials and other bureaucrats. The Russian government simply lacks the administrative capacity to use those funds effectively and neither good intentions nor the use of Western firms under contract to dismantle the weapons can change this reality. Thus, the more Western leaders worry openly about Russia's nuclear weapons, the more Russian leaders are likely to fan public fears in the West as a way of securing access to funds that they can skim for personal gain.

Besides, Russia stands to lose as much from nuclear proliferation as the United States, more so in the cases of Iran, Iraq, and North Korea. That the Russian government actually supports nuclear programs in some of these countries is evidence that it often cannot act even in its own national interest. This says very disturbing things about what one can expect any Russian government to do, even if it promises to be cooperative.

Nor do nuclear weapons really convey all that much power to their owners. The Russian military cannot invade Europe or South Korea or Japan with nuclear weapons alone. That would require a large offensive capability in conventional forces. Nor could nuclear weapons add much to a defense against a concerted Chinese invasion in the Far East. Nuclear weapons do nothing for Moscow in its war in Chechnya and its involvement in the periodic civil war in Tajikistan.

In today's strategic context, the coin of nuclear weapons has declined in an objective sense, but this new reality has yet to be fully recognized. The United States, therefore, is wise to accelerate that devaluation by simply treating these weapons as not all that important anymore. The administration is therefore quite right to want to extract the United States from the constraints that arms control treaties and the negotiating processes that achieve them impose against unilateral deep U.S. reductions and the restructuring of its arsenal. The record of nuclear arms control to date has mainly been to codify increases in weaponry or, at best, to drag out the time required to achieve reductions. Much can be said for making those reductions early rather than dawdling through another ten years of U.S.-Russian negotiations. If Russian leaders prefer to keep their large, aging and increasingly unreliable stockpile of nuclear warheads for years to come, let them.

The Weimar Analogy Myth

If Russia's nuclear arsenal is in truth a wasting asset, can Russia restore its conventional military power? Can it overcome its military weakness, as would be essential for the Weimar Germany analogy to make any sense? The answer is "no"; it cannot do so soon because the defense ministry effectively evaded systemic reform under Mikhail Gorbachev, successfully continued this strategy under Yeltsin, and appears to be following it against Putin, as well. The personal interests of senior military officers take priority over reversing the decline in Russian military power, something that would require large personnel reductions, particularly in the senior ranks, radical organizational change, and new relations with Russian defense industries. As long as the generals succeed in blocking reform, therefore, Russian conventional military forces will remain weak. The path-dependence phenomenon has a grip on the Russian military just as it does on the Russian economy and political system.

What if systemic military reform is nevertheless successfully imposed from above? Russian military power will still remain greatly constrained, first by the country's weak economy and second by adverse demographic and health trends. Russia is not Weimar Germany, with a healthy, young, expanding population. It does not have a world-class industrial economy that has competed effectively in global markets, as Germany did. It lacks a proud, unified and professionally competent officer corps, as the Reichswehr had. A strong Russian military, rising phoenix-like from the ashes of the Soviet collapse, is improbable. Still, a modest increase in military capabilities is possible—enough to pose a menace to those CIS countries that resist Moscow's dictates.

What, then, are we to make of the apparent increases in the Russian GDP over the past year? Is the economy truly recovering, as senior Russian officials claim and as some Western observers believe?

In the first place, all measurements of the Russian GDP are suspect. Russian officials have repeatedly and skillfully manipulated GDP figures to please the IMF. But they have done this so often that it is now doubtful that they themselves know which figures are accurate. Second, sharp reductions in imports of Western consumer goods after the 1998 financial crisis undoubtedly boosted domestic production in some sectors, but it did not lower transaction costs or improve factor productivity across the board—the real keys to economic growth. Meanwhile, commodity exports, especially oil at rising world prices, have brought more Western currency into Russian coffers, but this may only be temporary, and probably harms Russian institutional development. Countries living on oil export revenue, such as Nigeria, Venezuela and others, are notoriously poor at tax collection and mired in official corruption—key symptoms of the weak state syndrome. The present oil boom, therefore, is double-edged for Russia as well as for the other CIS oil-producing states, both a boon and a menace.

Moreover, the apparent good news on the Russian economy is in fact mixed. The Russian State Statistics Committee calculated capital flight for the first quarter of 2001 to exceed foreign direct investment by about $400 million. That means that for every foreign dollar coming in, more than one dollar flees the country—not a good sign for growth. Moreover, most foreign investment comes from Cyprus and the Netherlands, favorite places for Russians to hide their capital abroad.[11]   In other words, most of the money coming in is not really foreign investment, but recycled plunder from oligarchs and others. Western investors actually provide only a tiny fraction of the capital coming into Russia, hardly a vote of confidence in the Russian economy. Finally, President Putin's economic advisor, Andrei Illarionov, has consistently warned that the failure of institutional reforms portends economic stagnation, and that growth in 2001 is likely to be close to zero. Optimistic reports on Russian economic performance, therefore, should be taken with a heavy dose of skepticism.

Russia is no longer a great power and is unlikely again to become one over the next several decades. Treating it like one is neither in Russia's interests nor the West's. It increases Moscow's incentives for restoring a repressive regime, for abolishing the modest gains Russians have made in human rights, and for squandering resources on mischief-making in the international arena. Those Western enthusiasts for continuing to treat Russia as a great power are harming the very Russian citizens they claim to admire and desire to help. Ten years of Western policies based on that assumption, among others, have now disillusioned a large part of the otherwise pro-Western Russian intelligentsia. Well-meant financial largess is now widely seen as a CIA-directed scheme to weaken Russia. Creating a special arrangement for Moscow with NATO has given the Russian defense ministry one more lever for pumping up anti-American popular sentiment.

Many Russian scholars, journalists, and intellectuals clearly see the perversity of the present situation. The human rights activist, Sergei Kovalev, has explained how Putin successfully misled the Russian intelligentsia to support the war against the Chechens, a war that Elena Bonner has called "*de facto* genocide."[12] Mincing no words about the policies of the present Russian regime, she sounded like her famous husband, Andrei Sakharov, condemning the Brezhnev regime in the 1970s. Grigorii Yavlinskii, one of the few liberal politicians who survives in the present parliament, describes Russia's regime as a "pretend democracy" and warns that it is an illusion to believe, as some Russians do, that the West will not allow a return to dictatorship in Russia or its continued economic and social decline.[13] Putin's *de facto* censorship policies, however, are slowly reducing the number of Russian leaders who speak candidly on political issues. Anyone in the West truly wanting to know "what is reality" in Russia could do worse than listen to such voices—while they last.

Still Living with a Sick Bear

Many years ago, in the Winter 1985/86 issue of *The National Interest*, Henry S. Rowen wrote about the challenge for U.S. policy of "living with a sick bear." Rowen's was perhaps the first crystallized argument that weakness emanating from Moscow could come to occupy U.S. concerns as much as or more than Russia's strength. As it has turned out, a more or less permanently weak and trouble-making Russia is still a serious problem for U.S. foreign policy, but it is no longer a first-order strategic challenge. Other problems greatly transcend it: maintaining Western security alliances; managing international economic institutions; global pollution and other environmental issues; and preventing eastern Europe from lapsing into economic and political crisis. While Russia remains important, it is not all that important.

Adapting U.S. policy accordingly does not mean slamming the door on Russia, but it does suggest fewer U.S. efforts to shape Russian domestic developments through economic and technical assistance programs. It also requires candor about human rights and anti-liberal behavior by the Russian state. But the major change should come in how the United States treats Russia in the international arena. U.S. policy toward Russia should depend largely on whether Russia pursues a constructive foreign policy rather than one that engages in posturing and trouble-making diplomacy. If it chooses the latter, Russia would be slamming the door on itself.

One may anticipate an objection to this approach. It may be so that Russia is weak, but would it not be wiser to treat Russia as a great power than as a marginal one, lest we feed its resentment and be surprised by its still possible return to great power status? In light of the record of the past decade, the question is better put the other way around: Is it not wiser to end the pretense about Russia's status today even if we believed that it would return to great power status tomorrow? A decade of experience of including Russia in the circle of major powers has not been rewarding. Nor has it brought increasingly favorable Russian sentiments toward the United States—which is really no surprise, for the record of countries rewarding their former enemies for benevolent treatment is not good.

Even some observers who share the assessment of Russia presented here may fear that it is too harsh to present openly, too discouraging for the Russians to hear. They may worry that it will cause them to give up hope, to believe that they are permanently excluded from the West, and to behave even worse in the international arena than they otherwise might. But progress in relations between Russia and the West cannot be built on falsehoods and pretenses. It has to rest on genuine mutual understanding. One imperative understanding is that seven decades of Soviet rule are mostly to blame for Russia's present predicament, not the West. And escaping that predicament requires facing the facts, not pretending that things are otherwise by restoring the Soviet national anthem, insisting that the Baltic states voluntarily joined the Soviet Union in 1940, stirring nostalgia for the Soviet Union, and failing to purge the old nomenklatura and its KGB associates. Germany—the Western part, at any rate—was quickly and successfully reintegrated into the international order after 1945 because it faced the facts, not because the United States refrained from publicly acknowledging the truth about German fascism and its crimes.

Still others may object that the case made here is too fatalistic. Admittedly it has a strongly deterministic character. Yet it does not entirely rule out a role for political voluntarism of the sort that Yavlinskii and a few others have urged Russian leaders to exercise. Rather, it explains what these leaders are up against and how poor the odds are that they can quickly produce a significantly different outcome. Russian leaders may eventually find a way to escape their institutional path, and to alter it significantly for the better. Political leaders have broken their countries from path dependence in a few cases. But if it happens in Russia, as it did in Meiji Japan and Kemalist Turkey, it will be a homegrown affair, not one induced by Western ventriloquy, largess, pretenses and toleration of international mischief-making. It is more likely to happen earlier, moreover, if the United States insists on building its relations with Russia on the uncomfortable realities of the present day. In the meantime, the West can help marginally by keeping Russia's international role to a level commensurate with its power; to do otherwise would be to reinforce Russia's perverse path dependencies.

Notes

1. Strobe Talbott, quoted in the *Washington Post*, March 23, 2001.
2. Tayler, "Russia is Finished," *Atlantic Monthly*, May 2001, p. 35.
3. North, *Institutions, Institutional Change and Economic Performance* (New York: Cambridge University Press, 1990). Mancur Olson in *The Rise and Decline of Nations* (New Haven: Yale University Press, 1982) also offers a structural explanation, based on neo-classical economic analysis, as to why economies rigidify and decline. But unlike North, he does not really deal with why some countries have sustained effective economic performance while others have not. In his posthumously published *Power and Prosperity* (New York: Basic Books, 2000), Olson took a much wider view of the role of institutions, but North provides the more comprehensive treatment.
4. North, p. 59.

5. For perhaps the most egregious example, see Stephen F. Cohen, *Failed Crusade* (New York: W. W. Norton, 2000).
6. Putnam, *Making Democracy Work: Civic Traditions in Modern Italy* (Princeton, NJ: Princeton University Press, 1993).
7. Dahl, *Democracy and Its Critics* (New Haven, CT: Yale University Press, 1989), pp. 312-17. By Dahl's criteria, new democracies need at least twenty years to qualify as "mature."
8. See Joel Hellman, "Winners Take All: The Politics of Partial Reform in Postcommunist Transitions," *World Politics* (January 1998).
9. Hedlund, *Russia's "Market" Economy* (London: UCL Press, 1999).
10. See Joel Migdal, *Strong Societies and Weak States: State-Society Relations and State Capabilities in the Third World* (Princeton, NJ: Princeton University Press, 1988), for descriptions of the weak state and explanations of its origins and persistence.
11 Robert Cottrell, *Financial Times*, June 8, 2001.
12. Kovalev, "Putin's War," *New York Review of Books*, February 10, 2000; and Bonner, "The Remains of Totalitarianism," *New York Review of Books*, March 8, 2001.
13. Yavlinskii, "Vremya nazad," *Obshchaya gazeta*, February 14, 2001.

18

Odom's Russia: A Forum

Martin Malia, Jack F. Matlock, Jerry F. Hough,
Geoffrey Hosking, Alexey K. Pushkov, Robert Legvold,
Henry Trofimenko and William E. Odom*

Martin Malia:

In the bogged-down debate about post-Communist Russia's tribulations, William Odom has the merit of clearly identifying the chief villain of the story: "seven decades of Soviet rule are mostly to blame . . . not the West." Among works written as if Yeltsin's "young reformers" had inherited a thriving society from communism, he appropriately calls Stephen F. Cohen's *Failed Crusade* "egregious." The same must be said of Peter Reddaway's *Tragedy of Russia's Reforms*, which places the blame on "Thatcherite market bolshevism" (sic!).

---

*Martin Malia is a professor of history (emeritus) at the University of California, Berkeley, and is author of *Russia Under Western Eyes: From the Bronze Horseman to the Lenin Mausoleum* (2001). Jack F. Matlock, Jr. was formerly U.S. Ambassador to the Soviet Union. Jerry F. Hough is James B. Duke Professor of Political Science at Duke University and the author, most recently, of *The Logic of Economic Reform in Russia* (Brookings Institution). Geoffrey Hosking is Leverhulme Research Professor in Russian History, School of Slavonic & East European Studies, University College, London, and author of *Russia and the Russians: A History* (Harvard University Press, 2001). Alexey K. Pushkov is a member of the Russian Council on Foreign and Defense Policies and the anchor of Postscript, a news and analysis program aired on Russian Television Channel 3. He also serves as a member of the editorial board of *The National Interest*. Robert Legvold is professor of political science at Columbia University. Henry Trofimenko is a senior researcher at the Institute for the Study of the USA and Canada, Moscow. William E. Odom is a senior fellow at the Hudson Institute and an adjunct professor of political science at Yale University and served as director of the National Security Agency from 1985 to 1988. This forum first appeared in *The National Interest*, No. 66 (Winter 2001/02).

Odom is again right to claim that it is not enough to decree neo-liberal economic measures to create a true market economy, or to hold a few elections to produce a genuine democracy. For a successful market democracy, a strong institutional foundation is necessary: "rules for deciding who rules," guaranteed individual freedoms, an independent judiciary, stable property rights, and so on—all "deficit" items in post-Soviet Russia. Thus Putin has inherited "a mix of old and new institutions," a scaffolding of market democracy around a society still half-Soviet and with a holdover nomenklatura elite. Indeed, a decade after communism's collapse, Russian reform is clearly stuck in the mud, and the facile optimism of the days of "Boris and Bill" now appears juvenile and naïve.

At this point, however, Odom's analysis bogs down in a pessimistic version of the "Washington consensus" equation of free markets with democratic politics that he otherwise rejects. For the main burden of his article is that Russia will remain arrested in a neither-fish-nor-fowl state for decades to come, a position he argues with such plausible state-of-the-art social science models as "path dependence lock-in" (meaning set ways are hard to break) and "weak state" syndrome (meaning reformist initiatives from above cannot make any difference). On this basis, Odom concludes that it is pointless for the Bush administration to continue the Clinton administration's efforts to move Russia forward. In particular, he says, we should not treat Russia as a great power, or even take it seriously as an international actor beyond its ability to cause trouble for weak neighbors. Nor should Russia's stock of decaying nuclear weapons move us to give undue importance to such joint security efforts as the Nunn-Lugar program (though the program's first purpose is to protect us against nuclear proliferation).

It should hardly be necessary to say that the globequake of September 11 rendered these conclusions nugatory overnight. Russia is back in the game, and our ally to boot. Yet even without that spectacular reversal, Odom's argument fails for the more fundamental reason that his social science lacks proper historical grounding. His gold standard for measuring progress is the usual one: that most lucky of modern European nations, insular England in 1688. Albion then "broke out of its old institutional pattern based on absolute monarchy" thereby finding its "effective economic path," one "that *also took hold in Holland* (my emphasis) at about the same time. Meanwhile, France [and] Spain . . . remained . . . chained to absolutist institutional arrangements . . . trailing the booming English and Dutch economies for the next three centuries." This simply will not do, even as a rudimentary summary of how Europe modernized.

The first "modern" economy was obviously seventeenth-century Holland (building on the antecedents of medieval Northern Italy and Flanders), for which Jan de Vries' prize-winning *The First Modern Economy* (1997) gives the full story. Throughout the century, moreover, the English imitated the Dutch—

as in the creation of a national bank—not the other way around. And in 1688 the *Stadtholder* of Holland, William of Orange, mounted the English throne with the aid of Dutch and French Huguenot troops in order to contain Europe's premier power, France. Thus, with Dutch help, Britain was set on its way to becoming, by the mid-18th century, the continent's leading model for what we now call "modernity."

These remarks are no pedantic quibble about remote events without relevance to twenty-first century conditions. Rather, these developments defined the Atlantic matrix out of which modernization, both institutional and economic, later came to Central and Eastern Europe. Indeed, among the earliest sovereigns to take the cue was Peter the Great, in 1697–98. Significantly, he went first to advanced Holland and only later to William III's more recent dominion, England. So St. Petersburg came to be laid out in imitation of Amsterdam; and Peter for a time considered making Dutch the official language of his empire (William said the Czar spoke it "like a Dutch sailor").

Similarly, and in fact somewhat earlier, the Great Elector of Brandenburg-Prussia had imported Dutch craftsmen and Huguenot exiles to develop his backward realm; and later the Stein-Hardenberg Reforms introduced into Prussia a watered-down version of the French Revolution's innovations. As for Russia, from Alexander II's Great Reforms of the 1860s down to Sergei Witte's industrialization of the 1890s and his Duma Constitution of 1905, it was successfully plodding its way to both the economic and the institutional foundations of a more open order, this despite a notable "path dependence" of autocracy and serfdom—progress annulled by seventy years of communist pseudo-modernization.

The great social science model for this West-East dynamic of development is, of course, given by Alexander Gerschenkron in his *Economic Backwardness in Historical Perspective* (1962). Its central thesis is that backward societies modernize not by retracing their predecessors' exact steps, but by compressing and telescoping them through state action from above: *ergo* Peter, Alexander II and Witte; and, in his perverse and ultimately disastrous way, Stalin.

Could it be, then, that the new Petersburg boy, Vladimir Putin, is contemplating a Petrine-like leap to lift Russia out of its present humiliation? This is surely suggested by the way he was energized by September 11 to face down his stuck-in-the-mud military and gamble his Kremlin tenancy on the West. Witness the ardor of his embrace of Bush, his Lorelei song to the German Bundestag, and his economic wooing of the European Union in Brussels—all this at a time the Russian economy is at last picking up. It is most unlikely that such radical defiance of his earlier domestic base is merely a Potemkin ploy to lull us again into naiveté. So perhaps Russia's "path dependence lock-in" is not as tight as Odom thinks. And perhaps the organic coupling of the market and democracy may yet turn out to have merit, even in darkest Muscovy.

Jack F. Matlock, Jr.:

General Odom tells us that Russia is not a great power, probably cannot be one for a very long time, and therefore should not be treated as one. He does not, however, explain what a "great power" is in today's world, or how U.S. behavior should be influenced by the power hierarchy he imputes to the international scene. He implies that since Russia is no longer a great power it should be sharply demoted in significance, since its willingness and ability to support American interests are limited and its ability to harm those interests is not much greater.

Odom's perception of the world, of Russia, and of American interests differs from mine. The world I see is one in which states are no longer the sole players (if they ever were). It is a world in which non-state actors have seized part of the stage, acting sometimes as tools, sometimes as partners, but sometimes also as scourges of governments and the states they rule. It is a world in which success and failure do not depend entirely or even primarily on the size of a country, or its military strength, or the affluence of its population, or any other single factor—or, for that matter, on any simple combination of factors. States can be comparatively powerful in some respects and weak in others. In today's world, it is impossible to conjure up some litmus test that will usefully distinguish a "great power" from other states. One must first ask, "Power for what?"

Presumably, the power that is relevant to U.S. foreign policy is that which can affect American interests. Defining these interests and assigning priorities among them is a tricky exercise on which reasonable people can disagree. Nevertheless, one interest normally trumps all others: the defense of a country's territory against attack from abroad. On that score Russia is more likely to help than harm the United States, and these days we need all the help we can get.

Don't forget: The Cold War ended with Russia's help. (The Soviet Union was not Russia writ large but a Communist empire that Russia's leaders helped demolish.) When the Soviet Union disappeared from the geopolitical map, the United States became the unchallenged military power in the world, so much so that other states could no longer pose a plausible threat to American territory. Only non-state actors—terrorist networks, to be precise—can do that, by employing forms of asymmetrical warfare that operate below America's deterrence capabilities. The sort of defenses and alliances that were necessary during the Cold War have become of limited utility in dealing with the new threat. Russia, however, irrespective of its success or lack thereof in creating a stable, democratic society, was and remains relevant. It has been a target of these same malign forces and its geographic location provides indispensable assets for combating the most direct threat to American security.

That is why, ultimately, debating whether Russia is a "great power" is a pointless exercise. We need cooperation with Russia to secure our most fundamental security interests. If such cooperation were not in Russia's interest it would be futile (or too costly to other interests) to try to enlist it, but it is in Russia's interest. It would be irresponsible to reject security cooperation with Russia just because it has not yet and may never mirror image our own political and economic institutions.

I do agree with General Odom that past U.S. policy toward Russia has been mistaken, but the mistake was not the one he cites. The very limited economic support the United States offered Russia could not have been decisive in creating a transformation that at best will take more than a generation and, for better or for worse, it was not the most important element of Clinton administration policy.[1] Far more important, mostly for worse, were other decisions: NATO enlargement; bombing Serbia without Security Council approval; and the erratic use of military force to solve problems for which force was ill suited.

The fundamental flaw in Clinton administration policy was the absence of a strategy to meet the challenges of the post-Cold War world. Too many obsolescent Cold War practices were continued. American economic and military strength fed the illusion that the United States was invulnerable and could use its military forces to whatever purpose it chose so long as it limited American casualties. The administration failed to build the sort of alliances needed to meet the terrorist threat and dissipated American power by intervening in disputes with little relevance to its security, but that created or nurtured pockets of determined and dangerous enemies.

Finally, General Odom exaggerates Russia's current defects. His is the attitude of a hanging judge prepared to accept any allegation of wrongdoing as valid, while ignoring contradictory or qualifying facts. Indeed, the caricature General Odom draws of current conditions in Russia forms a precarious platform for his confident predictions. That caricature is reminiscent of others based on partial evidence and the "straight-lining" of temporary trends out into the distant future. Examples abound: the predictions in the 1970s that Japan would outstrip the United States in GDP by the 1990s; the "new paradigm" theorists' overblown projections of stock market valuation during the price bubble in technology stocks just a few years back; and the estimates, right through the 1980s, that Communist Party rule in the Soviet Union was so entrenched that it could not be seriously undermined from within. The prediction that Russia is "trapped" into some "weak state" syndrome has no more logical validity than one positing that Russia will gradually adapt its institutions to support a capitalist economy and an open society.

Neither outcome is inevitable, but several things should be clear. One is that only the Russians themselves can build the institutions and develop the attitudes they will need to fulfill their potential in a globalizing world. The second is that it is in the interest of the United States, its allies in Europe and the entire world that Russia becomes a full and responsible member of the civilized world community. The third is that U.S. policy can influence developments in Russia at least at the margins. Russia is much more likely to become a modern, productive and friendly state if its leaders see the country's future served by close association with western Europe and the United States. But they are likely to sustain that view only if the United States and its allies take Russian interests into account and cooperate in dealing with common problems.

This is not a prescription for treating Russia as an exception, or for excusing those shortcomings still apparent in its governance and some of its actions, but only for continuing policies that have proven successful in the past in other cases. We did not exclude Portugal, Spain, or Turkey from NATO membership on grounds that they were no longer "great powers" or that they were insufficiently democratic. The fact that Portugal was a member of the Western alliance played an important role in the evolution of a stable democracy when Antonio Salazar passed from the scene. Spain's basing agreements with the United States while General Franco was still running a fascist dictatorship helped rather than hindered the subsequent inclusion of Spain in NATO and the establishment of democratic institutions there. Would we or Turkey be better off today if we had refused to ally ourselves with that country because its armed forces razed Kurdish villages and intervened in Cyprus? In fact, the U.S.-Turkish alliance has helped preserve a secular government in Ankara and has encouraged political solutions in Kurdistan and Cyprus. Are there not useful lessons here when we consider relations with a Russia that, like the United States, faces the threat of terrorist attack?

General Odom wrote "Realism About Russia" before September 11 and, to be fair to him, I have written my critique as I would have on September 10, 2001, not going beyond views I have expressed publicly for nearly a decade. Let the reader judge whether the world today better fits his concept of realism or my perception of reality.

Jerry F. Hough:

For those of us who were engaged in debate with General Odom twenty years ago, his recent article in *The National Interest* brings a smile to the lips. Then, too, he was convinced that the Soviet present and future were determined by its past. Then, of course, he saw the Soviet Union as a strong state, dominated by its military and driven by that military to world domination. The dovish argument that the Soviet elite "only" wanted defense and equality with the West he denounced as naiveté; the possibility that social forces within the Soviet Union would produce evolution he dismissed out of hand.

As General Odom sees it, Russia is still incapable of any improvement or evolution, but now it is eternally a weak state, and its military officers are absorbed only with personal gain. None has any sense of national pride, professionalism or desire either for defense or national expansion. Defense against a rising China no longer occupies the thinking of any Russian, although in the past the historic fear of Tatars was said to make all Russians paranoid about China.

There is no question about the policy of Russia's current rulers. Anatoly Chubais, along with other Leningraders like Putin working with him, simply use the state to steal. These men do not seek economic growth because domestic stagnation gives them more oil, fertilizer, and natural resources to export, and they can easily receive a percentage of the proceeds for their personal gain. They do not invest their money at home, but keep it safely abroad.

In the short run, at least, this development is much more advantageous to American foreign policy than General Odom acknowledges. The United States can and does bribe Russian leaders to accept virtually anything—the expansion of NATO, an American sphere of influence in Serbia or Uzbekistan, assistance in Afghanistan, modification of the ABM Treaty, and so forth. The United States should not be criticized for sugarcoating what it is doing by treating Russia as a great power; that is, after all, a small price to pay for the privilege of suborning Russia's national interest.

The most fundamental problem with General Odom's analysis, however, is that it lacks perspective on the very long and difficult process of the development of markets and constitutional democracy. What we call corruption is a key part of this process, for it builds a network of people in different elite groups who have an interest in property rights, and in a government that both promotes economic growth and restrains the ruler. If a businessman brings a politician and a military officer into his project, then the government will protect and promote growth for personal reasons, and the military will support it. Members of the elite will support property rights so they can retain their wealth after they leave office, and so that their children can inherit it.[2]

But such investment-oriented corruption must be broadly based to be a positive factor in development. In Russia, major corruption has been too narrowly concentrated. Broad corruption has been limited to forms such as bribes that are dependent on a person remaining in office. The military let the Soviet system fall because its leaders had received none of the economic benefits of an American junior officer. Yeltsin's allowing the top generals to "privatize" the Ministry of Defense dachas in 1991 was crucial. The failure of Putin to bring Russian officials and military officers into the kind of development-centered corruption found in other Third World countries makes the Putin regime very susceptible to a military coup unless it changes its economic policy.

The notion that well-educated Russians cannot have China's rate of economic growth is silly. Douglass North, whom General Odom misinterprets, and Joseph Stiglitz, who just received a Nobel Prize, were directing their fire at the policy of Larry Summers at the Treasury Department, at his faith in neo-liberal economics and at the Russian leadership's willingness to adopt this policy in order to receive Western money. North and Stiglitz rightly said that this policy was totally inappropriate for market building. The policy will go down with pre-1941 Comintern support for Hitler as a classic case of the ability of dogmatic ideology to cause human suffering on a massive scale.

But just as the failure of Russian reform was the product of policy, so a change of policy can produce a different outcome. If the Russians adopt the advice of Alexander Gerschenkron and Joseph Stiglitz, if they re-adopt the policies of Nicholas II and Count Sergei Witte, they too can and will have rapid and stable growth. There are too many in the civilian and military elite with a vital personal interest in that development for it to be postponed for much longer.

We lose perspective about time when we live through torturous periods. We forget that thirteen years passed between the Declaration of Independence and General Washington's inauguration. We don't discuss the fact that the Constitutional Convention was the result of Washington's threatened military coup against the Continental Congress and that threats to his property rights in western Virginia were one of the factors driving him. It will be December 2004 before a similar period passes in Russia. It would be surprising if Russia were not following something like America's time framework. The determination of Russia's current rulers to keep their money abroad shows that they have a similar expectation. Let us hope that the result will be a George Washington and not the Napoleon Bonaparte produced by the nearly simultaneous French Revolution.

Geoffrey Hosking:

According to Odom, the "transition" in Russia is well and truly over. The country has become trapped in "path dependency": a vicious and ineluctable circle of corrupt authoritarian rule, economic stagnation and irresponsible behavior abroad. Its government cannot collect taxes, its oligarchs drain resources out of the economy instead of investing in it, and the army tries to dominate Chechnya by violence and intimidation.

One cannot deny the verisimilitude of Odom's picture. But the inferences he draws from it smack of American arrogance and exclusivity that increasingly alarm and repel the outside world, including some of America's closest allies. According to his model, only a few virtuous countries in the world are able to combine liberal democracy with a properly functioning market economy. These depend on having institutions of the kind created in England following the "Glorious Revolution" of 1688–89 or in America after it declared independence. All other countries have "weak states" and an "ineffective economy," and are unlikely to escape from this condition since "once a country has put in place a set of institutions—formal and informal—they are difficult to change." Among their number is Russia, which differs from the others only in claiming a great power role. We should reveal that claim to be hollow and abandon our attempts to integrate Russia into major international institutions. Thus Odom.

Odom derives his notion of "path dependency" from Douglass North, who has indeed made a major contribution to economics by demonstrating that political and social institutions play decisive roles in generating sustained growth. But it is caricaturing North's work for Odom to draw such heavily determinist conclusions from it, and doing so suggests an exclusivist Anglo-American version of modernization and globalization that threatens the stability of societies when thoughtlessly applied—as it often is nowadays. Countries can modernize in different ways, and with different institutions. France, as Odom notes, did not in the 18th century adopt the same institutions as did England in the Glorious Revolution; nevertheless, despite the destructive wars fought on its territory over two centuries, it did not get mired in "path dependency." The French economy today is at least as prosperous and productive as that of Britain, and its democracy is no less stable. The same could be said of several other European countries as diverse as Italy, Germany and Sweden.

Russia's economic performance during the first post-Soviet decade has unquestionably been very disappointing. However, it could be argued that it was precisely adherence to an Americanized model of development, imposed through the IMF, that best explains the failure. I would not take that argument too far, since the Soviet legacy would have been difficult to overcome in any event. But it is worthy of note that Russia's economic performance has improved markedly since the crash of 1998 and its *dis*engagement from some IMF-sponsored programs. Russia's potential was and is considerable. Its resources are abundant and still insufficiently mobilized. Furthermore, despite the degradation of the last decade, it still has a relatively low-paid and highly skilled workforce, well-qualified professional staffs, and a science and technology base capable of being restored to its previous high international level. This is a combination of resources not commonly found in foundering Third World economies.

Odom's accusation that Russia plays an irresponsible and unconstructive role in world affairs is also overdone. Its record is far from irreproachable: the brutality of Russia's attempt to subdue Chechnya has created massive devastation and has probably reinforced terrorism. Russia has not always behaved constructively elsewhere, either—for example, in Abkhazia (but that was at least in part because international institutions did not respond to its request for help with peacekeeping there) and in the Balkans during the lead-up to the Kosovo crisis (but that was because NATO did not genuinely consult with it about a region in which Russia has traditionally taken a close interest). But all the same, during the last fifteen years the Soviet Union and then Russia dismantled huge quantities of weapons, dissolved a military alliance, and withdrew from Afghanistan and most of central and eastern Europe, including the

Baltic states and Ukraine which were once parts of its sovereign territory. I should have thought this a record to praise.

It is true, as Odom asserts, that Russia is no longer a great world power with claims to rival the United States. It remains, however, a very significant regional power, without whose active involvement none of the major security problems of Europe or Central, North, and East Asia can be solved—not to mention international terrorism. It borders on more countries that any other state in the world. Its aging and degrading nuclear arsenal is in some ways more dangerous in that condition than if it were being properly maintained and controlled. All these factors suggest that we should integrate Russia into international decision-making institutions, not dismiss it with a condescending wave of the hand.

Odom is right that there is much to be gloomy about in Russia today. But there are also countervailing factors. No one can be certain about the country's future, but writing off such a major power as one to be shunned because it is condemned to decades of the "weak state" syndrome and economic stagnation is to help generate the unfortunate situation it describes. Russians are very sensitive to insults to their honor, and they are at their most formidable when their backs are against a wall. It is much better to regard Russia as a power capable of standing up for itself, willing and able to play a responsible role in world affairs when it is treated as a potential partner. This approach may turn out to be unrewarding, but it is preferable to err in that direction than in Odom's.

Alexey K. Pushkov:

A strong trend in Western thinking about Russia rejects Winston Churchill's definition of it as "an enigma wrapped in a puzzle" in favor of a clear-cut verdict that Russia is just a failed country incapable of contributing to international order and constantly engaging in trouble-making diplomacy. This is the position taken by William Odom. If ten years ago pro-Russian enthusiasts were painting its future in blue and gold, nowadays the opposite school of thinking paints it mainly black.

General Odom praises Germany after World War II for "facing facts"; this, he asserts, helped Germany to be more easily integrated into the international order. Let us face some facts, too. Germany was made to face facts because it was defeated in a hot war and occupied by foreign powers. Russia, however, was not defeated in a war; rather, it rejected communism through its own internal evolution—to the evident amazement of the United States and others. The fact that the Soviet Union lost a cold war but not a hot one is crucial: Russia simply could not have been expected to behave or evolve as did occupied Germany or Japan.

Odom is certainly right to say that Russia is still far from being a Western-type liberal democracy. But if one compares today's Russia not with an abstract ideal, but with the reality of only ten years ago, one finds tremendous positive changes. The scope and depth of such changes are surprising for a country weighed down by ten centuries of authoritarian history and seventy years of communist rule, a country that—to repeat—has not undergone a foreign occupation to force upon it a market economy and democratic political institutions. Hence Odom's conclusion, using a phrase borrowed from Jeffrey Tayler, that Russia is fated to be "Zaire with permafrost," is neither fair nor instrumental for a realistic understanding of Russia's future. Not only does Odom ignore the slow but important progress Russia is making, but his approach to realism is limited to an exercise in building worst-case scenarios. The main burden of Odom's pessimism lies in his reading of Russia's international behavior. By focusing on Russia's ties with China, India, and Iran, Odom overlooks the most significant dimension of Russian foreign policy, its Western dimension: Russia's ever-growing ties with the European Union and its persistent movement into the world economy. President Putin's decision to support the U.S.-led coalition against terrorism is clearly based on the desire of a leading part of the Russian political class, and a growing part of the Russian public, to see Russia as part of Europe and—politically—as one with the Western world. Without a serious basis for such a pro-Western choice, President Putin would not have risked such a stand.

In real strategic terms, too, Russian assistance to the United States has been, so far (as of mid-November 2001), more important than that given by the majority of its NATO allies. Russia is the largest and one of the two most powerful nations in Eurasia, as the crisis surrounding Afghanistan made clear, even for all those who failed to notice it before. One may well compare the Russian GDP with that of the Netherlands, but when one comes to geostrategic terms the comparison stops. Can the Netherlands talk to Central Asian countries about accepting U.S. military forces on their soil, or send troops to Tajikistan to counter Taliban incursions?

Russia's role in Asia is bound to grow further in coming years as China emerges as a leading international actor. In this light, Russia's special ties with India should not be criticized but applauded, especially in the light of a possible Indian-Pakistan confrontation in which Russia as a nuclear power can exercise a sobering effect on both sides of the conflict, perhaps together with America. Finally, as the events of September-October 2001 demonstrate, Russia does not use its ties with former Soviet republics to coerce them into an anti-American policy. Russia does exercise influence on those countries, but in the same way that the United States exercises influence on its Arab allies and partners. Why should Russia be condemned for pursuing a policy similar to one adopted by the United States?

One of the reasons Russia is seen as a troublemaker in the West is that America's present strength has created a propensity—among some Americans, at least—to equate "responsible" international behavior with that which corresponds to American interests. But Russia cannot automatically espouse U.S. foreign policy interests, for two very good reasons. First, Russia's geopolitical setting requires it to deal pragmatically with a number of regimes that the United States dislikes, such as China and Iran. Second, since Russia is not a member of a U.S.-led Western alliance, and does not enjoy the shared security of NATO members or the protection of the American nuclear umbrella, it must guide itself according to a different set of security and political interests. Whether those interests will conflict or comport with those of the United States depends on U.S. foreign policy as well as on Russia's. After all, the events of September 11 have made clear that even the United States, with all its might, cannot successfully conduct a policy in Eurasia that is not based on a shared-interests approach with key countries of the continent, Russia being one of them.

While General Odom has chosen to remove Russia from the ranks of the great powers, President Bush has chosen otherwise. When President Putin offered to assist the United States in the war against terrorism, he did so not as a supplicant, but as the leader of the great power he believes Russia to be. So it was that, on October 7, 2001 President Bush called President Putin to inform him in advance about the impending U.S. strike against the Taliban. Putin took the call and offered support. Could they both have been wrong?

Robert Legvold:

Although the point may not come through clearly, the essential issue raised by Bill Odom's essay is whether—for good or ill—Russia matters to the United States. He says, for the most part, no; but where it does matter it does so largely for ill. If Odom has reached the wrong conclusion, it is because either the argument is wrong or it is the wrong argument (or perhaps both). Let us begin with the argument.

Few observers, either in Russia or on the outside, would disagree with Odom's judgment that Russia's problems flow from its sad transformation into a "weak state." Nor would there be disagreement over the hurdles obstructing its escape. Disagreement would begin over how hopeless the prospects are. Odom settles for a rather wooden and simple dictum for why Russia will not shake free. His theory notwithstanding, if Russia does progress, it is likely to do so in small steps that begin to salvage the state, cleanse and strengthen key institutions such as the judiciary, put in place supports and practices that facilitate sustainable growth, and work around retrograde special interests.

Over the last two years, significant progress along these lines—albeit partial and incremental—has occurred. Nothing guarantees that this advance will reach critical mass, propelling Russia on to a swift and secure path to democracy and a revitalized economy. Odom could yet be right (and not only about Russia, but about a majority of the post-Soviet states), but the fragmentary trends of the moment remind us that path dependency works two ways. It may also lead Russia out of its hole. A prudent judge would pause and await more evidence before deciding.

The other half of Odom's argument raises sharper objections. Again, few analysts in the United States would disagree that Russian behavior at times, in places, and on certain problems has been "unconstructive," perhaps intentionally so. This is true of the way it has dealt with its immediate neighbors, sold nuclear technologies, pursued cooperation with states from China to Cuba, and reacted to NATO enlargement, national missile defense and other pet American ideas.

To treat this as the whole story, however, does considerable violence to the truth. Russia has also been capable of constructive behavior, even, at times, when in a larger context we have seen it as unconstructive, such as the ultimate role that it played in the 1999 Kosovo crisis. Long before September 11, and in many respects—from its dealings with North Korea on the nuclear issue to the dialogue with the European Union; from its long-standing collaboration with the United States on Afghanistan to its handling of Ukrainian debt—Russian actions, by any fair-minded judgment, have been constructive. Russia's behavior has been neither uniformly disruptive nor impervious to the influence of other states, including positive U.S. incentives when, on occasion, they have been offered. Odom's claim that Russia's waywardness stems from inherent political and psychological factors unsusceptible to U.S. influence is, at best, debatable.

Whatever one thinks of the accuracy of Odom's argument, however, the more serious drawback derives from its questionable utility or aptness. Russia matters to the United States not because it is a great power now but because it remains a significant factor on the world stage. To wind ourselves around our own axle over whether Russia should or should not be treated as a "great power" misses the point. Russia is not a distant tenth planet. It is located at the heart of the crucial landmass between Europe and Asia. Not only is this part of the world blessed with more natural wealth than any other, it also contains the potential for some of its gravest instability. Russia's fate and its actions remain the single most decisive factor determining the impact that the post-Soviet space will have on us all.

Not that Russia's 45 percent share of the world's nuclear weapons does not also matter, and is hardly to be written off as Odom suggests, while the United States unilaterally attempts to design a new strategic nuclear regime. Not that the role that we have discovered for Russia in the new overriding struggle against global terrorism ought not also to be in the picture. But the kind of relationship that we, the Europeans, Chinese, and Japanese work out with

Russia for coping with the challenges (or benefiting from the opportunities) in the netherworlds between NATO-Europe and Russia, and in the Caucasus and Central Asia, will shape the peace of mind and welfare of the two arenas that do indisputably matter to the United States—Europe and East Asia. It seems unlikely to me that we will get far in building the right kind of U.S.-Russian relationship for these purposes—let alone prosper in dealing with nuclear weapons and global terrorism—if we frame the issue in terms of Russia's twisted ego or write Russia off on narrow semi-deterministic grounds, not to mention making it our goal to keep "Russia's international role to a level commensurate with its power."

Henry Trofimenko:

General Odom's analysis of the "Russian question" (which is of perennial interest to the United States) is undoubtedly very important for the new administration in Washington. With great sadness, I confess that many Russians would agree with his dissection of the problem.

The key to his analysis lies in the concepts of "path dependence" and the "weak state" syndrome. As he himself points out, the theory is not new; as applied to the USSR, in particular, it was developed by such American Sovietologists as Richard Pipes and Seweryn Bialer, both of whom argued that the Soviet regime was in most respects a continuation of the imperial Russian regime—indeed, one that saved the Russian empire. Similarly, there is much evidence to suggest that the post-Soviet Russian regime has not changed as much as many suppose, neither as a result of so-called *perestroika* or even as a result of the dissolution of the Soviet Union. The ruling class of the "new country" remains the same—the old Soviet *nomenklatura* now bedecked with new titles and new fashions. During the Soviet period this class managed the resources of the state that belonged to it collectively. Now it (mis)manages the same resources that, through the mechanisms of privatization, were distributed to members of the same ruling elite. It is too much to expect that the members of this class, who continue milking former state property for personal gain (in amounts thousands of times greater than under the *ancien régime*), would actively hamper the continual process of their personal enrichment. Thus too, sad to say, Odom is correct to suggest that nearly all the assistance that was provided to Russia from the outside world has been appropriated largely by the ruling thieves for personal gain. Regretfully, many foreign consultants, especially the Americans, used their influential positions in Moscow for similar purposes.

One may hope that a new generation of leaders soon to replace the present aging elite will change Russia's path, but it is unlikely. The simple reason is that in Russia today the same old method of co-opting persons to high government positions is at work: only those reliably devoted to personal enrichment have a chance to ascend the ladder. Meanwhile, the rotting education system makes it very difficult for those not of the traditional establishment to move up.

Every state in the world is a living organism of sorts—the longer it exists, the more its old values (habits, culture, institutions, attitudes) are consolidated. Americans were extremely lucky to start with a relatively clean slate, but even so, it took seventy-five years to ban slavery and another century to rectify its legacy. Indeed, the continuing popularity of Louis Farrakhan suggests that the full integration of blacks into American society lies still in America's future rather than in the present. The point is that cultural patterns hang heavily over new generations of citizens—if not over their leaders—and the older the state culture, the heavier the burden. To change existing ways and attitudes requires great courage and boldness from truly outstanding leaders. And even with the best of intentions and a supportive international environment, significant changes take a long time.

Odom is also correct to argue that, whatever changes might be eventually executed in Russia and in the other newly independent states (most of which are still ruled by "popularly re-elected" oriental despots), the result will not be liberal democracy as it exists in the West. The present Russian embodiment of one of the main institutions of liberal democracy—the popularly elected parliament—came into being after the previous one, also duly elected, was crushed by the "democrat Yeltsin" tank gunfire, with the connivance of President Clinton. The new one, however, is a mockery of common sense: the members of its upper chamber are now appointed by the Russian president, and democratically-elected members of the lower house—the Duma—outdo each other in their collective frenzy to demonstrate absolute loyalty to the "higher authority," the un-elected Kremlin clique. This is the continuing heritage of ages of Russian history.

All that said, General Odom has trouble finding his ballast when discussing the particularities of contemporary Russian politics.

First, freedom of the media really does exist in Russia for the first time in hundreds of years, the insinuations of media magnates like Messrs. Berezovsky and Gusinsky notwithstanding. The regular, unhampered publication of such rabidly anti-government weeklies as *Zavtra and Duel*, as well as the daily rebroadcasts of the U.S. *Radio Liberty* on domestic Russian fm frequencies, confirms this fact. Media freedom is curtailed to a certain extent, but not because of official censorship or other restrictions. Rather, in contrast to the U.S. experience, the private ownership of most newspapers and TV stations mitigates against objectivity because the media is used in turf struggles among elite factions.

Second, the dyed-in-the-wool democrats like Sergei Kovalev and Elena Bonner now have zero influence in Russian politics. Grigorii Yavlinskii, who exists on foreign donations, is just a political chatterbox who surpasses even the superdemagogue, Mikhail Gorbachev, in his irrelevance to current events.

Third, Russia, despite its predicament, remains a great power by the fact of its still tremendous (if mismanaged) economic potential, its political influence in Eurasia and its place on the UN Security Council. Moreover, if Russia's leaders abandon their rhetorical flourishes in favor of real talks on the future of the ABM Treaty (as Defense Minister Sergei Ivanov has recently suggested), Russia's international image will certainly improve—as it has already by dint of Russia's response to the events of September 11.

Fourth, the Russian military does not shun constructive reform. But its leaders do oppose idiotic non-stop reorganizations of the kind that has almost liquidated the only really battle-ready Russian force—the airborne troops. However, it is true that the immense quantity of newly created generals and admirals (through protection and patronage) continues to wreak havoc in the command structure.

Fifth and most important, while weakened, Moscow has no real desire to unleash mischief in the international arena. The tragic events of September 11, which evoked a great deal of sympathy for the United States among Russians, demonstrate that there are still convincing reasons for the United States to pursue close and constructive cooperation with Russia to achieve shared and common goals. Russia's national interests are not identical to those of the United States, but that hardly makes Russia different from, say, France, as far as U.S. foreign policy is concerned. Or have some of us still not gotten over the bad habits of the Cold War?

William Odom Replies:

Let me thank all the respondents for their commentaries. To generalize about them, they agree with most of what I say about Russia's institutional development and economic performance, but they either do not like the way I reach my conclusions or do not like the conclusions themselves—occasionally both.

Because Professor Malia's reaction is the most interesting and complex, a proper reaction to it requires "more than a pedantic quibble" about his reading of Russian history. By his account, Russia has always been about fifty years behind Europe. By 1785, its nobility achieved institutions like France's *ancien régime*. The Great Reforms in the 1860s brought Russia up to Prussia's reforms of 1807–12. And the October Manifesto of 1905 was virtually a constitutional breakthrough. This interpretation is not universally accepted. The late Michael Florinsky would reject Malia's assertion that the Charter of the Nobility of 1785 instituted property rights in Russia similar to those in France at that time. Stefan Hedlund would probably deny that such rights were observed in Russia a century later. The Prussian reformers built on longstanding legal institutions deriving from Justinian's Code. Russia first introduced European code law in 1864. Ignoring key institutional realities, Malia can feel much cheerier about Russia's prospects.[3]

That is one reason he is so upset that I put the seventeenth century English experience before the Dutch. Indeed, the Dutch economic take-off was somewhat earlier than England's, but that does not damage my argument. Political power in the Dutch provinces rested on the wealth of their towns, which were never fully subordinated by an absolute monarch, as was the case in England and France.[4] The wealthy cities of southern Germany might have put that region on the Dutch path if they had not been weakened by princely wars against Charles V, the Holy Roman Emperor, and later devastated by the Thirty Years War.[5] The English case is more instructive for Russia because it involved changing absolute monarchy to limited monarchy. In Russia today, the problem is still limiting the state and making it assume the "third party enforcer" role.[6] Can "the Petersburg boy" accomplish this in less than five decades?

I agree with Malia that Russia must turn West because it is welcome nowhere else. Our difference is over Russian institutional realities, a matter on which there is still much to be discovered.

Turning to Ambassador Matlock, although he does not really challenge my analytical scheme, he does reject its implications, leaving me little to say. Since he once again complains about NATO enlargement, however, I must recall his oft-made prediction that it would bring the worst people to power in Russia. Presumably, then, Putin is an awful fellow who should not now be cooperating with the United States.

Professor Hough's wide-ranging comments can only be treated eclectically. His recipe of widespread corruption for creating a liberal regime is a sure formula for keeping Russia locked into its present path dependency. As for his charge that I have never acknowledged change in Russia, given his own record of predictions, one should not be surprised that he failed to read mine carefully. I confine two examples to a footnote.[7] And for Russia's sake, let us hope its leaders do not heed his suggestion that they adopt the policies of Witte and Nicholas II. Nicholas died believing that the entire empire was his "patrimony," and Witte shared Nicholas' suspicion of "limited liability corporations," neither view being very helpful for economic performance.[8]

Professor Legvold correctly notes that my arguments are equally applicable to most other post-Soviet states, not just Russia, but his belief that countries can incrementally creep out of predicaments like Russia's needs a few examples to be convincing. Wars and domestic upheavals more often bring such change. On the importance of Russia to the United States today, Pakistan and Uzbekistan are more important, but that does not make them great powers or permanently important to us. By his own standard these are "arguments that are wrong, not wrong arguments." I concede a point to him, however, and other respondents. I did not believe that my points about Russia's international role ruled out all cooperation with Moscow. If they did, then Legvold is right to emphasize that we do need Russian cooperation today.

Will it last? Has it suddenly become the same as the cooperation among all G-7 members? I remain skeptical, September 11 notwithstanding.

Professor Hosking dislikes my style, not my arguments, accusing me of "American arrogance and exclusivity." He has a point. Perhaps I should have put them more softly, but the tone was meant more for Westerners than Russians. On the "exclusivity" charge I feel less vulnerable, having suggested the Meiji restoration and Kemal Atatürk's handling of Turkey as ways that Russia might escape its present path. The American "free framer" route to liberal democracy (Robert Dahl's term) is difficult to imagine for Russia.

Neither Henry Trofimenko nor Alexey Pushkov rejects my case outright. They even approve much of it. Beyond that, Trofimenko's defensive remarks about freedom of the press and certain Russian liberals reveal an understandable sensitivity. So do Pushkov's comments about Germany. Pushkov does, however, evoke my humility by reminding us how far Russia has come in such a short time, throwing off the Soviet regime by itself and making unprecedented attempts at reform. I have acknowledged as much in the Russian press, asserting that the Soviet peoples, not the United States, won the Cold War.[9]

My article is intentionally provocative, and had I been a critic of it, I would have asked me if I really believed it. My answer? I would bet on Russia remaining in its present institutional path for at least several decades. After all, look at the expectations held in 1950 or 1960 for Brazil, Indonesia, Nigeria, Peru, and other richly endowed states that have received Western tutelage and assistance. Have any of them really "made it"? Something extraordinary would have to happen to make Russia different.

One change, of course, has eased Russia's traditional predicament: most of the minority nationalities have been off-loaded. They were an obstacle that no liberal reformer could overcome, certainly not Nicholas II and Count Witte. Without the nationalities, Russia's military requirements drop drastically, another positive sign. Still, Russia's institutional legacies in property, law, and state power present monumental barriers to change. Malia can justly claim that by his fifty-year lag thesis, Russia will break them by mid-century. Because its only real alternative is to join the West, it might do so, but it could take much longer than fifty years.

Notes

1. Odom also exaggerates its extent. It was hardly "massive": the grant aid could have come out of Bill Gates' after-tax income without significantly affecting his lifestyle. The IMF infusions (at no cost to the U.S. taxpayer) were loans, half of which have already been repaid.
2. See Hough, *The Logic of Economic Reform in Russia* (Washington, DC: Brookings, 2001).
3. See Malia's *Russia Under Western Eyes* (Cambridge, MA: Harvard University Press, 1999). The cornerstone of his case may be found on page 146: "The pressure

generated by Europe's advance, combined with the drag of native backwardness, would continue to complicate Russia's way to modernity. It is the action of these two forces, not the hoary memory of the Sacred Palace of Byzantium or the Mongols' Golden Horde that constitutes the true anomaly of Russia's modern history." Grant his "two forces," but by brushing off the Mongol period, Malia ignores the persistence of key Mongol institutional legacies, particularly the deeply ingrained practice of no limits on state power and no system of private property rights. A few other Mongol legacies endured in Muscovy's secular institutions; Byzantium provided its lasting cultural institutions. See Donald Ostrowski, *Muscovy and the Mongols: Cross-cultural influences on the steppe frontier, 1304–1589* (New York: Cambridge University Press, 1999), p. 47, for this evidence. Unless Malia can dispose of Ostrowski's evidence and interpretations, his dismissal of Mongol and Byzantine institutional legacies in modern Russia is difficult to accept. See also, Michael T. Florinsky, *Russia: A History and an Interpretation* (New York: Macmillan, 1960), pp. 570–1; and Stefan Hedlund, "Can Property Rights Be Protected by Law?" *East European Constitutional Review* 10 (No. 1, 2001).

4. Jonathan I. Israel, *The Dutch Republic: Its Rise, Greatness, and Fall 1477–1806* (New York: Oxford University Press, 1995). Jan de Vries' excellent book, mentioned by Malia, is not as comprehensive on the political history as is Israel's.

5. See Thomas A. Brady, Jr., *The Protestant Politics of Jacob Sturm (1489–1553) and the German Reformation* (Atlantic Heights, NJ: Humanities Press International, 1995), for details of the politics of these cities and their struggle to keep their institutions from being destroyed by either Charles V on the one hand or the local princes on the other.

6. Charles Tilly, *Coercion, Capital, and European States, AD 990–1992* (Oxford: Blackwell, 1992), also offers historical grounding for this point.

7. In 1987, I wrote that "the paradox remains that great central control is required to achieve major decentralization of economic control and power. If Gorbachev succeeds, he will lose his centralized power to forces that could undercut the political authority of the regime to a degree that could lead to the breakup of the empire." See my "How Far Can Soviet Reform Go?" *Problems of Communism* 36 (No. 6, 1987). Hough also might want to look at my "Choice and Change in Soviet Politics," *Problems of Communism* 32 (No. 3, 1983), where I pointed out that the only problem Andropov could not put off indefinitely without systemic implications was "the declining vitality and responsiveness of the party cadres." Failing to address it was "to risk eventually greater dangers for the system—dangers of the kind that developed for the Polish party." I saw change in the USSR as political decay. Hough saw it as transformation to a pluralist system.

8. Thomas C. Owen, *The Corporation Under Russian Law: 1800-1917* (New York: Cambridge University Press, 1991). As this account shows, economic development in the last decades of the Russian Empire encountered huge institutional difficulties, but these were obscured by the impressive growth rates of that period.

9. Interview in *Argumenty i fakty* (July 1998).

19

The Higher Police

Laurent Murawiec and Clifford Gaddy*

So much has changed in Russia since the fall of the Soviet Union that it is easy to overlook some things that have not changed. One of the most significant of these constants is the continued importance of an intelligence elite that has existed within the Russian state for nearly 200 years, both as a corporate body and, more importantly, as a current of thought endowed with a distinctive identity. This elite calls itself "the Higher Police" and, as things have turned out, it is largely in charge in today's Russia.

As it happens, the historical continuity of this elite can be traced, its self-conception can be charted, and its impact on the action of the Russian state, yesterday as well as today, can be assessed. Such tasks are critical to understanding Russia and Russian foreign policy today. It is to such labors that this essay is directed.

Grafting the Roots

In 1997, the FSB (*Federal'naya Sluzhba Bezopasnosti*, or Federal Security Service), the contemporary incarnation of the Russian intelligence service—most popularly known as the KGB[1]—convened the first of what was to be a series of annual seminars on the history of the intelligence craft and intelligence organizations in Russia. Dubbed the "Historical Lectures at the Lubyanka"—since they were held at the old headquarters of the KGB—the seminars took place under the auspices of the Andropov Institute. In-house KGB historians and invited outside academics gave presentations on such sub-

*Laurent Murawiec is a senior policy analyst with the RAND Corporation, Washington, DC. His book, *L 'Esprit de Nations—Cultures et géopolitique* (The Spirit of Nations—Cultures and Geopolitics) has just been published by Odile Jacobs (Paris, 2002). Clifford Gaddy is a fellow at the Brookings Institution. He is a co-author of *Russia's Virtual Economy* (Brookings, forthcoming).

jects as "The Founding of the *Cheka*: A New View," "On the Intelligence Activity of the Russian Ministry of Foreign Affairs at the Beginning of the 20th Century," and "The Department of Police and Secret Agents (1902–1917)." Remarkably, KGB historians have been focusing on pre-1917 intelligence work and organizations. While they do not reject eighty years of Soviet intelligence history—that of the *Cheka*, the GPU, the NKVD, and the KGB[2]—their focus points to a continuous corporate identity harking back to pre-revolutionary predecessor organizations that defined themselves as a "Higher Police" that transcended ideology itself.

The modern history of the Higher Police dates back to the early 19th century. The Decembrist *putsch* of 1825 failed to overthrow the newly enthroned Czar Nicholas I. After it was put down, the Czar established a new organization that soon "became the most powerful force in the country," the Third Section of His Majesty's Own Chancellery.[3] Designed not merely as a command center for repression of subversive machinations, it was also tasked with "the study of Russia's condition." Gathering the best and the brightest of the nobility, its brief was virtually unlimited. It was subordinate to the monarch only. Such was the *vysshaya politsiya*, or, in the French preferred by the aristocracy of the time, *la haute police*. Its chief was General Count Alexander Khristoforovich Benckendorff (1783-1844), a soldier who rose from the ranks of the Baltic-German nobility that had provided so many of the Czars' servants.

Under Benckendorff's stewardship, which stretched from 1825 through 1844, the Third Section devoted itself to social engineering on a grand scale. Far from being merely a political police, it conceived of its role as "eradicating abuse" wherever it might be found in Russian society. Its 1839 report to the Czar boldly stated: "All Russia impatiently awaits changes. . . . The machine requires to be reworked afresh. The keys to this necessity are to be found in Justice and Industry. . . . [The Section is] convinced of the necessity, even of the inevitability, of the liberation of the serfs."[4] One could barely cite so explosive and sensitive an issue in the Russia of the time. Had such words been published in a journal, uttered in public, or even whispered in private—by anyone other than a member of the Third Section—it would have been cause for instant imprisonment or exile. Yet the Third Section regularly issued such reformist policy recommendations without fear. The 1838 report advocated the development of railways in Russia; the 1841 report called for special attention to public health; the 1842 report advocated lowering tariffs to foster economic development. The Section's Annual Reports on the State of Public Opinion were the Czar's eyes and ears. (While these extraordinary reports have in general been available to historians, their import has not been properly understood. As "police" reports, they are only of passing interest; as traces of the Higher Police's social engineering ambitions, they are of primordial importance.)

The Third Section represented the emergence of a technocratic elite that pursued its mission of serving the Russian state from within and with the use of "enlightened" methods of social control and engineering. They were not a gaggle of thugs, or the jackbooted shock troops of autocratic repression. They conceived of themselves as the best, purest and most loyal servants of "a certain idea of Russia," and it is a concept that set deep roots.

It recurred several decades later in the 1870s, when the reformist course followed by the "czar-liberator" Alexander II faltered and terrorists besieged the regime. In a desperate bid to regroup, reorganize and streamline the forces of counter-revolution to defend the tottering regime, the Czar nominated General Prince Mikhail T. Loris-Melikov as head of the Third Section.

The prince, an Armenian warlord who had met signal success as commander of the Army of the Caucasus, applied liberal "techniques" to a difficult situation. He enlarged public liberties in the hope of rallying the enlightened segments of public opinion. The slogan that inspired and symbolized Loris-Melikov's policy was a call for a "dictatorship of the heart." (It seems that even in matters of the heart, Russians cannot do without dictatorship.) Loris-Melikov soon acquired and exercised sweeping powers, virtually controlling all aspects of government except foreign policy, to the point of being nicknamed the "vice-czar" by Russian-society.[5] Still, this could not save the Czar's life: Alexander II was brutally assassinated in 1883 and the short-lived "liberal era" came to an end. The Third Section was soon replaced by the "security section," the *okhrannoye otdeleniye*, or Okhrana.

In sharp contradistinction to the "enlightened" rule of Loris-Melikov, a powerful group of aristocrats advocating instead a regime of brutal repression organized their own form of support for the threatened autocracy. Representing a temporary abandonment of the social engineering ethos, and organized as a secret society, these families formed a quasi-military "volunteer guard" of more than 10,000 in the name of and for the sake of protecting the Czar. They called themselves the "Sacred Brotherhood" (Svyashchennaya Druzhina), an allusion to the medieval Russian lords' and princes' elite guards, or bands of companions, the Druzhina. The Brotherhood also operated an international intelligence apparatus that later became the seed-crystal for the Okhrana's own foreign department.

In a way, the Brotherhood was too successful. The ferocious policies it advocated were adopted in full by the new Czar Alexander III and his influential adviser, the Procurator of the Holy Synod of the Russian Orthodox Church, Konstantin Pobedonostsev, who has been called, not without reason, the most influential reactionary in Russian history. Moreover, the Brotherhood's independent strength bothered Pobedonostsev as the ideologue of a supreme Czardom. As a result of Pobedonostsev's ascendancy, however, the Czar dissolved the Brotherhood. Its heritage nevertheless lived on in the later establishment of the violent, militantly anti-Semitic "Black Hundred" organization (the Chernaya Sotnya)—the forerunner of modern Russian fascism.

If the Sacred Brotherhood represented both the high nobility and the brutality of the Russian intelligence elite, the figure of Colonel Sergei Zubatov (1863-1917) stands for the return of social engineering of the highest sophistication. Originally a revolutionary student who was "turned," Zubatov rose meteorically to become the head of the Moscow Okhrana, where he applied refined methods comparable to "brainwashing" for turning revolutionists into Okhrana agents. In the end, his police organization controlled much of the Russian Left's political organizations, even up to the leadership level. Father Georgi Gapon, the priest and labor organizer who led the early phases of the 1905 Revolution, was originally Zubatov's agent.

Zubatov single-handedly created Russia's trade-union movement. As his biographer put it, "The idea of a pure monarchy . . . [as] the sole force working for the common good" guided him, the aim being the "taming of the bourgeoisie. . . [and] gaining the favors of the workers and the peasants." What mattered was "not so much the statics of autocracy as its dynamics." Zubatov's inspiration in his effort to "re-educate Russian society"—re-engineer it, that is—was that "the free Russian people do not wish their country to become another France or United States." The innate desire of the Russians, he believed, was the fulfillment of "the Russian Idea." To that end, Zubatov advocated paternalistic governance over the working masses, to include better working conditions, healthcare, social security benefits, and so on—all to be gouged out of the industrialists. His doctrine, though not explicitly socialist, was strongly anti-capitalist.[6]   It was, in a way, a kind of coerced *noblesse oblige.*

World War I derailed Zubatov's plan. It changed not only the rules of the game but the game itself. Once again, history overwhelmed the careful design of the enlightened intelligence elite. No amount of social engineering could contain Russia's chaotic transformation. When news of the February 1917 Revolution reached the retired Zubatov in his Petersburg home, he committed suicide.

The Higher Police under Bolshevism and Beria

The new era posed the strongest challenge yet to the very survival of the upper-nobility elite notion of the Higher Police. How could their self-conception as the best and the brightest, the servants of Russia according to the Druzhina ideal, the social engineers and master manipulators, endure under Bolshevik rule? Of course, many creatures of the old Okhrana did survive and prosper under the new regime. Countless former agents—Stalin being most probably one of them—were now on the loose, in leadership positions in the Soviet Communist Party and the state apparatus. In addition, members of the "Black Hundreds" flocked into the Bolshevik Party; the anti-capitalist, anti-Western, anti-liberal outlook of proto-fascist mass movements like the Black Hundreds easily accommodated the Bolsheviks' own ideology, while the latter welcomed the aroused masses in their own ranks. As a result, many senior Okhrana functionaries joined the newly established Bolshevik secret police, the "Extraordinary Commission" (Cheka).

It was clear that the functions ascribed by Lenin to the new Cheka had less to do with social engineering than with social deconstruction by means of the extermination of non-approved social categories. The Cheka's incentive structure emphasized murder, torture, brutality and atrocities of all stripes, not sociological investigation. The Higher Police yielded to another current, which has also recurred throughout Russian history: the sheer violence exerted by the state against all, the war by government against society. Just as Ivan the Terrible's personal guard, the Oprichniki, had visited unspeakable brutality upon nobles and the general populace during the sixteenth century, Lenin's Oprichniki slaughtered millions of Russians with little regard for higher-police methods. "Cruelty is the Russians' principal trait," Maxim Gorky once wrote.

Still, even in this most brutal chapter of the history of the Russian secret services, there is evidence of the less coercive, social-engineering approach to the intelligence function. Interestingly, the founder of the first Bolshevik security organization after Lenin's putsch of October-November 1917 was not, as is often assumed, Feliks Dzerzhinsky, the Savonarola of mass-murder—it was rather Lenin's old friend and confidante, V. I. Bonch-Bruyevich, a professional anthropologist.[7] Although a shroud of secrecy still surrounds the inner workings of Soviet intelligence in its initial period (from 1917 through 1939), there was a full-fledged social science research department inside the NKVD, at least in the 1930s. Staffed by sociologists, economists, anthropologists and others, it was tasked to study and report independently—independently of both party and NKVD hierarchies—on the state of affairs in the Soviet Union, including the morale of the population. A very unusual freedom of thought reportedly prevailed within the unit.[8]

A more critical development in the historical continuity of the Russian intelligence services took place in the 1940s. Dzerzhinsky and his ferocious successors, Genrikh Yagoda and Nikolai Yezhov, who organized the purges of the 1930s that resulted in the death of millions, were primarily concerned with terror as the principal means of government. This changed when Stalin appointed his fellow Georgian, Lavrentii Beria, to head the NKVD in 1939.

Beria was no boy scout, to be sure, but neither was he a monster. Indeed, his once execrable reputation has been thoroughly revised in Russia in recent times. The traditional portrayal of a bloodthirsty psychopath and monstrous sex maniac has been replaced by a "new Beria." The new narrative relies in large part on the memoir of Beria written by his son, missile engineer Sergo Beria. It is an extraordinary book whose center stage is the inner recesses of Soviet power under Stalin.[9] The version of the elder Beria displayed there is of a Georgian who is not a Communist, a senior party leader who loathes Communist ideology and who places efficiency and rationality above all other values.

In truth, Beria did save the lives of many top Soviet scientists and technologists otherwise doomed by Stalin's crass repression. These included the nuclear scientist Igor Kurchatov, the aircraft designer Andrei Tupolev, and many others who were often employed in the jail-laboratories—the "luxury" Gulag for scientists, the famed *sharaga*. During World War II, Stalin entrusted Beria with leading the Soviet crash program to develop nuclear weapons. Beria delivered. He rallied the scientific and technological intelligentsia in part by effectively protecting it. Further, he created within his Ministry of the Interior (MVD) a string of research institutes. The mission of these think tanks was to elaborate full sets of policies, both domestic and international. As was later claimed, Beria wanted supreme power, and to that end he prepared alternative policies. A foreign policy proposing a neutralized Germany as the first step to drive a wedge between Europe and the United States is one of the best-known planks in Beria's program.

"Enlightened" and pragmatic though he was, Beria lost out in the power struggles that followed Stalin's death, and was executed by the Politburo. In all likelihood, Beria, who terrified all the other Soviet leaders, fell victim to a coalition of the frightened. Nikita Khrushchev, who ended up as the head of the coalition that eliminated Beria, reduced the size of the "organs"—the secret police in Soviet parlance—lest they threaten again to take over the system as a whole. But the ideas, plans, and programs that had been associated with Beria kept resurfacing in the Soviet Union for thirty years and more after his death: the debate over economic decentralization identified with economists Yevsei Liberman and Vadim Trapeznikov; the Kosygin policy of giving more power to enterprise directors; and the liberation of political prisoners (Beria had halved the number of concentration camp inmates, *zeks*, in the late 1940s). Beria protégés kept on rising, too; Dimitri Ustinov as defense minister was but one example.

The rise of KGB head Yuriy Andropov (1914-1984) under Khrushchev's successor, Leonid Brezhnev, heralded a new era in the history of the Higher Police. Early in his reign, Andropov summoned Sergo Beria to his office and, according to the latter, told him: "Sergo, I've studied your father's file, the materials and the policy: they're good and I'm going to implement them." It was Andropov who turned to the Siberian branch of the Academy of Sciences, to the prestigious research institutes associated with it, and thus to some of the country's brightest minds: Tatiyana Zaslavskaya of the Institute of Sociology in Novosibirsk, Abel Aganbegyan and his Institute for the Study of Industrial Organization, Leonid Abalkin and the Institute of Economics. [10] He asked them, often personally, to devise new policies and new strategies to save the Soviet system. In effect, Andropov asked these scientists (who were generally not members of the KGB themselves) to do the think tanking for the new course he was plotting—perestroika. The top-down transformation envisioned by Andropov was perhaps the apex of Russian *hubris* in matters of social engineering; not only was the country going to be turned upside down and its economy thoroughly restructured by a self-appointed leadership, but the country was not even going to be told about the plan.

Only Andropov's unexpected death and the premature elevation of a leader who commanded little following and loyalty forced the matter into the open. Mikhail Gorbachev appended glasnost to perestroika as the substitute for the authority Andropov could have wielded through the intelligence and security apparatus. The rest is, as they say, history.

The Post-Communist Higher Police

The Soviet Union crashed as soon as the regime center's coercive resolve failed it. The Communist Party, which revealed itself as nothing but a coalition of rent-seekers leveraging power for its member's own ends, crashed too. The once almighty State Planning Commission—the Gosplan—that monument to artificial, arbitrary mismanagement, vanished. Deprived of their right to claim a permanent blood transfusion from the economy, the armed forces faltered. What survived amid all this wreckage, despite the shrinking of its perimeter and the escape and removal of whole areas of national life from its brief, was the intelligence service. Overcoming a brief initial period of shock and disarray from the old regime's collapse, the intelligence elite has by all indications steadily regrouped throughout the 1990s, both within government and the newly formed private sector.

By 1998, the intelligence elite emerged openly into positions of authority, especially in the presidential apparatus. To mention but a few examples, Sergey Ivanov, Putin's Minister of Defense, spent 18 years in the KGB-FSB. Oleg Chernov, Deputy Secretary of the Security Council; Aleksandr Manzhosin (First Deputy Head of the President's Directorate for Foreign Policy), Igor Sechin (Putin's chief secretary and deputy chief of the Kremlin administration) and Viktor Ivanov (deputy head of the Kremlin administration in charge of personnel), are all long-time veterans of the KGB, where they served in senior positions. In their view, the current circumstance is the fulfillment of their historical destiny. Listen to how it is explained by one of these proud contemporary upholders of the "true" Russia. Nikolai Leonov (b. 1928), a former deputy head of the KGB's First Main Directorate (foreign intelligence), was for years the controller of all KGB terror and subversion networks in the Americas. In a recent interview he was asked why so many former and current KGB operatives have assumed positions of power in Russia today. Leonov replied:

First of all, the demand today is precisely for such tough, pragmatically thinking politicians. They are in command of operative information, they have a broad field of view, and they're open to new ideas. But at the same time, they are patriots and proponents of a strong state grounded in centuries-old tradition. *History recruited them* [emphasis in original] to carry out a special operation for the resurrection of our Great Power [*Derzhava*], because there has to be balance in the world, and without a strong Russia the geopolitical turbulence will begin. Second, it was only representatives of the System that were prepared to carry out that task. It turned out to be too much for the others. But then again, what is a KGB officer? He is, above all, a servant of the state. . . . Experience, loyalty to the state, strong intellectual capabilities, an iron will—where else are you going to find cadres? So there's nothing surprising about the fact that representatives of the System were demanded by Russia. The only people that can bring order to the state are state people [*gosudarstvennyye lyudi*].[11]

With these remarks as the immediate background, the figure of Russian President Vladimir Putin acquires an interesting relief. Putin's hallmark, his signature phraseology, has been associated first and foremost with "the Russian idea," and with notions of efficiency and pragmatism: greatness of the State (*derzhava* in traditional Russian political language) through competent management, but without totalitarianism and a centrally planned economy. But for those who know history, Putin also raises eerie echoes from the past. Prince Loris-Melikov spoke of a "dictatorship of the heart"; Putin talks of a "dictatorship of the law." Colonel Sergei Zubatov explained that "the free Russian people do not wish their country become another France or United States"; Putin argues that "Russia cannot become the second edition of, say, the U.S. or Britain in which liberal values have deep historic traditions."[12] The Higher Police are in charge.

In his landmark "Millennium Message," delivered via the Internet in the dying days of 1999, Putin presented a comprehensive program for what his administration was going to be. To date, it is the most far-reaching programmatic document to have come from the Russian presidency, and is therefore a source of considerable weight. Russians today, he asserted, must again become Servants of the Russian Idea:

The public looks forward to the restoration of the guiding and regulating role of the state to a degree which is necessary, proceeding from the traditions and present state of the country." They must work on behalf of "the greatness of Russia. Russia was and will remain a great power. It is preconditioned by the inseparable characteristics of its geopolitical, economic, and cultural existence. They determined the mentality of Russians and the policy of the government throughout the history of Russia and they cannot but do so at present.[13]

Many questions remain to be studied. The relationship within the intelligence services between a Higher Police committed to managing Russia by means of social engineering, on the one hand, and those we have labeled the

Oprichniki, who rely on brute force and power, must be better understood. Their rivalry and interplay will shape much of the domestic sources of Russia's future evolution. As crises strike and as key issues become more sharply defined, opposition between these tendencies will likewise become more focused. Diverging agendas will clash, and contending currents will be at daggers drawn. Further, the version of Russia's polity presented here is stylized, an ideal type. Shades and nuances must be added to bring the model closer to everyday realities in Russia. But there are means to test the validity of the hypothesis we present. For instance, what is the treatment meted out to Beria in documentary and fiction, in film, television and literature, and the media? What kinds of heroes are presented for the adulation and identification of the masses in thrillers and other popular culture movies? Are the principal tenets of the Higher Police's doctrines spreading in policy circles, among contemporary manufacturers of ideology? From answers to such questions it may be possible to adduce the directions taken by Russia's ruling elites. They seem to be firmly on a Higher Police course for the time being. What history holds next for the noble elite, no one can say.

Notes

1. This article uses the term "KGB" as shorthand for post-1917 Soviet intelligence organizations, including their post-1991 incarnations, while the term "Chekisty" will be used as the generic term for members of these organizations.
2. The "Cheka" was created in 1917 and stands for the Russian initials for the term "Extraordinary Commission." The GPU (Glavnoe Politicheskoe Upravleniie, or the Main Political Administration) was created in 1922. In 1934 its functions were assigned to the NKVD (Narodnyi Kommisariyat Vnutrenikh *Del*, or the People's Commissariat for Internal Affairs). In 1954 the KGB (Komitet Gosudarstvennoi Bezopasnosti, or Committee for State Security) was created. It was dissolved in 1991.
3. P. S. Squire, *The Third Department: The Establishment and Practices of the Political Police in the Russia of Nicholas I* (Cambridge: Cambridge University Press, 1968), p. 2.
4. Squire, p. 205.
5. Michael T. Florinsky, *Russia: A Short History* (New York: Macmillan, 1964), p. 309.
6. Jeremiah Schneiderman, *Sergei Zubatov and Revolutionary Marxism: The Struggle for the Working Class in Tsarist Russia* (Ithaca, NY: Cornell University Press, 1970).
7. Bonch-Bruyevich was Russia's premier authority on the religious schismatics, the Old Believers, who comprised about twenty percent of the Russian population at the time. The legacy of government persecution, the role played by Old Believers in rebellions against czarist rule, and the secretive and conspiratorial nature of some Old Believer sects fascinated Russian revolutionaries.
8. A new source documenting the work of this unit has started appearing in Moscow as a book series, *Top Secret: The Lubyanka to Stalin on the Situation in the Country (1922-1934)*. Publication is jointly sponsored by the Russian Academy of Science's Institute for Russian History and the Central Archives of the FSB. The foreword to

the entire series, by G. N. Sevast'yanov, is available on the FSB website, http://www.fsb.ru.

9. Sergo Beria, Ed. Françoise Thom; trans. Brian Pearce, *Beria, My Father: Inside Stalin's Kremlin* (London: Duckworth, 2001).

10. The "Siberian Academy," established in Novosibirsk, was created to provide scientists a degree of breathing space and relative freedom from Communist Party inquisitors and ideologues, and played a crucial role in the advancement of both the natural and the social sciences in the former USSR.

11. Pavel Yevdokimov, "Russkaya pravda generala Leonova" ("General Leonov's Russian Truth"), *Spetsnaz Rossii* (May 2001). Online edition available at http://www.specnaz.ru.

12. Vladimir V. Putin, "Vystupleniye na zasedanii kollegii Ministerstva yustitsii RF" ("Speech at the Meeting of the Board of the Ministry of Justice of the Russian Federation"), January 31, 2000. Available online at http://www.president.kremlin.ru.

13. Vladimir V. Putin, "Rossiya na rubezhe tysyacheletiy" ("Russia on the Threshold of a New Millennium") (December 1999). Available online at www.government.ru.

20

Moscow Nights, Eurasian Dreams

*Nikolas K. Gvosdev**

In 1918, sitting amid the ruins of the Russian Empire, the poet Alexander Blok symbolically expelled Russia from the Western community of nations, renouncing Russia's claim to be the heir and successor to Rome:

> We shall abandon Europe and her charm.
> We shall resort to Scythian craft and guile.
> Swift to the woods and forests we shall swarm,
> And then look back, and smile our slit-eyed smile.
> Away to the Urals, all!

Blok must have struck a chord, for three years later, a group of émigré intellectuals urged an "Exodus to the East." They had in mind lands between the Vistula and the Amur that to them were neither Europe nor Asia, but a distinct "Ocean-Continent" they called Eurasia. Genghis Khan, the unifier of the steppes, was their hero; Peter the Great, the man who tried to "open a window onto Europe," they despised.

The so-called "Eurasianists," however, never found a receptive audience among ordinary Russians. When Charles de Gaulle visited the Soviet Union in 1966 to proclaim a Europe stretching "from the Atlantic to the Urals," most Russians were more than happy to think of themselves as belonging within a common European home. The lands beyond the Urals (Siberia, Central Asia, and the Caucasus) were instead dragged symbolically toward the west, becoming "European" through their association with Russia—especially so after the signing of the Helsinki Final Act in 1975.

---

*Nikolas Gvosdev is executive editor of *The National Interest* and a senior fellow at *The Nixon Center*. This article originally appeared in *The National Interest*, no. 68 (Summer 2002).

With the disintegration of the Soviet Empire, however, the non-Russian republics once referred to as "the Soviet Union in Asia" found themselves spinning in a geopolitical void. Time-sensitive designations (former Soviet republics, "newly-independent states") lose relevance with each passing year. Thus, the term "Eurasia" is being revived, sometimes to refer to the entire ex-USSR, but often to designate only the Caucasus and Central Asia—those countries lying beyond the pale of any realistic prospects of being included in NATO or the EU. An old term has met a new history head on.[1]

Blok prophesied that Eurasia would be the host for a major clash between civilizations:

> Quick, leave the land,
> And clear the field for trial by blood and sword,
> Where steel machines that have no soul must stand
> and face the fury of the . . . horde.

And so, in the aftermath of September 11, Eurasia has become the principal front in the war against terror—the crucible where Islamist terrorism and a far more ecumenical system of organized crime merge. Two well-traveled smuggling routes for all types of contraband—drugs, weapons, dirty money, and illegal migrants—crisscross the region. The north-south corridor runs from Afghanistan into European Russia via the Central Asian republics; the trans-Caspian route connects Central Asia with Georgia and Azerbaijan, with further extensions via Chechnya and Dagestan (into Russia and Northern Europe) and through Turkey and the Balkans (into Southern Europe). Call them, for short, the Sleaze Road and Grifter Avenue. Russian law-enforcement sources estimate that the drug trade alone in Eurasia generates up to $12 billion in income and assets. In places like Uzbekistan (where the average monthly wage is $20) or Georgia (where 60 percent of the population lives below the poverty line), that kind of money buys about as much political "access" and police "protection" for all sorts of nefarious activities as anyone could reasonably require.

Seen in this light, the optimism radiating from the Oval Office about the "deepening of regional integration" as the sine qua non for the security of the entire region—as a joint U.S.-Kazakh statement in December put it—seems a little misplaced. The weak post-Soviet successor states of the Caucasus and Central Asia are in no position to develop effective multilateral regional institutions capable of effectively meeting the challenges before them. Over the past decade, several organizations have been created with much fanfare—the Central Asian Union, the Collective Security Treaty of the Commonwealth of Independent States (CIS), the Eurasian Economic Community, GUUAM [Georgia-Ukraine-Uzbekistan-Azerbaijan-Moldova] and the Shanghai Cooperation Organization among them. They have accomplished little beyond providing work for underutilized diplomats who excel at making speeches and penning declarations. The newest contender—the Central Asian Cooperation Organization, whose charter was signed on February 28, 2002—is unlikely to break the mold.

Strengthening the states that lie along the southern periphery of Eurasia, especially those that abut centers of Islamic radicalism in southwest Asia, will take time and hard work. Such strengthening would nevertheless appear to be a logical course of action that is in the interest of both Washington and Moscow. How to do this is less clear. Secretary of State Colin Powell envisions a joint effort: "We know that this is something we cannot do without the Russians and something that increasingly they realize can't be done without us, and without the full participation of the countries in the region."[2] The Secretary assumes, however, that Moscow, Washington and the governments of the "Eurasian" republics share a common interest in pursuing such cooperation. Alas, things are not so simple.

Russia finds itself in a Eurasian quandary. For the past decade, it has benefited from the weakness of the post-Soviet successor states in order to maintain its influence within and among them. Facing internal unrest or external threats, several post-Soviet states (notably Tajikistan) have requested the continuing deployment of Russian troops on their soil. Separatist movements in places like Abkhazia or Trans-Dniestria have given Russia the opportunity to deploy its forces in other republics under the guise of peacekeepers. Moscow has played both ends against the middle by giving refuge and succor to political opponents of existing regimes (such as the former president of Azerbaijan, Ayaz Mutalibov and the former foreign minister of Turkmenistan, Boris Shikhmuradov), while cultivating links with dissatisfied ethnic minorities (the Lezgins of Azerbaijan, for instance) and regional politicians often at odds with their own central government (such as Aslan Abashidze, the leader of Adjaria, an autonomous region within Georgia). The Russian special services have also been accused of fomenting coups and assassination attempts against leaders inclined to move their states out of Moscow's orbit.

This, then, is the paradox of Russia's Eurasian policy: the unconsolidated states to the south have been unable to act as an effective barrier between Russia and the maelstrom of Islamic radicalism emanating from southwest Asia, but that same weakness makes these regimes susceptible to Moscow's own reduced means of influence. In the wake of September 11, therefore, any significant financial and security assistance extended from the United States to the nations of the Caucasus and Central Asia, while it would stand to enhance Russia's own security, could also undermine Russia's Eurasian sphere of influence.

That is why the Russian political elite is anxiously trying to divine American intentions in the region. Washington, however, is sending contradictory signals. Last October, Defense Secretary Donald Rumsfeld assured Central

Asian leaders that it was "safe to be associated" with the United States, since the administration was prepared to be engaged for the long term. This view was reiterated from the Democratic side of the aisle by Senate Majority leader Tom Daschle during his visit to Tashkent in January, when he declared that "our presence and our relationship with . . . the countries in the region is one that we look upon in long terms." And yet, barely a month later, on February 11, Assistant Secretary of State Elizabeth Jones stated that "we don't want U.S. bases in Central Asia" since "our goal with the Russians is to make sure that they understand we are not trying to compete with them in Central Asia, we're not trying to take over Central Asia from them." If, as Secretary Powell has observed, the "way we are approaching Central Asia is symbolic of the way we are approaching the [U.S.-Russia] relationship as a whole," then America's inconsistent behavior thus far is disconcerting news indeed.

Disregarding Blok's advice to "keep our distance and . . . observe the deadly conflict raging on the field," Vladimir Putin pledged full and enthusiastic support for the anti-terrorism coalition that Washington assembled after September 11. The Russian political elite was initially ecstatic, for it assumed that the United States would task Russia, as a "regional superpower," to keep order in Eurasia. Instead, the United States has opted for direct aid to the post-Soviet republics—including the deployment of its own military forces into Eurasia—rather than asking, and funding, Russia to act as America's proxy.

Georgia is a particularly sore case in point. For years, Georgian President Eduard Shevardnadze rebuffed Moscow's requests for joint military operations to secure the Pankisi gorge, or for Russian troops to operate on Georgian territory to combat Chechen rebels. After 9/11, Moscow assumed that, as Washington's partner in the war on terrorism, the United States would support Russia's demands vis-à-vis Georgia. On February 18, Russian Defense Minister Sergei Ivanov called for a Russian-led counter-terrorist operation against suspected terrorist training camps in the Pankisi gorge. Three days later, the chief of the Russian General Staff, Anatoly Kvashnin, said that the likelihood of any American involvement in such an operation would be "very small," and reiterated Moscow's position that "Russia and Georgia should jointly eradicate this terrorist center in the Pankisi gorge." Then came the announcement that the United States would dispatch a mission to train and equip Georgian forces, which the Russians claim took them unawares. This forced the Russians to backpedal. On February 27, the Speaker of the Duma, Gennady Seleznev, tried to spin American aid to Georgia as an extension of the "international antiterrorist coalition." He reiterated, however, that any "decision on what should be done in the Pankisi gorge can and must be made only within the framework of tripartite consultations between Georgia, Russia and the United States of America."

So far, however, the administration has shown no inclination to involve Russia at all, even in a symbolic fashion, in its Caucasian deployment—

though the Russian complaint about the lack of prior U.S. consultation is much exaggerated. The U.S. posture has led two prominent members of the Duma, Dmitry Rogozin (chair of the International Affairs Committee) and Boris Pastukhov (chair of the CIS Affairs Committee) to warn that the administration's unwillingness to involve Russia in the plans for the deployment of U.S. advisors in Georgia would have "a negative impact on bilateral cooperation in the fight against terrorism."

Some in Russia—and not only in Russia—have concluded that the Bush team views "partnership" with Russia along the lines outlined by Zbigniew Brzezinski in these pages two years ago: namely, that the United States must help Russia divest itself of imperial baggage so that it can be join Western institutions as a major, if not a predominant, actor.[3] The continuing eastward expansion of NATO as well as other post-September 11 developments—from the basing of American forces in Central Asia to the announcement of new aid packages for the post-Soviet states of the region—look to many in Moscow like Brzezinski's recommendation in action: the incipient American "encirclement" of Russia via deployments in the south and NATO expansion to their west.

If this is the case, then why has Putin reacted so dispassionately to this turn of events? It is not simply to cultivate goodwill in the West—although he keeps a portrait of Peter the Great in his office—and it is not only for the enjoyment that annoying his own chattering classes brings. Rather, it is because, in his calculation, the entry of the United States into Central Asia and the Caucasus, far from representing a defeat or a threat, actually constitutes a no-lose situation for Russia.

Take the "train-and-equip" mission to Georgia. The Bush Administration has reportedly given private assurances to the Russian government that U.S. assistance will not be diverted by the Georgians to compel a military solution to the separatist enclaves of Abkhazia and South Ossetia, both of which maintain close links to Russia. If the mission is successful—and the Georgians clear the Pankisi gorge—a major transit point for the Chechen rebels will be shut down and rear recuperation areas will be lost to them. If the Georgians fail to act, however, the United States, having verified the presence of Al-Qaeda operatives in the region, risks damage to its credibility in the war on terrorism. The United States would then have to contemplate a frontline combat role for itself, something it is loath to do, or compel Tbilisi to permit Russian forces to deal with the threat. For Putin, at least, U.S. involvement in Georgia is not, in his words, a "tragedy" for Russia.

Putin apparently views George W. Bush (in terms of his administration, not on a personal level) as an overbearing yet wealthy uncle whose tedious holiday visits can be endured because he presents a lucrative gift at the end of the day. Consider this: the United States did in a matter of weeks what years of Russian aid to the Northern Alliance was unable to do—decapitate the Taliban regime. Washington removed a major threat to the stability and territorial integrity of the Russian Federation. Russia cannot afford to state-build in Eurasia, while the United States can offer one country, Uzbekistan, long-term financial aid, loans and investments that could easily reach $8 billion—a sum equal to Russia's entire annual military budget. Therefore, while the United States takes on the lion's share of the costs to revamp Eurasia's security architecture, "we are increasing our security, saving the lives of our soldiers, and gaining time for our own rearmament," declared Putin advisor Gleb Pavlovsky.

Putin is gambling that U.S. guarantees, such as the one extended to Uzbek president Islam Karimov during his visit to Washington this past March, will be of short duration, especially as the threat from Al-Qaeda recedes and the United States seeks to extricate itself from the region. Even though the United States can easily outbid Russia, Washington's concerns about how its assistance might be misused—either by authoritarian regimes seeking to crack down on opposition movements, or by corrupt local officials to improve the quality of the protection they extend to criminal organizations—means that tensions between Washington and its new "partners" are inevitable. The United States will not endure them if the reward for doing so is already paid out.

For the locals, post-9/11 developments are simply one more set of steps in the "Eurasian shuffle," as regional leaders dance between Moscow and Washington to secure maximum advantage. Karimov himself is most adept at this waltz. When it appeared that the United States was prepared to play a more active role in Central Asia, especially in the energy sector, he declared, in 1995: "The presence of the United States in Central Asia is a guarantee of stability in [this] part of the world." When no large-scale Western investment materialized, and when Washington intensified its criticisms of his unreconstructed authoritarianism, Karimov made the pilgrimage to the Kremlin, where, in May of last year, he pronounced: "We favor Russia's presence in Central Asia. This is a fundamental guarantee of security and stability in the region." Karimov may be America's new best friend but when the relationship with the United States cools (whether over human rights, lack of democratization or corruption), Moscow will be waiting to receive the prodigal back into the common Eurasian home.

Even if the United States intends to establish a long-term presence in the region, the naval base at Guantanamo Bay is a telling example of how a military presence in an area can have virtually no impact at all on events in the host country. Given the U.S. penchant for "freezing" conflicts indefinitely rather than expending its own treasure and energy to craft final solutions, Russia can retain its forward "enclaves" in the region (such as peacekeepers in Abkhazia or Tajikistan, or the base at Akhalkalaki in southern Georgia) to counterbalance any American presence.

Moreover, the lack of substantial Western investment in the region, other than in the hydrocarbons sector in certain areas, allows Russia to retain a considerable degree of economic and political leverage in the new Eurasia. The Russian economy remains underdeveloped by Western standards, but Russia is an El Dorado for millions of legal and illegal guest workers who send remittances back to their families in the Caucasus and Central Asia.[4] After years of decline caused by the Soviet breakup, trade between Russia and its former Soviet republics grew by more than 40 percent in 2000, totaling over $25 billion. Finally, several years of continuous growth in the Russian economy—not to mention the enormous profits obtained by Russian corporations, especially in the energy sector—have enabled Russian firms to buy up assets, at bargain prices, in other Eurasian countries (as well as in Eastern Europe) where Western investors still fear to tread. An influential Ukrainian newspaper thus opined, "Moscow will not go anywhere. The old debts and old links that determine mutual dependence will stay."[5]

Putin has thus revealed himself as the consummate pragmatist. While the United States fixes its gaze on the open-ended, idealistic task of rooting out global terrorism (and dispenses its largesse in pursuit of that lofty goal), Russia has kept its eye firmly on the more earthy objective of resurrecting its power and influence among its neighbors. One result of the Russo-American "partnership" in the war on terrorism is likely to be a revived and strengthened Russia as the dominant power in Eurasia, and this will cost Russia not a single kopeck in the coin of its institutional advance toward Europe. Putin can thus be both "Peter" (opening Russia to Western investment and technology, and further integrating Russia into Western institutions) and "Genghis" (rebuilding the groundwork for a Russian-dominated Eurasia)—if we let him.

Notes

1. President Nursultan Nazarbaev of Kazakhstan has been a staunch proponent of the "Eurasian" idea. He named the university in the new capital of Astana for Lev Gumilev, the historian and geographer who propounded the notion of Eurasia as a shared cultural and environmental space uniting Turk and Slav, Orthodox and Muslim. See, for example, his speech (December 15, 2000) at the VII session of the Assembly of the Peoples of Kazakhstan.
2. Testimony before the House Appropriations Subcommittee on Foreign Operations, Export Financing and Related Programs, February 13, 2002.
3. Brzezinski, "Living with Russia," *The National Interest* (Fall 2000).
4. This explains in part why an April poll conducted by "M-Vector" found that more than 60 percent of residents in Bishkek, the Kyrgyz capital, oppose the basing of U.S. military personnel in the republic, fearing a potential deterioration of relations with Russia.
5. *Holos Ukrainy, December 4, 2001.* Consider how Kyrgyz President Askar Akaev rushed to proclaim that the U.S. presence in Central Asia must not "conflict with Russian interests"—after Russia indicated it might not restructure Kyrgyz debt. Ahmed Rashid, "Russia, China Warily Watch for American Intrusions in Central Asia," *Eurasia Insight*, May 3, 2002.

Afterword

The U.S.-Russia Relationship
After the Iraq War

Paul J. Saunders*

It can be easy to think that the United States and Russia have moved beyond the dispute caused by disagreements in the run-up to the war in Iraq. The
summit between Presidents George W. Bush and Vladimir Putin in St. Petersburg this June, followed by the G-8 meeting in Evian, presented to the world a
public reconciliation between the two states.

Yet, this perspective can be dangerous. The fundamental questions that led
to the dispute have not been addressed, creating the very real possibility that
there will be further, similar disputes between Washington and Moscow. Indeed, we can ask: how many more such disputes can the U.S.-Russia partnership endure before the mood in Washington changes and Russia is seen as an
ungrateful and obstructionist country?

As the Iraq war was drawing to a close, President Vladimir Putin made two
widely publicized statements that appeared to demonstrate Russian interest in
beginning to repair the damage to the U.S.-Russian relationship caused by the
disagreements over how to deal with Saddam Hussein. While acknowledging
that Russia disagreed with the American decision to go ahead with military
action designed to forcibly remove Hussein from power, he nonetheless stressed
that Moscow and Washington had to continue to work together on important
issues such as terrorism and non-proliferation. American officials have made
similar statements.

It is very useful for the United States to work together with Russia. The
relationship with Russia is among America's most important, because Russia

---

*Paul J. Saunders is the director of The Nixon Center. (The Nixon Center co-publishes
The National Interest, along with Hollinger International. This afterword is adapted from
a presentation given at The Nixon Center on July 15, 2003.

261

is perhaps uniquely positioned in the world to exert either a positive or a negative influence on some of America's most vital national interests—ranging from the continuing war against Al-Qaeda to curbing the spread of dangerous technologies used to manufacture weapons of mass destruction.   A genuine partnership with Russia could advance a number of important U.S. interests

Still, the degree to which the Kremlin is prepared to work with the Bush Administration remains uncertain. After September 11, many in Washington and Moscow had come to believe that Mr. Putin had made a strategic choice to pursue a closer relationship with the United States. Though Russian officials continue to express interest in strengthening ties with the United States, it is not clear what precisely the current intentions of the Putin Administration are. Sergei Karaganov, chairman of Russia's Council on Foreign and Defense Policy, complained that his country "lacked a coherent strategic objective" in developing and implementing policy, pointing out the absence of an "underlying strategic line" that spelled out Russian national interests and the best way to achieve them.

Indeed, the Russian-American relationship is still largely predicated upon the personal bond between the two presidents, but it seems unlikely that this is a sufficient foundation for a close and lasting partnership. Despite the warm and friendly relations between Bush and Putin, it is difficult to see how the U.S.-Russian relationship can return entirely to pre-war business as usual. The optimism expressed by Robert Legvold in his contribution to this volume has been tempered by the degree to which Russia was prepared to publicly offer very critical rhetoric and to work with others to attempt to block American military action in Iraq. Still, Russia's potential influence on important American interests necessitates an effort to move the relationship forward. If Russian leaders appear committed to strengthening ties, Washington should be prepared to renew efforts to expand relations with Moscow. An urgent goal in any such efforts must be to build a solid foundation for a constructive and sustainable relationship with Russia.

However, since the advancement of U.S. interests—and not friendly relations for their own sake—is the paramount objective of this process, it is necessary to ensure that the relationship will indeed serve those interests. Russian behavior in the run-up to the war in Iraq indicates that this point is not self-evident to at least some members of the Russian political elite. Three lessons from "what went wrong" need to be fully digested before further progress can be made.

The first lesson for Washington is that Russia has its own interests and perspectives on foreign affairs. With regard to Iraq, Russian officials did not believe that Iraq had a substantial weapons of mass destruction (WMD) program or the links to international terrorism, both claims advanced by the Bush Administration. Nor did the Kremlin believe that Iraq posed such an imminent threat to regional and global security as to require immediate military action. Russia cannot be expected to accept U.S. assessments at face value.

The second lesson is that Russia has its own domestic politics that affect its foreign policy. While Russia may not be a full-fledged democracy, it does have domestic interest groups and constituencies. Moreover, elections to the State Duma will be held in December 2003. Certainly, the Kremlin can use its formidable administrative resources to affect the outcome of close election contests, but the regime is much more constrained in its ability to manage the electoral process when there are clear winners. Given than up to 90 percent of Russians opposed U.S. action in Iraq, and that clear opposition had been expressed even by long-standing U.S. allies such as France and Germany, the Putin Administration, which is hoping to solidify a pro-government majority in the next Duma, clearly sought to avoid alienating Russian public opinion.

Finally, the United States cannot take Russian support for granted. The personal connection between the presidents could not win out (in the case of Iraq) against a coordinated Franco-German lobbying effort to solicit Russian support. Given that the bulk of Russia's trade and investment is generated from the European Union, this development should not have been surprising.

Several of the essays contained in this volume have stressed the need for the United States to establish clear priorities vis-à-vis Russia. As the crisis over Iraq demonstrates, the foundation of the current U.S.-Russian relationship can sustain only a certain load. This means that, once the United States has prioritized what matters most in its relationship with Russia, Washington should work most aggressively to advance vital or very important interests in the relationship while seeking to avoid disputes over secondary or peripheral matters.[1] The Executive Branch must also work to develop bi-partisan support for this approach in Congress, to prevent individual agendas from disrupting the course of the relationship.

The key to deriving the maximum value from the U.S.-Russian relationship on a sustainable basis lies in structuring Russian choices by providing sufficient benefits through cooperation to outweigh the costs imposed by necessary and inevitable U.S. actions at variance with Russian preferences. This is not an abstract principle: Senior Russian officials made clear privately before the war that Moscow could have been more cooperative over Iraq in the context of a better relationship with Washington. Generating these benefits for Russia requires identifying areas of important convergent interests and pursuing them energetically while seeking creative solutions in areas where our interests are not inherently contradictory. Success should allow the United States to act independently (including in the face of Russian objections) when necessary without sacrificing the long-term advantages of a constructive relationship with Russia. We cannot avoid disagreements—so the objective of a U.S.-Russia partnership should not be to eliminate differences but to manage them, to compartmentalize them while focusing on issues of shared interest.

Three central issues—the war on terrorism, non-proliferation, and Russia's integration into the international economy—have the potential to offer significant mutual rewards to the United States and Russia and to serve as the foundation of a lasting relationship. Though there are many other areas of potential collaboration, these three offer immediately apparent and tangible benefits to both countries. They create the fabric of ties—between our militaries, our intelligence services and our business communities—that will help to solidify the partnership, so that we can reach the point where it is conceivable that Mr. Putin (or another Russian president) could justify cooperating with the United States even if the two countries do not see eye-to-eye on a particular issue; in other words, where the value for Russia of preserving the relationship outweighs many particular items on the agenda.

This could also be strengthened by more frequent and more comprehensive consultations with Moscow in advance of important American policy initiatives. Such an effort would give Russian officials—and the Russian public—a sense that the Bush Administration values Russian input and advice. After all, Moscow is unlikely to be with Washington for the landing if it was not at the takeoff. The United States, alternatively, does have the options of ignoring Russia or giving it much less priority among a multitude of foreign policy goals. But such an approach would have its own costs and could undermine important American objectives, most notably in fighting terrorism and proliferation, but also in rebuilding Afghanistan and Iraq, pursuing peace in the Middle East, and using the UN Security Council to advance U.S. interests.

Genuine partnership with Moscow will not be easy in the face of differing perspectives, priorities and institutional cultures. The U.S. -Russia partnership is likely to remain a high-maintenance relationship. But the rewards of success could be considerable. And though there is considerable asymmetry between American and Russian capabilities, Russia has made and can make a real difference in many circumstances, especially if U.S. ties with some traditional allies are further strained. In a complex and dangerous world, Russia can be an important friend. Pursuing such a partnership is worth the effort.

Note

1. One such area that needs to be re-examined is the U.S. support for GUUAM. Supporting the independence of the post-Soviet states is an interest of the United States; the question is whether a regional organization that appears to be directed against Russia is the best mechanism to achieve this. One can certainly argue that direct bi-lateral ties between the United States and the various post-Soviet republics could achieve many of the same goals without needlessly antagonizing the Russians.

For Product Safety Concerns and Information please contact our EU
representative GPSR@taylorandfrancis.com
Taylor & Francis Verlag GmbH, Kaufingerstraße 24, 80331 München, Germany